SAP° Extension Suite Certification Guide

T0100190

SAP PRESS

SAP PRESS is a joint initiative of SAP and Rheinwerk Publishing. The know-how offered by SAP specialists combined with the expertise of Rheinwerk Publishing offers the reader expert books in the field. SAP PRESS features first-hand information and expert advice, and provides useful skills for professional decision-making.

SAP PRESS offers a variety of books on technical and business-related topics for the SAP user. For further information, please visit our website: *www.sap-press.com*.

Banda, Chandra, Gooi
SAP Business Technology Platform: An Introduction
2022, 570 pages, hardcover and e-book
www.sap-press.com/5440

Acharya, Bajaj, Dhar, Ghosh, Lahiri
Application Development with SAP Business Technology Platform
2023, approx. 625 pages, hardcover and e-book
www.sap-press.com/5504

Aron, Gakhar, Vij
SAP Integration Suite
2021, 343 pages, hardcover and e-book
www.sap-press.com/5326

Bönnen, Jegadeesan, Mary, Vij
SAP API Management
2020, 365 pages, hardcover and e-book
www.sap-press.com/4928

Acharya, Debelic, Joshi, Dhawan
ABAP in the Cloud: Development and Operations
with SAP BTP, ABAP Environment
2021, 316 pages, hardcover and e-book
www.sap-press.com/5236

Krishna Kishor Kammaje, Mahesh Kumar Palavalli

SAP® Extension Suite Certification Guide

Development Associate Exam

Editor Rachel Gibson
Acquisitions Editor Hareem Shafi
Copyeditor Julie McNamee
Cover Design Graham Geary
Photo Credit Shutterstock.com: 1798739896/© Chursina Viktoriia
Layout Design Vera Brauner
Production Hannah Lane
Typesetting SatzPro, Germany
Printed and bound in Canada, on paper from sustainable sources

ISBN 978-1-4932-2239-1
© 2023 by Rheinwerk Publishing, Inc., Boston (MA)
1st edition 2023

Library of Congress Cataloging-in-Publication Data:
Names: Kammaje, Krishna Kishor, author. | Palavalli, Mahesh Kumar, author.
Title: SAP extension suite certification guide : development associate exam
 / by Krishna Kishor Kammaje and Mahesh Kumar Palaval.
Description: 1st edition. | Bonn ; Boston : Rheinwerk Publishing, 2022. |
 Includes index.
Identifiers: LCCN 2022029157 | ISBN 9781493222391 (hardcover) | ISBN
 9781493222407 (ebook)
Subjects: LCSH: Relational databases--Examinations--Study guides. | SAP
 HANA (Electronic resource)--Examinations--Study guides. | Software
 maintenance--Examinations--Study guides.
Classification: LCC QA76.9.D32 K36 2022 | DDC 005.74--dc23/eng/20220812
LC record available at https://lccn.loc.gov/2022029157

Contents at a Glance

Dear Reader,

I've recently taken up vegetable gardening. When I started planting in my small raised bed, it seemed like it would be a simple, relaxing hobby and an easy way to get local, organic produce. Oh, how wrong I was! Little did I know how many things can go wrong in a 10' × 6' box of dirt.

I unknowingly planted cold-weather vegetables in the dead of summer. I tried coaxing wilted kale back to life. I overwatered my quickly browning lettuce and fought to keep my rows of herbs from prematurely flowering in the warm sun. I successfully grew six whole heads of broccoli, but just as they were getting big enough to be picked, I woke up to find they had all been eaten overnight. (My prime suspect? The woodchuck that lives under our shed.)

Thanks to all of my setbacks, I've learned that gardens require a few different things to be successful: research, patience, and dedication. In that way, they're not unlike the skillset you need when studying for a test. Consider this book your field guide to SAP Extension Suite, where you can find all the tips and tools to use when studying for and taking your development associate exam. Let our expert authors Krishna Kishor Kammaje and Mahesh Kumar Palavalli help you build the knowledge base you need to successfully ace the test. And as you're studying, give yourself the same patience, dedication, and care you would a garden. You got this!

What did you think about *SAP Extension Suite Certification Guide: Development Associate Exam*? Your comments and suggestions are the most useful tools to help us make our books the best they can be. Please feel free to contact me and share any praise or criticism you may have.

Thank you for purchasing a book from SAP PRESS!

Rachel Gibson
Editor, SAP PRESS

rachelg@rheinwerk-publishing.com
www.sap-press.com
Rheinwerk Publishing · Boston, MA

Contents

1 SAP Business Technology Platform 25

2   Web Development Standards   63

3   SAP Cloud Application Programming Model   95

6   Authorization and Trust Management   229

7   Continuous Integration and Delivery   271

Foreword

Experience is so central to our very being, to the way we see and will see life as we travel through it. In your enterprise, your customers, vendors, and employees will all have some kind of experience when they use the applications you build, so I implore you to do your very best to apply everything in this excellent book to ensure the experience is thought through, well designed, and well built. You are embarking on a journey to become a developer in a technology that has such potential to create positive and effective user experiences, to free the SAP user community from the chains of confusing transaction codes that need significant training to operate, to simplify and streamline the enterprise user experience.

The value of a great user experience is tremendous to the enterprise in the speed with which change can be implemented, new systems and processes can be rolled out, and staff can move between job functions with minimal training on the system focusing instead on the business objectives and being guided to success by the tools and applications they use. Always remember to be guided by a consistent language, the SAP Fiori design guidelines, in how you craft your SAP applications to ensure they can be adopted quickly and easily. A great SAP Fiori experience will be guided towards a specific business goal, a task or an objective that should be simplified beyond the traditional transaction codes to the very essence of what the business needs to achieve. In some cases, a totally custom experience, perhaps a highly branded one, will be appropriate, and when this is the case, always remember to put the end user and ease of adoption over developer preferences.

Let's pause for a moment to think of a very specific example before and after SAP Fiori by looking to the app called Sales Order Fulfillment Issues, where previously over a dozen reports and transactions needed to be completed to get the basic information before action could be taken in following transactions. Now, with SAP Fiori, the issues are summarized with a simple button to resolve them. This is beautifully simple by comparison and a tremendous improvement in user experience, demonstrating thinking and design beyond the transaction and focusing on the desired business outcome of smoothly flowing customer sales orders. This level of simplification is likely only possible with an in-memory processing engine, so as with all your apps, think about how you too can help ask a better question and present the context and options for user decisions more effectively than the legacy spinning disk databases could allow. The responsiveness and depth of question is a key component of the user experience, and the opportunities to delight your end users with simplicity like this app are many.

This book will help you guide you through key concepts for designing and building great enterprise solutions, to share the art of the intended and the possible, then to craft excellent applications using BTP as it was intended. You will be able to confidently articulate how critical it is to invest in good solution design with a solid user experience design and how design research and iterations of the prototype application with input from real end users is critical to success. It is a sad reality that many enterprise applications miss the mark so widely, often because of a lack of good design and lack of input from real end users. Don't let your app be "that app" that no one uses. Advocate for and defend good user experience design, and be proud of how much more successful your applications will be when they are well designed.

You will quickly find, if you have not already, that SAP Business Technology Platform (SAP BTP) is much like PowerPoint. The toolset is very powerful, and the range of flexibility is immense while the experience of those consuming the end product can be intuitive and easy or frustrating and un-engaging. Take what you learn in this book and the associated reading to help your solutions be the engaging successful apps your end users and your organization deserve, giving them a well-designed and effective experience for the type of environment and device they will need to be successful.

By helping you understand the foundations of SAP BTP, this book will help you select and apply the most appropriate parts of the SAP BTP toolkit to bring great solutions to life. You will find tips to help make sure your application is scalable and thoughtfully designed from a security perspective, and that it aligns with the intended technical functioning of SAP BTP and the SAP solution stack. These sections will again help make sure you avoid building "that app" that needs your attention after go-live or an upgrade to make corrections or fixes. You have the opportunity to bring valuable and well-adopted solutions to life. This will always be more important than a badge or certificate since you will directly leave a positive impact on thousands of people's lives and your organization's success.

I hope you will seize this opportunity to become more than an SAP BTP developer, and instead become an SAP BTP solution creator, bringing more value to your enterprise than ever before.

Shaun Syvertsen
Managing Partner and CEO of ConvergentIS

Introduction

Techniques You'll Master

- Finding the content of the certification exam
- Learning about the exam pattern and scoring rules
- Understanding how to register for the exam and take the exam
- Exploring exam preparation sources
- Keeping your knowledge updated

In the following sections, we'll cover the SAP Certified Development Associate – SAP Extension Suite exam objective and structure, and then dive into test preparation resources and test-taking strategies to help you on the day of the exam.

Exam Objective

This exam is an associate level exam that aims to validate your knowledge in becoming an SAP consultant to work with SAP Extension Suite products and tools. It tests your knowledge in building OData services using the SAP Cloud Application Programming Model, Node.js flavor. It expects you to know how to add an SAP Fiori elements-based user interface (UI) to your application using annotations, as well as how to add enterprise features such as security and authorization to your SAP Cloud Application Programming Model projects. You'll be tested in your skills in deploying the developed application both manually and automatically into SAP Business Technology Platform (SAP BTP) using Continuous Integration (CI) and Continuous Deployment (CD) tools.

As this is a certification focused on the Node.js flavor of SAP Cloud Application Programming Model, you're expected to know the basics of JavaScript and other basics of web development. Basic knowledge of cloud concepts can greatly help as well.

Exam Structure

The online, multiple-choice exam can be taken from the comfort of your home. You can go to the homepage of the certification exam at *https://learning.sap.com* and searching for exam code C_CPE_13, as shown in Figure 1.

SAP provides a 15-minute mock test for you to prepare that contains six questions. This can give you some experience with the real-world exam, the answering process, and the assessment software. You access this sample test by clicking on **View sample questions ❶**.

In the following sections, we'll cover exam booking and how the exam is scored, as well as what to do if you don't pass the test on your first try.

Exam Booking

The first step toward registering for the certification exam is to purchase a subscription to the Certification Hub. There are two options here. You can either purchase six attempts or one attempt (in a 12-month period for both options) toward certification exams. Go to *https://training.sap.com*, and search for code CER001 for the one-attempt option or code CER006 for the six-attempt option.

Note
Even if you buy the SAP Certification Exam, Six Attempts option, a single exam (e.g., C_CPE_13) can be taken only three times. You need to use the remaining attempts for other exams.

The next step is to schedule your certification exam within the Certification Hub on the *https://learning.sap.com* site. Click on **Book your exam** ❷, and follow the instructions to schedule your exam.

After that, you'll get an email with all the instructions on how to start the exam on the exam day.

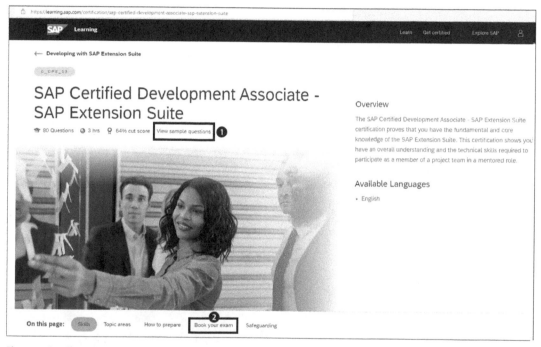

Figure 1 Certification Homepage

Exam Scoring

During the exam, you'll have three hours to answer 80 questions. You need to score 64% of the marks to pass the exam; that is, you need to answer 51 questions right. If a question has more than one correct answer, you need to choose all correct answers to get the question right. There is no negative penalty for wrong answers. You can submit your answers within the allotted 3 hours. If you don't turn it in, the exam will end at 3 hours automatically, and the score will be calculated. At the end of the exam, your marks and percentage will appear so you can see whether you've passed or failed the exam.

What If You Fail?

Keep calm! It's not the end of the world. A particular exam (e.g., C_CPE_13) can be taken up to three times. If you can't pass in those efforts, you need to wait for the upcoming version of that exam topic.

Test Preparation Resources

Traditionally, SAP Help was the only free learning resource available. However lately SAP has brought in multiple free learning resources to augment your learning and help you in clearing your certification exam. In this section, we briefly go through each of these resources.

SAP Learning Hub

During TechEd 2021, SAP made several SAP Learning Journeys free. One such learning journey is Developing with SAP Extension Suite, as shown in Figure 2. You can use your free personal SAP account to access this learning journey.

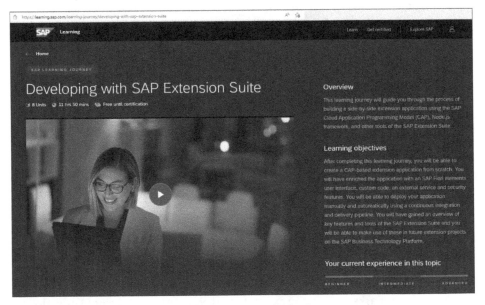

Figure 2 Free Learning Journey for SAP Extension Suite Certification

SAP HANA Academy's YouTube Channel

SAP HANA Academy is known for providing quality YouTube content on topics across SAP technology solutions (see Figure 3). Don't be misguided by the name into thinking that it has only SAP HANA-relevant content because the YouTube playlist contains 15 videos for various topics covering the certification syllabus (go to *www.youtube.com/c/saphanaacademy*). This can act as a quick recap of various exam topics. You can browse through several other videos on this channel to go deep into some of the exam-relevant topics and to keep your knowledge current.

Figure 3 SAP HANA Academy's YouTube Channel

SAP Tutorials for Developers

These tutorials are step-by-step, hands-on guides for realizing various use cases (available at *https://developers.sap.com/tutorial-navigator.html*). Based on the complexity of the tutorial, there are three levels: beginner, intermediate, and advanced. These are great places to get hands-on experience. You may not get enough theoretical knowledge in these tutorials, so we recommend you try these after you gain some theoretical knowledge (beginner-level tutorials can be an exception). Tutorials are grouped into **Groups** and **Missions** so that related tutorials are together and can be pursued sequentially (see Figure 4).

openSAP

openSAP provides useful, detailed training on the SAP Cloud Application Programming Model (see Figure 5). This course might feel slightly dated as it was originally run in May 2020. Nevertheless, most of its content is still relevant and can add a great deal of knowledge about SAP Cloud Application Programming Model. You can enroll in this course at *https://open.sap.com/courses/cp7*. Keep an eye out for new and updated courses at *https://open.sap.com*.

Figure 4 SAP Tutorials

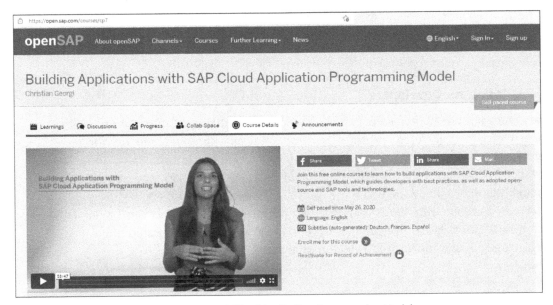

Figure 5 openSAP Course on SAP Cloud Application Programming Model

SAP Discovery Center Missions

SAP Discovery Center missions have several missions available that can help you achieve predefined goals (go to *https://discovery-center.cloud.sap/missions*). Missions provide step-by-step guidance along the best practice path to achieve your goal. In Figure 6, you can see a mission explaining how to build an SAP BTP application.

Figure 6 A Sample SAP Discovery Center Mission

SAP Community

SAP Community is a great place to browse topics, ask questions, and read blogs. You can also share your experiences by writing blogs and getting engaged with the community. The community has many helpful members who can answer your questions and help you solve any roadblocks in your learning journey. You can reach the SAP Extension Suite community at *https://community.sap.com/topics/extension-suite* (see Figure 7).

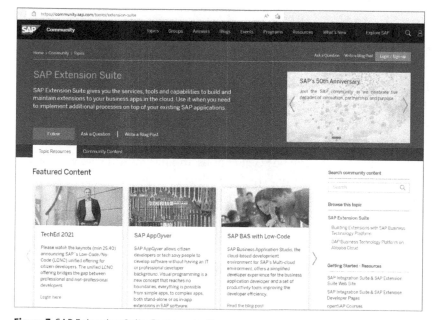

Figure 7 SAP Extension Suite Community Page

SAP Help

SAP has a comprehensive support page at *https://help.sap.com/docs/BTP* that provides official documentation for SAP BTP services, as shown in Figure 8. Best practices are defined for setting up the account model, security, and developing new applications.

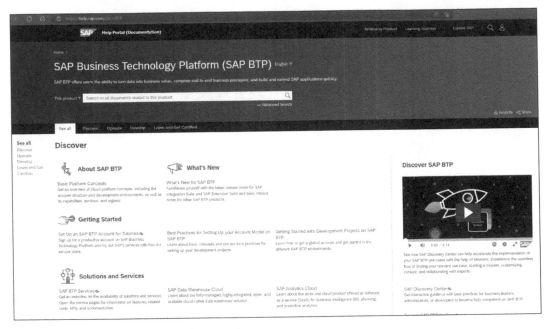

Figure 8 SAP Help Page for SAP BTP

Test-Taking Strategies

As you prepare for the certification and go through this book, we suggest you get some hands-on experience building a sample project using the trial account to reinforce the concepts taught here. All the code used to realize a sample scenario in this book is available in the Git repository at *http://s-prs.co/v540901*. There are several branches in this repository depicting various stages of development through various chapters.

When you take the exam, there will be 80 questions and 180 minutes, so you have more than 2 minutes to spend per question, which is enough time to reasonably answer the exam. During the exam, you need to keep intermediate goals to ensure you're on track. For example, you can aim to answer 30 questions every hour, so that you have enough time to see all questions. If you encounter an unknown question, don't get stuck at that point, rather you can flag that question and revisit it later. As there are no negative penalties for wrong answers, make it a point to answer all the questions to maximize your chance of clearing the exam. For questions that have more than one answer, take extra caution to pick all the right answers. If you get just one of the options wrong, the question will be marked as wrong.

Summary

In this introduction, we went through the steps for registering and scheduling the SAP certification exam. We described the exam structure and provided various other resources to augment your knowledge on the examination topics. We also explained a few strategies to ace the test.

We'll start covering the examination topics in the next chapter. See you there!

Chapter 1
SAP Business Technology Platform

Techniques You'll Master

- Describing cloud computing concepts, the need for cloud computing, and where SAP BTP fits in

- Understanding the SAP BTP account model and commercial model

- Recognizing the importance of the SAP BTP, Cloud Foundry environment, and its architecture and components

SAP Business Technology Platform (SAP BTP) is the central component of SAP's strategy for extending its various cloud and on-premise solutions. To appreciate SAP BTP's purpose in the modern digital enterprise, you need to understand cloud computing and the cloud service models. In addition, you'll learn about the account models and commercial models of SAP BTP so that you can confidently navigate the hierarchy inside and understand the impacts of subscribing to and consuming various services offered by SAP BTP. We'll also focus on the SAP BTP, Cloud Foundry environment, which is currently, by far, the most mature and feature-rich of the available environments.

Real-World Scenario

Conder a customer of yours is exploring SAP BTP as its digital transformation backbone. The customer wants to use SAP BTP as its extension platform but isn't aware of all the capabilities. The customer isn't sure where to get started or if SAP BTP can meet its business requirements. The customer is also wary of committing to SAP BTP as he isn't sure how to estimate the monthly costs involved in operating SAP BTP.

As an SAP BTP consultant, you need to be aware of various information sources available to guide a prospective customer. You need to be aware of various other platform-as-a-service (PaaS) offerings in the market and explain how the capabilities of SAP BTP can be advantageous when extending SAP solutions. You also need to know the technical components of SAP BTP to convince the prospective customer that there is no vendor lock-in or technology lock-in when you choose SAP BTP.

1.1   Objectives of This Portion of the Test

This portion of the test checks your understanding of the concepts regarding SAP BTP. It's important to understand the account model of SAP BTP along with its various available environments. Next, you're expected to have deep knowledge of the SAP BTP, Cloud Foundry environment, as well as its general related concepts.

Note
The SAP BTP topics make up more than 12% of the total exam.

1.2   Cloud Computing

Cloud computing is revolutionizing IT landscapes worldwide. Let's discuss what cloud computing is, the various as-a-service models, and where SAP BTP fits in.

Traditionally, enterprises owned and operated their computing resources within their premises. However, this strategy came with several problems:

- High cost of acquiring, installing, and configuring on-premise infrastructure
- Not optimum to purchase high configuration infrastructure for peak loads (e.g., during Black Fridays) and let it idle during nonpeak loads
- Inability to quickly try new software and hardware due to constraints in purchasing and configuring

Enterprises are using cloud computing as a solution to these problems. Cloud computing refers to the delivery of various computing resources over the internet. Computing resources can be servers, storage, applications, virtual machines, development tools, networking capabilities, and others. The provider of computing resources is called a cloud provider.

1.2.1   Types of Cloud Computing

Primarily, there are three types of cloud computing scenarios, depending on how the computing resources are provisioned:

- **Public cloud**

  In a public cloud scenario, a cloud provider's infrastructure is shared across its customers. This is called a multitenant environment where a cloud provider's computing infrastructure and other resources are partitioned based on customer (tenant) requirements. It's the cloud provider's responsibility to install, configure, update, and even scale on demand. Customers are charged only for the part of the infrastructure they consume, thus optimizing their costs.

  However, there are a few limitations to this option. Customers can't customize the resource because it's shared by other customers as well. In addition, a few customers have security concerns as their data might be sitting next to their competitor's data, and a software bug or attack might inadvertently expose their critical data to competitors. In addition, in industries such as finance and health care, legal compliance issues may prevent certain customers from using the public cloud.

- **Private cloud**

  A private cloud can solve the limitations of the public cloud, but at an extra cost. In a private cloud scenario, a customer gets dedicated computing resources, such as servers or databases, for customers' requirements. No other customer of the cloud provider will share these resources. Unlike public clouds, services are usually available only inside the customer's firewall, thus increasing the security of the applications.

  Private clouds were traditionally built and run on-premise. However, today, it's common to rent data centers owned by third parties (service providers).

- **Hybrid cloud**

  Enterprise needs are rarely completely met by either a private cloud or public cloud alone, and require a hybrid cloud approach. For example, parts of enterprise data are sensitive, requiring a private cloud. However, there might be another set of nonsensitive business processes and applications that can be efficiently hosted on a public cloud.

  A hybrid cloud refers to an IT landscape that is a mix of on-premise resources, private cloud resources, and public cloud resources. This is a very common approach with most customers these days to optimize their costs and tap into the advantages of both public and private cloud approaches.

A Typical Cloud Journey

For many enterprises, the cloud journey starts with a private cloud. Later, a few non-mission-critical services start moving to the public cloud, resulting in a hybrid cloud landscape. Gradually, as the enterprise gains confidence and the concept of the cloud becomes acceptable within the organization, more and more services move to the public cloud, retaining only a few resources on-premise or on a private cloud.

1.2.2   Cloud Computing Models

In the on-premise world, the entire IT infrastructure, starting from the server, storage, operating system, application runtime, and applications, is built and maintained by the enterprise itself. When the enterprise decides to go the cloud way, it need not be an all-or-none approach. That is, an enterprise can decide to source only a few resources via the cloud provider and can decide to take care of other resources itself.

Based on which resources are provided by the cloud provider, the cloud model can be classified into three types:

- **Infrastructure-as-a-service (IaaS)**

  In this option, as shown in Figure 1.1, the hardware part of the landscape, that is, physical application servers, networking between various servers, and storage servers are provided as resources by the cloud provider. The cloud provider is responsible for handling the virtualization and scaling the hardware when required. The customer is responsible for installing the operating system and the application runtime, and deploying the application. Amazon Web Services (AWS), Microsoft Azure, Google Cloud (previously called Google Cloud Platform), and IBM Cloud are a few popular IaaS providers.

  In a typical SAP landscape using IaaS, an enterprise customer would buy the required compute resources and memory as services from an IaaS provider, and then install their own SAP S/4HANA software on those. It's the customer's responsibility to maintain the SAP S/4HANA software, while it's the IaaS provider's responsibility to maintain the hardware and its performance, respond to scaling requests by the customer, and take care of the safety and security of the hardware.

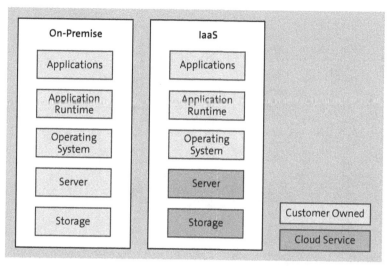

Figure 1.1 Comparing On-Premise and Infrastructure-as-a-Service

Note
SAP works with most of the popular IaaS providers and builds a partnership with them to provide prebuilt SAP-certified IaaS workloads, making it easy for SAP customers to confidently choose from the available options.

- **Software-as-a-service (SaaS)**
  In this model, as shown in Figure 1.2, the cloud service provider provides the entire application to the end users. The consumer uses the application to meet his needs, but the application acts as a black box to the end user. That is, the end user doesn't have to take care of any of the application development, development tools, application servers, databases, and hardware infrastructure.

  The email service that we use every day is an example of SaaS. When we use an email service such as Gmail, Outlook, or Yahoo! mail, we're not worried about how the application is built or where is the server running the application. A few examples of enterprise SaaS products are SAP S/4HANA Cloud, SAP Success-Factors, Salesforce, GitHub, Workday, and Zoho.

- **Platform-as-a-service (PaaS)**
  This option is a cloud model that provides services between PaaS and IaaS. In addition to IaaS, PaaS provides the operating system, databases, developer tools, various application runtimes, and platform services such as auditing and logging. PaaS providers can provide a multitude of services to improve developer productivity and, in some cases, provide focused domain and product-specific tools that differentiate them from other PaaS providers.

SAP BTP is one such example of PaaS. Other examples of PaaS products are AWS Elastic Beanstalk, Salesforce Platform, Microsoft Azure, IBM Bluemix, Red Hat OpenShift, Google App Engine, and VMware Tanzu Application Service (previously called Pivotal CF).

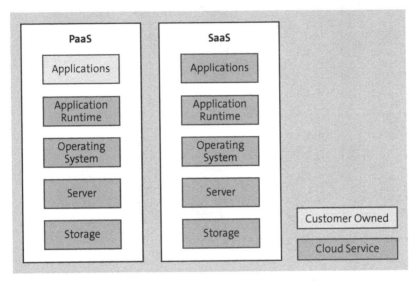

Figure 1.2 Platform-as-a-Service and Software-as-a-Service Models

1.3   SAP Business Technology Platform

As we discussed, the SAP BTP is SAP's technological foundation to aid customers' digital transformations into intelligent enterprises. It helps customers extend their on-premise and cloud solutions, integrate with third-party applications, and realize the true value of their data while providing the agility required for continuous innovation. This section covers SAP BTP's uniqueness, capabilities, and environment. We'll also discuss the SAP BTP cockpit, which is used for managing resources in SAP BTP.

1.3.1   The Uniqueness of SAP Business Technology Platform

Enterprises have a variety of options to choose from in a PaaS. Let's explore the salient features of SAP BTP and what makes it the go-to tool for SAP customers:

- **Unified experience**
  A customer might be using multiple SAP cloud or on-premise systems, but SAP BTP will be the go-to tool for integration, extension, and data-to-value scenarios. This uniformity means using common interfaces that result in better interoperability and reduced complexity. This unified experience and interoperability ensure that customers build innovative new solutions by mashing up data and processes from multiple backend systems.

- **Marketplace ecosystem**
  PaaS systems are usually focused on developers to provide tools, services, and application programming interfaces (APIs) to improve developer productivity. However, SAP BTP takes this to the next level by providing a platform for SAP partners to create new products for unique customer needs and makes it easy for customers to extend their industry solutions by consuming these partner-provided products and extensions.

- **Business focus**
  SAP BTP provides a multitude of business- and application-focused services, making it easy to add value to the business. For example, there are services for handling intelligent invoices and for handling country-specific business processes, as well as a semantic layer for business data providing a common data model for interoperability. These business services are continuously evolving, and SAP's strong domain knowledge is an advantage here.

- **Multi-cloud architecture**
  SAP BTP is built for openness, thus allowing flexibility to choose multiple industry-accepted hyperscalar providers for hosting your SAP BTP tenant. So, if you're a customer who is already using hyperscalers such as AWS, Google Cloud, Microsoft Azure, or Alibaba Cloud, you can choose the same hyperscaler and data center for hosting the SAP BTP deployment. Thus, SAP BTP will be near to your data and other hyperscaler-provided services. In the future, if you decide to change the enterprise hyperscaler for some reason, SAP BTP will be portable to your new hyperscaler without any lock-in.

  In addition to flexibility, multi-cloud architecture comes with an important capability to easily create mash-up applications using SAP data along with services offered by the hyperscaler's PaaS offering. For example, you can use Amazon SageMaker to create machine learning models from the SAP HANA Cloud or data lake services.

- **SAP product focus**
  SAP BTP focuses on SAP's on-premise and cloud solutions such as SAP S/4HANA and SAP S/4HANA Cloud, SAP SuccessFactors, SAP Customer Experience, SAP Business One, and others. SAP BTP has tools to extend the functionality of each of these solutions. SAP BTP also provides tools to uniformly connect to each of these SAP solutions and extract data to create data-to-value scenarios. SAP BTP provides several Software Development Kits (SDKs) and tools for developers to connect and build applications.

  Thus, SAP BTP's product focus helps SAP customers speed up their digital transformation in several ways.

1.3.2   SAP Business Technology Platform Capabilities

The SAP BTP capabilities can be broadly grouped into four categories based on the type of business value they add—database and data management, analytics, intelligent technologies, and application development and integration—as shown in Figure 1.3. These capabilities are also known as the four pillars of SAP BTP.

Database and Data Management	Analytics	Application Development and Integration	Intelligent Technologies
• SAP HANA Cloud • SAP SQL Anywhere • Redis on SAP BTP, Hyperscaler Option • PostgreSQL on SAP BTP, Hyperscaler Option • SAP Master Data Governance • SAP Data Intelligence • SAP Information Lifecycle Management • SAP PowerDesigner • SAP Landscape Transformation Replication Server	• SAP Analytics Cloud • SAP Crystal • SAP Data Warehouse Cloud • SAP Business Planning and Consolidation	**SAP Integration Suite** • SAP API Management • SAP Event Mesh • SAP Cloud Integration for Data Services **SAP Extension Suite** • SAP Business Application Studio • SAP AppGyver • SAP Launchpad • SAP Work Zone • SAP Mobile Services • SAP Workflow Management	• SAP AI Core • SAP Intelligent RPA • SAP Conversational AI • SAP AI Business Services • SAP IoT • SAP Edge Services

Figure 1.3 The Four Pillars of SAP BTP Capabilities

Let's dive further into these capabilities:

- **Databases and database management**
  SAP BTP provides multiple databases for both on-premise and cloud deployment. Based on your requirements (transactional or analytical), you can choose suitable databases. Figure 1.3 shows some of the available databases.

  SAP BTP provides data management solutions that help enterprises efficiently model, design, collect, analyze, manage the quality of, and replicate their data. Many of these products have overlapping features, so careful evaluation of these services is required to choose the right service for an enterprise's requirements.

- **Analytics**
  SAP BTP provides several services to analyze past performances and predict future business outcomes. Tools within SAP BTP help you connect to any data stored on-premise or in the cloud to fetch the data for performing analysis. *SAP Analytics Cloud* is one such solution that aims to become the go-to tool for all analytics needs. *SAP Web Analytics* is another product in SAP BTP that helps you to capture the usage data of various applications both on-premise and in the cloud.

- **Intelligent technologies**
  SAP BTP provides several tools to embed artificial intelligence into your business applications adding value and helping with effective decision-making.

SAP AI Core is an important service in this portfolio. It helps you create machine learning models, execute pipelines, and manage the lifecycle of an intelligent scenario.

SAP also provides several business services that focus on a specific business problem. For example, *Invoice Object Recommendation* helps to identify suitable general ledger accounts and cost objects to an incoming invoice. The *Document Classification* service helps to classify documents into user-defined tags.

- **Application development and integration**
  SAP BTP, as a developer platform, enables developers with tools and technologies for accelerating the development of new features, integrations, and extensions. SAP BTP services for application development and integration are grouped under two broad headings:
  - **SAP Extension Suite**
    SAP BTP provides several services for creating applications across channels such as desktops, tablets, and mobile phones. SAP Extension Suite is recognized as a Leader in *Gartner 2021 Magic Quadrant for Multiexperience Development Platforms*, as shown in Figure 1.4.

Figure 1.4 Gartner 2021 Magic Quadrant for Multiexperience Development Platforms

SAP Business Application Studio is a full-featured professional integrated development environment (IDE), while SAP AppGyver is a low-code, no-code application development platform.

SAP Mobile Services is a cloud service that helps developers create offline-enabled Android or iOS mobile user experiences.

SAP Launchpad, SAP Work Zone, and SAP Conversational AI help enterprises provide a digital experience and improve the productivity of their users.

- **SAP Integration Suite**
  SAP BTP provides several tools for achieving the integration of multiple SAP and non-SAP solutions. Per *Gartner Magic Quadrant for Enterprise Integration Platform as a Service*, as shown in Figure 1.5, SAP Integration Suite is recognized as a Leader.

Figure 1.5 Gartner Magic Quadrant for Enterprise Integration Platform-as-a-Service

A few important offerings of SAP Integration Suite are as follows:
- SAP BTP provides 160+ Open Connectors, which are prebuilt integrations that will speed up integration with non-SAP solutions.

- SAP API Management is a tool that allows enterprises to build and manage a uniform API layer so that various internal and external developer teams can have a uniform experience connecting with myriad solutions.
- SAP Event Mesh is a cloud service that allows applications to communicate via asynchronous events; for example, SAP and non-SAP products can publish and consume business events.

1.3.3   SAP Business Technology Platform Environments

Enterprises have diverse skill sets ranging from open-source technologies such as SAP BTP, Cloud Foundry environment and Kubernetes to SAP proprietary technologies such as ABAP. To accelerate the digital transformation journey, it's important to provide enterprises with multiple options so they don't have to rebuild their skill sets.

The other requirement for enterprises is the ability to create a variety of applications. Requirements can be creating a simple custom UI for existing APIs, extending the UI and data model of existing enterprise applications, creating multiple microservices, creating an application consuming those microservices, or creating a mash-up of multiple microservices for applications to consume.

To cater to this need, SAP BTP provides multiple environments for developers to develop and host applications. Each of these environments is a PaaS offering providing a runtime, services, and tools for developing and hosting an application.

At a high level, there are two technology stacks available on SAP BTP:

- SAP BTP, Neo environment
- Multi-cloud (or multi-environment) for SAP BTP

Neo was built using SAP's proprietary technologies. This is the foundation that was introduced along with SAP's foray into the cloud platform. It lets you create and host HTML5, Java, and SAP HANA extended application services. This technology stack is available only in SAP data centers and is called the SAP BTP, Neo environment, to compare it with other environments that were introduced along with the multi-cloud architecture.

SAP soon realized that managing data centers isn't its strength and is better managed by established IaaS solutions such as AWS, Microsoft Azure, and Google Cloud. This is how SAP BTP's multi-cloud architecture was born. SAP also decided to not reinvent the wheel by not investing in Neo, but rather looked for open-source platforms.

Within the multi-cloud foundation for SAP BTP, SAP decided to partner with the Cloud Foundry and other open-source technologies to provide multiple environments for its customers to choose from. With the multi-cloud strategy, Neo is no longer the platform of choice. SAP recommends Neo customers migrate to the multi-cloud foundation for SAP BTP, although there is no end-of-life or end-of-maintenance plan for the SAP BTP, Neo environment, yet.

There are three environments available in the multi-cloud foundation for SAP BTP:

- **SAP BTP, Cloud Foundry environment**
  SAP BTP, Cloud Foundry environment, is a PaaS offering based on the open-source platform managed by the Cloud Foundry Foundation. SAP BTP, Cloud Foundry environment, provides a layer of abstraction over the infrastructure provided by the IaaS providers so that developers need not worry about the infrastructure requirements for running the application. SAP BTP, Cloud Foundry environment, also allows you to develop applications using various standard or custom-built runtimes or build packs. Within SAP BTP multi-cloud environments, SAP BTP, Cloud Foundry environment, is the most mature and complete in terms of features, so there is a good chance that you might be picking it as the general platform of choice unless you have specific requirements.

  Because of its importance, we'll study the SAP BTP, Cloud Foundry environment, in greater detail in Section 1.6.

- **SAP BTP, ABAP environment**
  It's common for SAP customers to have huge in-house skill sets around ABAP technologies. To take advantage of these resources, SAP provides an ABAP PaaS option so that enterprises can create innovative applications using SAP BTP. Though a separate environment, SAP BTP, ABAP environment, is built using SAP BTP, Cloud Foundry environment, and is provided as a service to SAP BTP customers.

> **Tip**
> *Steampunk* is SAP's internal code name for SAP BTP, ABAP environment. Although you won't see this name in any official documentation, it's common to encounter this name in many SAP Community blogs and even in SAP TechEd keynotes.

Another important use case for SAP BTP, ABAP environment, is migrating your on-premise custom code to SAP BTP, ABAP environment, so that you can reduce the custom code on-premise but still reuse most of the custom code. Going forward, in upcoming releases of SAP S/4HANA, SAP will provide this ABAP environment within SAP S/4HANA and SAP S/4HANA Cloud so that it becomes simpler to build extensions by locally consuming released APIs.

- **SAP BTP, Kyma runtime**
  SAP BTP, Kyma runtime, is an environment based on the open-source *Kyma project*. Kyma is a cloud-native application platform that combines a Kubernetes cluster along with many best-in-class open-source components to develop and run cloud-native applications. You can connect multiple applications (e.g., SAP) to a Kubernetes cluster using an *application connector*. By doing this, you expose the applications' APIs and events. Next, you create serverless

functions and microservices to extend and integrate connected applications by consuming these APIs and events.

When you activate SAP BTP, Kyma runtime, you get the following:

- A fully managed Kubernetes cluster on the chosen IaaS and data center
- Open-source Project Kyma installed and provisioned via the cluster

1.3.4   SAP Business Technology Platform Cockpit

SAP BTP cockpit is a web-based tool for managing your resources, such as users and services, as well as monitor resource usage in SAP BTP.

You can log in to the SAP BTP cockpit via *https://cockpit.eu10.hana.ondemand. com/cockpit/*. In the URL, *eu10* refers to the region from which the cockpit is loading. You can replace that with the region that is closer to you so that there is less latency and better performance. You can use any of eu10 (Frankfurt), eu20 (Netherlands), ap10 (Sydney), us10 (US East), and us20 (US West). Once you log in to the cockpit, you see the **Account Explorer** page showing a list of directories and subaccounts within the global account. You can click on each of the subaccounts to navigate to the subaccount cockpit shown in Figure 1.6. In the subaccount cockpit, there is a navigation box to manage various features and resources ❶.

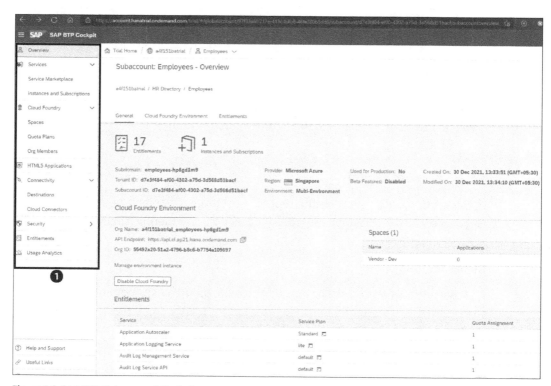

Figure 1.6 SAP BTP: Subaccount Cockpit

1.4   SAP Business Technology Platform Account Model

Resources inside SAP BTP are organized into various hierarchy levels. In this section, we'll discuss the various hierarchy levels and their purpose.

1.4.1   Feature Sets

The cloud management tools are provided for users to manage SAP BTP. This toolset, along with SAP BTP hierarchies, is undergoing an evolution as new features and tools are added. To ensure that users aren't inconvenienced, SAP has called the existing set of tools *feature set A* while building new tools and features into *feature set B*.

SAP automatically upgrades SAP BTP customers from feature set A to B in a phased manner. Customers can also request this transfer manually if they are ready for new features.

As of now, feature set B doesn't support custom identity providers (IdPs) for platform users. There is no other missing feature in feature set B compared to A.

Here are the important new features that are coming with feature set B:

- Introduction of a new optional hierarchy level called *Directory* that groups subaccounts inside a global account. It can be used to monitor resource usage and allocate entitlements as well.
- A new set of REST APIs to manage SAP BTP cockpit functionality
- A new set of command-line interface (CLI) tools to manage SAP BTP cockpit functionality
- Introduction of the ability to add a user-defined *label* to various hierarchy levels, so that they can be used to identify, search, and filter

1.4.2   Account Model

In this section, we'll cover the different account models available and walk through global accounts, directories, subaccounts, and user and member management.

Global Account

A global account represents a contract between an SAP customer and an SAP BTP customer. If you've signed multiple contracts with SAP, you'll see multiple global accounts when you log in to the SAP BTP cockpit. Customers can't manually create a global account unlike other hierarchy levels within SAP BTP.

Global accounts are independent of the IaaS provider, region, and environment. Global accounts can be of two types:

- **Enterprise account**

  An enterprise account is created when an enterprise signs a contract with SAP, which usually comes at a cost to the enterprise. Enterprises still have the option to use free-tier service plans. It's mandatory to have an enterprise account if you want to make productive use of SAP BTP.

- **Trial account**

  Any user or an enterprise can get a trial account online for test-driving SAP BTP features. This account doesn't incur any cost to the consumer, but it comes with several limits concerning the duration and amount of cloud resources the consumer can use.

Tip

Once a customer signs an SAP BTP contract, SAP creates a global account for the enterprise and sends the login details to the IT contact specified on the contract. This is how a customer gets the global account and starts accessing the SAP BTP cockpit to add more users and create an account model.

Directory

In feature set A, global account and subaccount are the only two hierarchy levels. In feature set B, the new Directory hierarchy structure is introduced. A directory is usually used to group multiple subaccounts and can have one or more subaccounts as its children. A directory can also contain one or more directories as its children. Example usages are as follows:

- Having a directory for each of the landscapes, that is, a directory for each development and quality subaccount.

- Having a directory for each of the departments; that is, finance departments and procurement departments have a directory each so that they can group their subaccounts and manage the costs.

- Having geography-wise (country/region) directories.

You can have up to five levels of directories. In that case, if you consider that the top level is a global account and the bottom level is a subaccount, by introducing five levels of directories, you can achieve up to seven levels of hierarchy in SAP BTP feature set B.

In addition to adding a hierarchy level to manage subaccounts, directories serve the following purposes:

- **Monitor usage**

  You can have a summarized usage view of all the directories and subaccounts inside a directory. For example, an enterprise customer using directories for each of its departments can now easily view the expenditure at the department level. Without this feature, it had to manually sum up all the usages.

- **Control entitlement and quota**
  You can assign entitlement and quotas to a directory so that it can be distributed further into its children (directories and subaccounts).
- **User and authorization management**
  You can maintain platform users and assign them predefined role collections to manage or view directory features. There is one role collection available to control administration (Directory Administrator) and one to view directory information (Directory Viewer).

Subaccount

Subaccount is an independent hierarchical structure that lets you group SAP BTP services. Data access and data visibility segregation are done at the subaccount level, so you may create a subaccount for each of the landscapes in your organization.

> **Note**
> In a productive landscape, SAP recommends at least three subaccounts, one each for development, testing, and production.

As a directory, a subaccount can also be used to represent an IT department or a part of it in many ways. A subaccount can represent a department (e.g., a separate subaccount for HR, finance, etc.), a separate subaccount for each landscape (development, testing), or a separate subaccount for a combination of landscape and department (HR-Dev, FI-DEV, HT-Test, FI-Test, etc.).

As shown in Figure 1.7, in feature set A, there can be only two hierarchy levels. A global account can have one or more subaccounts per the requirement.

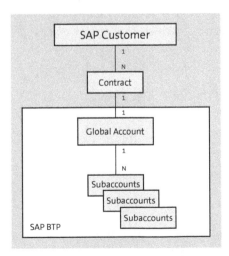

Figure 1.7 Account Model in Feature Set A

In feature set B, as shown in Figure 1.8, a subaccount can be created either as a child of a global account or as a child of a directory.

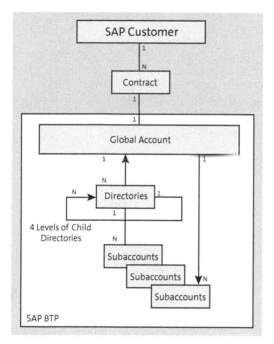

Figure 1.8 Account Model in Feature Set B

When you create a subaccount, you need to choose an IaaS provider and exactly one supported region. Choosing a region is an important decision and is dependent on many factors, as follows:

- **Location of end users**
  Choosing a subaccount in the region nearer to the physical location of your end users can help you deliver a better response time to them.

- **Location of other related services**
  If you need to create applications by mashing up SAP services with other services hosted on an IaaS, hosting them on the same IaaS and the same region can make the integration easier and result in better performance.

- **Availability of services**
  As of writing this book, according to SAP Discovery Center, there are 94 services on SAP BTP. Out of this, 84 are available on AWS, 49 are available on Microsoft Azure, 35 are available on Google Cloud, 28 are available on SAP, and 14 are available in Alibaba Cloud data centers. It's better to have an overview of the type of services that are going to be needed for your project so that you can make the right decision.

Tip

Creating a new subaccount doesn't incur any costs. But too many subaccounts can increase administrative tasks such as creating destinations for backend systems, so it's important to carefully design the account model.

User and Member Management

Two types of users use SAP BTP:

- **Business users or end users**
  These users log in to SAP BTP (most of the time via the enterprise's IdP) and make direct use of services and applications that are deployed on SAP BTP. These users are mostly business users performing the daily transactions of the enterprise. However, they can be developers as well, in which case, they are using developer tools such as SAP Business Application Studio. Typically, these users access the SAP BTP applications via a URL and aren't worried about how and where these applications operate.

- **Platform users**
  These are the users who log in to SAP BTP to manage the services and applications offered by SAP BTP. They don't directly consume the services. These are predominantly enterprise infrastructure teams (usually the SAP Basis team), security teams (to take care of authorization for both business and platform users), or developers (to troubleshoot and deploy services). These users use the SAP BTP cockpit UI, APIs, and CLIs to manage SAP BTP resources.

User management refers to managing role collections of a business user. To manage users, you need to go to the subaccount cockpit (Figure 1.9 ❶), click on **Users** ❷, click on a target user along with the right **Identity Provider** ❸, and then assign **Role Collections** ❹ relevant to the service or the application they need to access.

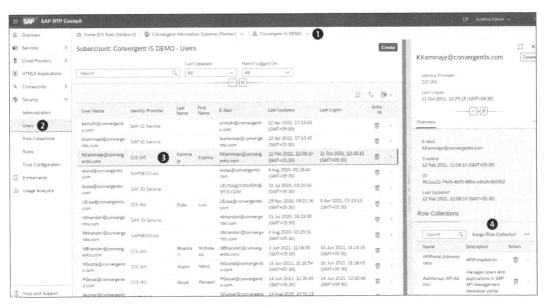

Figure 1.9 Role Collections in SAP BTP Cockpit

Member management refers to managing the authorization of platform users. In feature set A, at the global account level, there is a menu item for maintaining members. All members maintained here are assigned as global account administrators. In feature set B, you explicitly choose the user, select the IdP, and assign one of the **Global Account Administrator** or **Global Account Viewer** role collections. As you see in feature set B, SAP is making the experience of member management consistent with the experience of user management.

1.5   SAP Business Technology Platform Commercial Models

SAP BTP commercial models refers to the pricing involved in consuming SAP BTP services. In this section, let's explore the different pricing models available for enterprise accounts.

Commercial models are created per SAP's understanding of customer needs based on the business and commitment requirements of customers. There are two types of commercial models for SAP BTP:

- **Consumption-based commercial model**
  In this commercial model, you're charged based on the amount of cloud services you use.

- **Subscription-based commercial model**
  In this commercial model, you subscribe to one or more cloud services at a fixed cost per year.

In the following sections, we'll delve into these commercial models in detail. We'll also discuss the free-tier model, trial accounts, and different service plan models available.

1.5.1   Consumption-Based Commercial Model

The consumption-based commercial model charges you for your consumption. All SAP BTP services are allowed for usage in this model. Customers can switch on and off SAP BTP services as required and will be charged only for consumption. However, there are two options within this commercial model:

- **Cloud Platform Enterprise Agreement (CPEA)**
  This commercial model is suitable if you're familiar with SAP BTP services, how they are metered, and what your enterprise's requirement will be for a year. You can sign an agreement with SAP with a commitment to consume a specific amount of SAP BTP services, and SAP will throw in a price discount for your commitment to consumption. These are volume-based discounts and vary based on your commitment.

  When you pay for your yearly commitment (minimum of $10,713 USD per year, as of now), you get cloud credits, which can be thought of as a currency for using SAP BTP services. Every month, you get a statement of your usage and remaining cloud credits.

If you don't have enough cloud credits, you'll still be able to continue to use the SAP BTP services, but you'll be invoiced at the end of the month for the overage. In addition, for the overage usage, you won't get the discount that you got earlier when you signed the contract. You have to pay per the list price for those overages. However, you can purchase and top up your cloud credits so that there are no overages. So it's important to keep an eye on cloud credit consumption and plan well to get better pricing.

At the end of the year, if you have unused cloud credits remaining, those will expire as you had signed a contract with a commitment to consume a certain number of cloud credits.

Tip

CPEA is the most popular commercial model among SAP BTP customers.

- **Pay-As-You-Go for SAP BTP**
  What if you're very new to SAP BTP and not familiar with how many cloud credits you would require for a year? Pay-As-You-Go for SAP BTP can be the ideal way to start your journey with SAP BTP. There is zero commitment in this commercial model, and you get invoiced every month for the usage. The minimum contract duration is for three months, and the contract is auto-renewed at the end of it. Pricing can be expensive compared to CPEA because you don't get the discount that you get for the usage commitment. However, there is no risk of unused cloud credits expiring in this case.

  As you try SAP BTP with this commercial model and feel confident in your usage projection, you can transition to the CPEA licensing model.

1.5.2   Subscription-Based Commercial Model

Unlike the consumption model, only subscribed services are allowed for usage in the subscription-based model. When you sign a subscription-based contract, you choose which services to subscribe to and the usage amounts up to a predefined limit. At the end of every billing period, you'll incur the agreed charge irrespective of the actual consumption. In addition, you'll have the option to consume any service that isn't part of the subscription-based contract.

In a subaccount, you can activate both consumption-based and subscription-based models. In that case, whenever you consume a service, if that service is part of the subscription-based contract, no other consumption-based cost will be incurred. If the consumption goes beyond the metric specified in the subscription contract, then the consumption-based cost/contract (CPEA or PayG) will come into play.

1.5.3   Free-Tier

SAP BTP provides a free tier model for enterprise customers on a consumption-based commercial model (both Pay-As-You-Go for SAP BTP and CPEA). Even if you don't have an existing contract with SAP, as an individual or as an enterprise, you can opt for SAP BTP free tier. However, free-tier options are available only in selected geographies. In the free tier model, customers can use the eligible services without incurring any charge. The free tier plan for each service comes with limited features and consumption units.

When you instantiate an SAP BTP service, you need to specify a *service plan* (you'll learn more about the service plans in Section 1.5.5). You can specify the service plan as **Free** to ensure that you don't incur any charges.

If a service has a free service plan available, it will come with its own set of restrictions that can be accessed via SAP Discovery Center. If you need to use the service beyond the free limits, you need to select the subscription or instance and update the service plan to a non-free service plan.

If you're not an existing SAP customer, you can go to SAP Store and sign up for a PayG account, which is valid for three months. The account gets auto-renewed at the end of the duration. You need to submit credit card details so that SAP can charge you for using any services with paid plans. With this account, you can try various services with free tier plans. There will be no charges unless you consume a paid service.

When you decide to go for a paid plan, you can do so without signing any new contract or without any need for rebuilding your account hierarchy and redeploying your applications.

1.5.4   Trial Account

A trial account is for individuals to explore SAP BTP. It comes with a limit of 365 days. This can be a good option to explore various SAP BTP services and build and deploy applications. You can self-register for a trial account at the SAP Store website.

However, if you decide to use SAP BTP for productive usage, there is no direct path. You have to sign up for a production account (regular, non-trial account) and manually recreate your account model and deploy your applications.

Tip
While the trial account isn't intended for productive use, free tier service plans of SAP BTP services can be used for productive use cases.

1.5.5   Entitlements, Service Plans, and Quotas

All resources within SAP BTP are offered as services. Quotas and entitlements are used to control the delivery and measure the usage of these services. Quotas and entitlements are provided at the global account level, and administrators allocate them to directories and subaccounts.

Let's try to understand quotas and entitlements in SAP BTP by considering the context of the internet service that we receive at our homes.

Service Plans

Consider an internet provider providing four plans, as shown in Table 1.1.

Plan Name	Plan Detail	Cost
Home – Basic	40 Mbps, 100 GB 24-hour issue resolution	$30/month
Home – Premium	100 Mbps, 500 GB 24-hour issue resolution	$40/month
Office – Basic	1 Gbps, 1,000 GB 4-hour issue resolution	$80/month
Office – Premium	5 Gbps, 5,000 GB 4-hour issue resolution	$100/month

Table 1.1 Sample Internet Plans

In this example, each internet plan provides an internet connection at a specific speed while providing a data download bandwidth up to the specified limit. If you cross the allowed data limit, you'll be charged extra for additional data consumed. Each plan also comes with a service agreement to resolve any issues within 4 hours or 24 hours based on if you've chosen an office plan or a home plan.

Consider the first plan, Home – Basic. If you choose this plan, you can receive the internet at a speed of 40 Mbps for $30/month. You're also entitled to download data up to 100 GB and get any issues resolved within 24 hours. These rights come to you by choosing the *service plan*.

Similarly in SAP BTP, each service offers multiple service plans to its consumers. When you choose a service plan, you get to use the service with specified qualities. Table 1.2 shows SAP BTP's current pricing plans for CPEA for the SAP Application Logging service for SAP BTP, which is similar to Table 1.1. These specific numbers might be different when you read this book, and this is given only for reference.

Plan Name	Plan Detail	Cost
Lite	Logging data up to 10 MB/h	Free
Standard	Logging data up to 250 MB/h	$840/month
Large	Logging data up to 1,000 MB/h	$1,092/month

Table 1.2 SAP BTP Plans for the Application Logging Service

Entitlement and Quota

Entitlement specifies *which* service plans can you choose from and *how many* units of a specified service plan you can use. This quantity or unit of a service plan is defined as the *quota*.

Going back to our internet service example, the internet provider can specify that for a business premise, only office plans can be subscribed to. This can be compared to SAP BTP's entitlement concept. In the internet example, consider there is a maximum of five connections to a business premise. In that case, five can be interpreted as the quota.

Entitlements can be specified at the global account level, directory level (for feature set B), or subaccount level. Entitlements defined at a higher hierarchy level are by default available at lower hierarchy levels unless limited by specifying smaller entitlements (both service plans and quota) at the lower hierarchy level.

1.6   Cloud Foundry

In this section, we'll deep dive to understand the open-source Cloud Foundry project and how it's an important part of SAP BTP's multi-cloud strategy. Cloud Foundry is an open-source technology that is used by industry leaders to build their multi-cloud PaaS offerings. The Cloud Foundry Foundation (CFF) is a nonprofit organization set up to develop, maintain, and evangelize Cloud Foundry as the industry standard for delivering PaaS solutions.

Cloud Foundry allows developers to focus on developing cloud-native applications and not worry about the infrastructure. This is one of the main focuses of the Cloud Foundry project along with being a go-to technology for building cloud-native applications.

Cloud Foundry provides an abstraction layer above the IaaS providers, thus making it easy to port between public or private cloud providers. Cloud Foundry uses container technology to run your application and takes care of infrastructure configuration, management, securing, and scaling, thus letting the developers focus on code.

As of writing this book, CFF has certified seven distributions of Cloud Foundry. Each of these seven distributions uses the Cloud Foundry platform to deliver a multi-cloud PaaS for its customers. These are SAP BTP, IBM Cloud Foundry, Atos

Cloud Foundry, Cloud.gov, SUSE Cloud Application Platform, Swisscom Application Cloud, and VMware Tanzu.

Cloud Foundry uses BOSH, an open-source tool to connect to various IaaS providers to deliver a multi-cloud offering. Currently, CFF has certified 10 IaaS providers to run Cloud Foundry PaaS. A few popular ones are Google Cloud, AWS, and Microsoft Azure. In addition to using these IaaS providers, you can also choose your on-premise infrastructure to run Cloud Foundry to host applications. This would make it easy for you to move to IaaS providers in the future.

> **Note**
>
> Red Hat OpenShift is another comparable and popular PaaS platform, similar to Cloud Foundry.

1.6.1   Architecture

Cloud Foundry has several components that interact with each other for its efficient functionality. Figure 1.10 shows a list of the most important components, which are also described here:

- **Gorouter**
  Any requests to the Cloud Foundry system are handled by this component, which forwards the call to available application containers or the cloud connector component. It acts as a reverse proxy and a load balancer.

- **OAuth server**
  The OAuth server takes care of the authorization and other identity management functionality.

- **Cloud Controller**
  Cloud Controller is in charge of deploying the applications. When you push an app to the Cloud Foundry, Cloud Controller stages and runs the applications by triggering the processes in the Diego layer.

- **Service broker**
  Service brokers are responsible for providing the instances of all the bound services to each application.

- **Blob store**
  Cloud Foundry needs to store various binary files, such as application code, build code as droplets, and build packs for various supported runtimes. The blob store stores these artifacts.

- **Diego/Garden**
  Every app that is deployed to Cloud Foundry is run inside a Garden container. A Garden container provides an isolated environment to run processes, dedicated memory to run applications, and an isolated file system. Diego is a container orchestration component that manages the Garden containers inside Cloud Foundry. Diego accepts requests to run an application, creates and restarts

required containers, manages the container lifecycle, monitors containers, and logs the status.

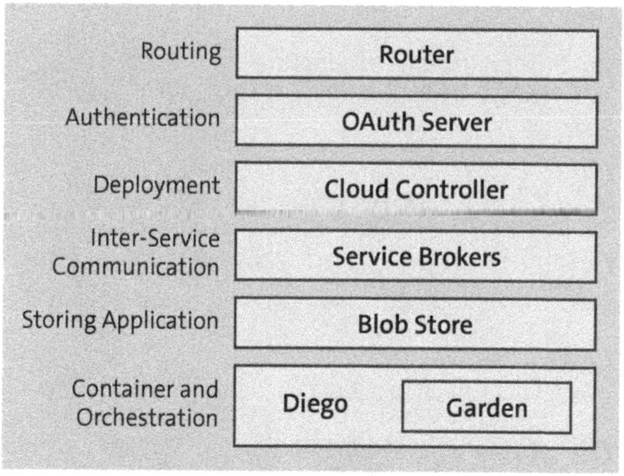

Figure 1.10 Cloud Foundry Components

Each of these Cloud Foundry components interacts using HTTP and Neural Autonomic Transport System (NATS) protocols. There are a few other components to perform logging, metrics capturing, and streaming logs.

1.6.2   Cloud Foundry Layers

A Cloud Foundry environment is organized as *orgs* and *spaces*. Let's understand their purpose and find out how to create these levels:

- **Org (organization)**
  Within Cloud Foundry, *org* or *organization* is a hierarchy level where resource quotas, services, applications, and users exist. Billing for resources happens at the organization level. In an enterprise, if you need a separation of resources and users, and if there is a need to monitor and control costs, then enterprises can create multiple organizations as needed.

  When you create a Cloud Foundry environment by clicking on **Enable Cloud Foundry** in an SAP BTP subaccount, it creates a Cloud Foundry organization. Because you can create only one Cloud Foundry instance within an SAP BTP subaccount, an SAP BTP subaccount and Cloud Foundry organization have a 1:1 relation.

- **Space**
  An organization is further divided into spaces. A space can have its quota. An organization's quota can be subdivided into space quotas. By assigning a separate quota at the space level, you can control and monitor the resource usage at the space level. If you don't assign a quota at the space level, then the space can use resources up to the parent org's quota limit.

> **Example**
> An example of a Cloud Foundry org and space hierarchy is as follows:
> - An org for each line of businesses (LoBs)
> - Three spaces for each org, one each for dev, staging, and production

1.6.3   Enabling Cloud Foundry in SAP Business Technology Platform

Within an SAP BTP subaccount, the Cloud Foundry environment isn't active by default. From the subaccount cockpit, you need to click on the **Enable Cloud Foundry** button, as shown in Figure 1.11 ❶.

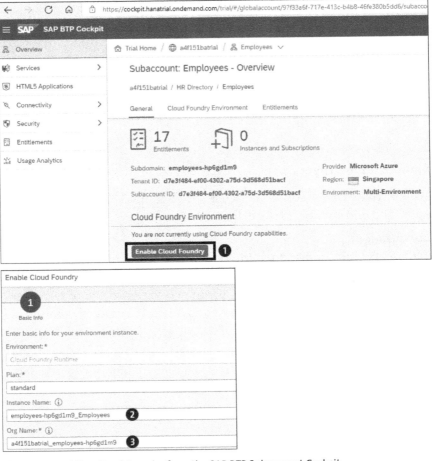

Figure 1.11 Enabling Cloud Foundry from the SAP BTP Subaccount Cockpit

You need to provide an SAP BTP-specific **Instance Name** ❷ and an **Org Name** ❸ that will be used as the name of the Cloud Foundry organization. Upon clicking on the **Create** button, a new Cloud Foundry organization will be created within a couple of minutes.

Within an organization, you need to have at least one space to consume or deploy any services.

1.6.4   Cloud Foundry Command-Line Interface

Cloud Foundry provides a CLI (client) to be used with various terminal tools. This CLI tool allows you to manage various Cloud Foundry resources such as services, applications, orgs, spaces, routes, and users.

Before you start using the Cloud Foundry CLI tool, you need to download and install the following CLI tools for your operating system from the official Cloud Foundry website:

- `cf login`
  The first command to be used in Cloud Foundry CLI is `cf login` to log in to the Cloud Foundry environment. As part of the login process, you need to provide the **API Endpoint** of your Cloud Foundry installation, which is the URL of the Cloud Controller component of your Cloud Foundry installation. You also need to choose an **Organization** and a **Space**. This is called the *target*. All further commands will be executed in the context of this target.

- `cf push`
  This is one of the *trademark* commands of Cloud Foundry. With this one command (after logging in to Cloud Foundry), the application gets uploaded into Cloud Foundry, gets staged, gets started, and becomes available on Cloud Foundry.

- `cf deploy`
  Many times, it's common to have multiple modules in your solution. For example, you may have a UI, a server, and database modules for your solution to work. Therefore, for making your solution available to users, you need to `cf push` each of these modules separately. But as they are logically related, SAP wanted to group them into one application (called a multi-target application [MTA]) and manage its lifecycle with one command. The result is the `cf deploy` command.

  This command comes from a Cloud Foundry CLI plug-in by the name *MultiApp*. Through this CLI plug-in, SAP provides multiple commands to manage an MTA. `cf deploy` can be used to deploy or sync an MTA.

1.6.5   Scaling a Cloud Foundry Application

One of the main advantages of running an application on the cloud is easy scalability. Scalability refers to the ability to handle higher loads in terms of concurrent traffic and processing demand.

When you deploy an application into Cloud Foundry, it creates a single instance of it on the cloud by default. This single instance has a fixed disk quota (disk space) and a fixed memory assigned. If you want your app to handle additional concurrent users performing multiple complex tasks, you need to scale the application. There are two options available, as shown in Figure 1.12:

- **Vertical scaling**
  Vertical scaling is all about making the current application instance more powerful by allocating more disk space and providing more memory (or even a powerful CPU) to handle higher loads. Vertical scaling usually involves downtime so that the container running the application instance is upgraded.

  In the Cloud Foundry CLI, you can use command `cf scale <application name> -k <disk space>` to set a disk space. For altering the memory limit, you can use the command `cf scale <application name> -m <memory>`.

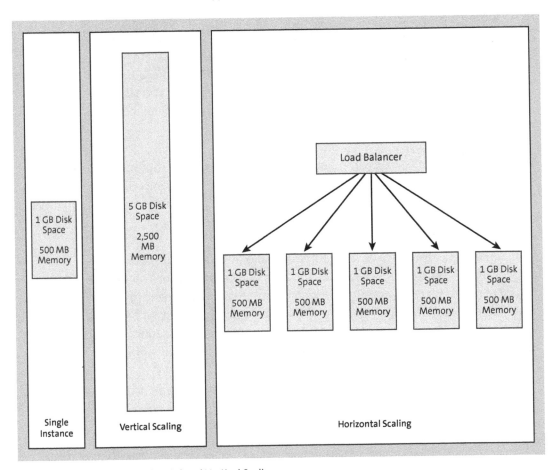

Figure 1.12 Horizontal and Vertical Scaling

- **Horizontal scaling**
  In the case of horizontal scaling, you add more instances to your application. This step requires a load balancer that can route and distribute the load equally among the application instances. As the current instance is undisturbed, adding

more instances doesn't need any interference with the running instance. Thus, horizontal scaling doesn't need any application downtime.

In the Cloud Foundry CLI, you can use the command `cf scale <application name> -i <number of instances>` to set the number of instances to run the application. Cloud Foundry uses a load balancer and distributes the load across the created instances.

Tip

SAP BTP provides the *Application Autoscaler* service that can be used to automatically increase or decrease the number of instances based on a schedule or based on various application parameters such as response time, memory, and resources used.

1.6.6   Past and Future of the Cloud Foundry Platform

Cloud Foundry was born as a small open-source project started by a few employees at VMWare in 2009 and named Cloud Foundry in 2011. In 2015, the Cloud Foundry Foundation was launched to manage the Cloud Foundry project and the project came out of VMWare. In 2017, Cloud Foundry official training and Certified Developer courses were released.

Cloud Foundry uses Docker containers along with the Diego container orchestration engine. However, Kubernetes is the alternative open-source, industry-leading, latest-technology container orchestration engine, so it's natural for Cloud Foundry to embrace Kubernetes to make Cloud Foundry lighter, easier to maintain, and less expensive. There have been several efforts to bring Kubernetes to Cloud Foundry. These projects aim to replace the Diego and Gardner toolchain with the Kubernetes-based toolchain.

Community efforts to bring Kubernetes to Cloud Foundry started with the project KubeCF. KubeCF approaches the goal with an outside-in approach, that is, keeping the developer experience of Cloud Foundry intact while changing the internals.

Then came the community project cf-for-k8s. The cf-for-k8s project follows an inside-out approach; that is, it's a pure Kubernetes native approach that would result in a change in the current Cloud Foundry developer experience. KubeCF was the first project, but it lost popularity, and cf-for-k8s gained traction.

The community learned from the previous iterations of KubeCF and cf-for-k8s and recently launched a new project, Korifi, in May 2022. Korifi, which is currently in a beta version, is a completely different implementation rewritten to resolve some of the architectural limitations of cf-for-k8s. Korifi aims to take away the complexities of Kubernetes and make it easy for developers to use. The industry hopes Korifi is successful so that the benefits of both Cloud Foundry and Kubernetes reach customers and their projects.

1.7   SAP Discovery Center

SAP Discovery Center is your go-to tool for discovering, planning, learning, and kick-starting your SAP cloud projects (*https://discovery-center.cloud.sap/*). On a high level, it contains two types of content:

- **Missions**
  Cloud journeys for enterprises usually involve steep learning curves and high skills for successful cloud projects. Missions are a catalog of common use cases (technical and business) involving SAP BTP. Click **Missions** on the homepage to see the step-by-step guides on how to achieve those use cases along with videos and documentation. The best part is that for each mission, there are dedicated experts assigned from SAP with whom you can talk and seek guidance on best practices.

- **Services**
  Under **Services** on the homepage, the SAP Discovery Center provides a catalog of all the services available on SAP BTP. This list can be filtered by the commercial model, IaaS provider, and the regions for each IaaS provider.

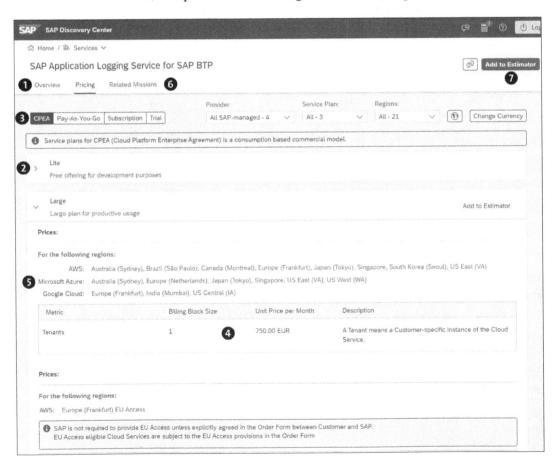

Figure 1.13 Features of SAP Discovery Center

For each service, you'll find the following information, as shown in Figure 1.13:

❶ Description and further resources of the service

❷ Available service plans

❸ Available commercial (license) models

❹ Pricing details for each commercial model

❺ IaaS provider and region

❻ Related missions using the service, and featured customer success stories using the service (located inside **Related Missions**)

❼ Ability to add the service to the Estimator tool

1.8   Important Terminology

In this chapter, the following terminology was used:

- **Cloud Foundry**
  Cloud Foundry is an open-source PaaS solution that can be deployed on various IaaS providers, providing a multi-cloud experience. It aims to let developers concentrate on coding and not worry about infrastructure and scaling.

- **Cloud-native**
  This refers to a way of building applications targeting cloud providers to take advantage of cloud deployment, namely scalability, speed of development, agility, fault tolerance, and openness for integration.

- **Cloud Platform Enterprise Agreement (CPEA)**
  A CPEA is signed with SAP when a customer knows the number of resources that will be consumed and can commit to a specified amount of consumption of SAP BTP. Customers will get a volume-based discount on the cost of the commitment. Any unused consumption quota will expire at the end of the agreement duration. All resources of SAP BTP are available for consumption in this model.

- **Consumption model**
  This is a commercial model available in SAP BTP where the customer is charged based on the consumption of resources.

- **Garden and Diego**
  Garden is a containerization technology that Cloud Foundry relies on. Diego is the container orchestration tool that manages Garden containers. Garden is one of the first containerization technologies that came about much before the arrival of Docker. In the same analogy, Diego can be compared to Kubernetes.

- **Hybrid cloud**
  This is a scenario where a consumer's IT infrastructure is made up of both on-premise and public cloud resources. This can let the consumer take advantage of both flavors of cloud computing based on the requirements.

- **Infrastructure-as-a-service (IaaS)**
  In this cloud model, computing infrastructures such as databases, compute resources, networks, and virtual machines are made available as a service. Consumers can easily scale up or scale down their subscriptions and also be free from maintaining this infrastructure.

- **Kyma**
  Kyma is one of several platforms available for running your applications in SAP BTP. It's a serverless option built on the industry-standard Kubernetes runtime.

- **Pay-As-You-Go for SAP BTP model**
  The Pay-As-You-Go for SAP BTP model is a consumption model where there is no commitment of usage. Customers can choose this model if they aren't confident with SAP BTP pricing. Customers will be charged per their consumption. However, there are no commitment-based discounts in this model.

- **Platform-as-a-service (PaaS)**
  This is a cloud model where the developers are the primary consumers. This offering provides the developers with all the tools and technologies to build new applications and develop extensions to current applications.

- **Private cloud**
  In this scenario, the computing resources are dedicated to a consumer and not shared with others. As the resources are dedicated, consumers can customize the resources according to their needs without affecting other consumers.

- **Public cloud**
  This is a type of cloud-computing option where computing resources are provided over the public internet and shared by all of its subscribers. The cloud service provider takes the responsibility of owning, setting up, and maintaining these cloud resources.

- **SAP Business Technology Platform (SAP BTP)**
  SAP BTP is a PaaS offered by SAP to build extensions to SAP's portfolio products. It also lets developers create new applications and integrate SAP products with third-party solutions.

- **Software-as-a-service (SaaS)**
  This is a cloud model in which a functional software application is offered for subscription. Consumers can use this software to meet their business requirements and are free of developing, maintaining, and running the software.

- **Subscription model**
  In this commercial model, the customer is charged a fixed subscription cost for specific SAP BTP services. The actual consumption doesn't affect the cost. Customers can't use any services that aren't part of the subscription agreement unless they have other consumption-based agreements for using them.

1.9 Practice Questions

1. Within SAP BTP, a region is chosen at which level?
   - ☐ **A.** Global account
   - ☐ **B.** Directory
   - ☐ **C.** Subaccount
   - ☐ **D.** Space

2. What are the features for the Directory hierarchy level in an SAP BTP account model? (There are two correct answers.)
   - ☐ **A.** Entitlements and quotas can be assigned at the directory level.
   - ☐ **B.** A commercial model can be assigned at the directory level.
   - ☐ **C.** A region can be assigned at the directory level.
   - ☐ **D.** Usage can be monitored at the directory level.

3. With this commercial model, you'll get charged a fixed amount every billing cycle.
   - ☐ **A.** Pay-As-You-Go model
   - ☐ **B.** CPEA model
   - ☐ **C.** Subscription model
   - ☐ **D.** Prepaid model

4. Which SAP BTP environment gives you a Kubernetes cluster when activated?
   - ☐ **A.** SAP BTP, Kyma runtime
   - ☐ **B.** SAP BTP, ABAP environment
   - ☐ **C.** SAP BTP, Neo environment
   - ☐ **D.** SAP BTP, Cloud Foundry environment

5. Which resource is NOT available on a subaccount?
   - ☐ **A.** Application
   - ☐ **B.** Virtual machine
   - ☐ **C.** Services
   - ☐ **D.** Subscription

6. Who is NOT a platform user in SAP BTP?
   - ☐ **A.** Administrator
   - ☐ **B.** Security admin

☐   **C.** Developer

☐   **D.** Business user

7.   What does an SAP BTP environment provide you? (There are three correct answers.)

☐   **A.** Runtime

☐   **B.** Tools

☐   **C.** Services

☐   **D.** Virtual machine

8.   A contract between SAP and an SAP customer is represented by which of the following?

☐   **A.** Global account

☐   **B.** Subaccount

☐   **C.** Directory

☐   **D.** Space

9.   Within SAP BTP, which environment would you use if you want to build serverless functions and containerized microservices?

☐   **A.** SAP BTP, Cloud Foundry environment

☐   **B.** SAP BTP, Kyma runtime

☐   **C.** SAP BTP, Neo environment

☐   **D.** SAP BTP, ABAP environment

10.   If you don't assign a quota at the space level, then which of the following is true?

☐   **A.** No resources can be consumed at the space level.

☐   **B.** There is no limit to the number of resources that can be used by the space.

☐   **C.** Space can consume resources up to the parent org's quota.

☐   **D.** Space can use only free services.

11.   What is true about a Cloud Foundry space? (There are two correct answers.)

☐   **A.** One space gets automatically created when you activate Cloud Foundry within an SAP BTP subaccount.

☐   **B.** You need to manually create a space.

☐   **C.** Space is mandatory if you want to deploy an application to Cloud Foundry.

☐   **D.** Space isn't mandatory for subscribing to a service from SAP Service Marketplace.

12. To not incur any charges if I don't consume SAP BTP services in a billing cycle, which commercial model should I use?

☐ **A.** Pay-As-You-Go model

☐ **B.** CPEA model

☐ **C.** Subscription model

☐ **D.** Prepaid model

13. What is NOT true about the SAP free tier?

☐ **A.** You need to submit credit card details to get it.

☐ **B.** It has no expiry date.

☐ **C.** There is an easy path to consuming paid plans.

☐ **D.** It's available only for existing SAP customers.

1.10   Practice Question Answers and Explanations

1. Answer: **C**

   A region is a physical location where the data center is located. When you create a subaccount, you need to choose a region that is provided by the IaaS providers. You can optimize the overall performance of your applications by selecting a region that is closer to your users and other IT infrastructures.

2. Answer: **A and D**

   Entitlement and quotas can be assigned at the directory level, and the usage of those resources can be measured as well. The commercial model is assigned only at the global account level. A region is assigned at the subaccount level.

3. Answer: **C**

   The subscription model allows you to access predefined services at a fixed cost. CPEA and Pay-As-You-Go are consumption-based models, so there is no upper limit on the billing.

4. Answer: **A**

   Kyma is an open-source project used to provide an environment on SAP BTP that will create a fully managed Kubernetes cluster when activated.

5. Answer: **B**

   A virtual machine is an IaaS service and is usually not part of a PaaS offering, so an SAP BTP subaccount doesn't provide a virtual machine. The subaccount provides resources to develop, deploy, and run various applications and services. It also allows you to subscribe to SAP and other third-party-built multi-tenant applications.

6. Answer: **D**

   The business user is an end user of applications hosted on SAP BTP. A platform user manages the SAP BTP platform by deploying applications, managing resources, and assigning authorizations to end users.

7. Answers **A, B, and C**

   Each environment provides a runtime and the required infrastructure for running applications. Next, it provides various services for building the application. It also provides tools such as a Software Development Kit (SDK) for making it easy to consume and expose services.

8. Answer: **A**

   An SAP BTP contract between SAP and its customer is represented by a global account. A global account won't be created by the customer; it's created by SAP upon signing a contract.

9. Answer: **B**

   SAP BTP, Kyma runtime, is built for creating containerized microservices and serverless functions.

10. Answer: **C**

    Assigning a quota at the space level is optional. If you don't assign a quota at the space level, then space can consume resources up to the org's quota limit. By assigning a quota at the space level, you can limit and monitor the costs at the space level.

11. Answer: **B and C**

    Space is an additional hierarchy level within Cloud Foundry that can be used to limit resource usage and control costs. Once you've enabled the SAP BTP, Cloud Foundry environment, an organization gets created. You need to manually create each space that you need. A space is mandatory for subscribing to any services and deploying any applications into Cloud Foundry.

12. Answer: **A**

    In the Pay-As-You-Go model, there is no minimum charge. You get charged only for the consumption of the resources. In CPEA, you have to commit and pay for a predetermined quota of consumption. In the subscription model, you have a fixed cost per billing cycle despite your actual usage.

13. Answer: **D**

    When you register at the SAP Store and choose the Pay-As-You-Go commercial model, you need to provide your details along with credit card details. You get an account with a default validity of three months that will get auto-renewed. There are no more expiry dates as you would see in a trial account. You can keep the cost as zero as long as you consume only free plans of SAP BTP services. If you're an existing customer with an existing SAP BTP account, you'll automatically have free plans available. However, you can register to get these benefits even as a new SAP customer.

1.11   Test Takeaway

Cloud computing is all about providing and using various computing resources via the internet for a fee. SAP BTP is one such cloud service for SAP's customers where a platform for developing new and extension applications is on offer. SAP BTP provides several hierarchical levels to maintain and organize resources within it. Once you start accessing SAP BTP, there are several commercial models for purchasing the various resources and features offered as services. Several platforms are available in SAP BTP, including the open source and industry-accepted Cloud Foundry.

1.12   Summary

In this chapter, you learned the pain points of the traditional on-premise IT infra-structure and how cloud computing is the way forward as a solution. We covered the types of cloud computing and models of cloud computing based on the type of service offered via the cloud.

You also learned the concept of a platform and how SAP BTP provides multiple PaaS offerings and provides more choices. We discussed the importance of multi-cloud and its advantage to customers, and then we set on to discover the capabilities of SAP BTP based on the various services offered.

You can now recognize the importance of Cloud Foundry to SAP BTP in enabling the multi-cloud approach, as explored the Cloud Foundry concepts and how it's integrated within SAP BTP.

You also learned how the SAP BTP account model allows users to easily manage the cloud resources. The commercial model was also discussed to explain how to optimize the costs associated with consuming SAP BTP services.

In the next chapter, we'll explore various web development standards and concepts.

Chapter 2
Web Development Standards

Techniques You'll Master

- Understanding web development standards
- Using APIs and the importance of REST and OData
- Working with JSON and YAML data formats.
- Building a twelve-factor app

Web technologies are evolving at a fast pace. Web development standards are established by various independent bodies specifying how the developers must build products, how they interact with other standards, and how usability and accessibility features are used. This chapter covers different web standards and data formats you use for configuration files and data transfer over the internet. You'll also learn about the twelve-factor app principles for building and designing resilient applications.

Real-World Scenario

You're developing a modern, enterprise-grade resilient web application and need to deploy this application to an industry-standard cloud provider. You then need to understand which types of application programming interfaces (APIs) are required and the guidelines to develop resilient applications.

2.1   Objectives of This Portion of the Test

This portion of the test checks your understanding of the web development standards. Application programming interfaces (APIs) play a significant role in moving data to and from user interfaces (UIs). You're expected to know about representational state transfer (REST) principles in API design and development. You'll also have to learn about Open Data Protocol (OData), a REST-based protocol for building and consuming RESTful APIs. You'll learn about Yet Another Markup Language (YAML) and JavaScript Object Notation (JSON), which are useful for defining configuration files, as well as the best practices for developing resilient applications.

Note
Web development standards topics make up less than 8% of the total exam.

2.2   Application Programming Interface, Representational State Transfer, and Open Data

For different systems to communicate with each other to exchange data, you need an interface called an API. There are various ways to architect the APIs, and REST, Simple Object Access Protocol (SOAP), and OData are the most popular formats. We'll discuss these in detail in the following sections.

2.2.1   API

APIs enable companies to securely connect their internal applications or external partners to transfer data both ways. An API will have a set of protocols that defines the rules of how it's accessed. Consumers don't need to know how an API is implemented; they only need the documentation that is explicitly provided or comes automatically with the API.

The role of an API is to act as an interface or an intermediate layer that transfers the data between multiple partners, as shown in Figure 2.1. The actors and their responsibilities in Figure 2.1 are as follows:

- Consumers, who can be the end users and third-party companies, request the API to access the data from their applications.
- API producers take care of creating, hosting, and managing the API.
- The API gets the request from the consumers, validates it, and queries the database to fetch the data.
- Data is processed and sent back to the consumer applications.

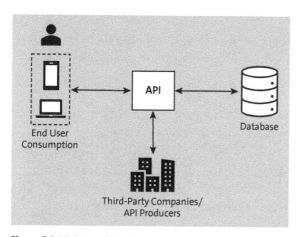

Figure 2.1 High-Level API Design

APIs should not expose all the data of the database or the server; they should only show the required and authorized information when they are accessed. For instance, A bank application only lets you access your account details; it should not show other users' accounts. So it's recommended to include robust security protocols while designing an API.

There are different ways to architect the APIs, and the widely used architectures are SOAP and REST. SOAP is a stricter protocol with defined security rules and is standardized by the World Wide Web Consortium (W3C), which uses XML payload to transfer the data between systems. Although SOAP used to be popular, the REST protocol is now used mainly for developing APIs. In the next section, we'll cover REST in detail, which is the most used architecture today.

2.2.2   REST

REST is a famous web API architecture that is mainly used for lightweight web services and mobile applications. Unlike SOAP, which has stricter protocols, REST comes with guiding principles, and the APIs that implement these guidelines are referred to as RESTful APIs. Following are the guiding principles and constraints that a RESTful API should have:

- **Client-server architecture**

  The client-server architecture enforces the separation of client and server, which allows them to be updated and evolve independently. The client will only request the server for the data using an API, and the server can only return the data via HTTP requests without interacting with the clients.

  For example, consider a mobile bank application (client), where only the application is available in the user's mobile phone, but not the database or the business logic of the bank process. Users can only see their account details via the API provided by the bank. The business logic and database reside in the server, where the requests coming from the API are authenticated and processed.

- **Statelessness**

  Statelessness requires that all the requests originated from the client be unconnected, and each request should have all the information to complete the request.

- **Cacheability**

  Cache ability suggests that, when required, resources should be cacheable on the client side or server side to increase the performance of applications.

- **Layered system**

  The layered system in a server takes care of the request in different stages (firewall, load balancing, security, etc.). The server should hide all these processes from the client and only respond to the request by returning the data.

- **Uniform interface**

  Uniform interface mandates that all API requests should have a standard format. The following multiple constraints should be applied while designing an API:

  - All the resources requested from the client must be uniquely identifiable.
  - Server responses should have uniform representations, including metadata, which API consumers can use to modify the resources in the server.
  - Response messages from the server should be informative enough for the client to process them.
  - Hyperlinks to different actions should be available in the server response to discover the available resources the API needs.

- **Code on demand**

  Code on demand is the ability to send the executable code to the client to customize different functionalities. For instance, the client can use Java applets or JavaScript code to extend its functionality.

2.2.3 OData

OData is a REST-based protocol approved by International Organization for Standardization/International Electrotechnical Commission (ISO/IEC) and used for building and consuming RESTful APIs. It helps you focus on business logic without needing to worry about the different API approaches in defining your request, response, status codes, URL conventions, query options, and so on. OData supports XML-based AtomPub and JSON formats.

OData protocol follows these design principles to achieve the uniformity of both the data and the data model:

- Follow the REST principles as OData is the best way to REST.
- Support the API extension without breaking the client's functionality.
- Keep it simple by addressing the common functionalities and providing the extensions wherever required.
- Prefer mechanisms that work on a variety of data sources. Don't assume a relational data model.
- Build incrementally—a basic, compliant service should be easy to build, and additional work should be necessary only to support additional capabilities.

In SAP, the OData protocol is primarily used to generate the APIs. For example, SAP S/4HANA uses the ABAP RESTful Application Programming Model (RAP) to generate OData V2 and V4 services, and in SAP BTP, the SAP Cloud Application Programming model is used for generating the OData services. Even the UI, SAPUI5, has built-in libraries to consume OData V2 and V4 models, which use metadata and annotations to construct the UI dynamically. A typical OData service looks like Figure 2.2.

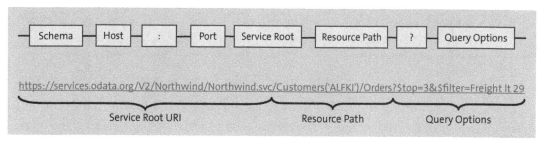

Figure 2.2 OData URI Components

Let's look at the OData request URL and its components in detail:

- **Service root URI**
  The service root URI is the root of an OData service through which different resources can be accessed and created. OData services provide two types of metadata documents, as follows:

– A *service document* has all top-level feeds so clients can discover them and access only those required (see Figure 2.3). The service document is available by accessing the service root URI directly.

```
<service xml:base="https://services.odata.org/V2/Northwind/Northwind.svc/">
<workspace>
<atom:title>Default</atom:title>
<collection href="Categories">
<atom:title>Categories</atom:title>
</collection>
<collection href="CustomerDemographics">
<atom:title>CustomerDemographics</atom:title>
</collection>
<collection href="Customers">
<atom:title>Customers</atom:title>
</collection>
<collection href="Employees">
<atom:title>Employees</atom:title>

.
.|
.

.
</workspace>
</service>
```

Figure 2.3 Service Document

Example
To see an example of an OData service, go to: *http://s-prs.co/v540902*.

– A *service metadata document* is usually referred to as metadata. This document describes the Entity Data Model (EDM) for a given service. You can get all the information about different resources, associations, and properties from the EDM.

Example
To access the metadata of an OData service, you must add *$metadata* to the end of the service as shown in this URL: *https://services.odata.org/V2/Northwind/Northwind.svc/$metadata*.

As you can see in Figure 2.4, the metadata document provides all the entities, properties, and relations (navigation properties). Along with the properties of the individual entity, it also returns the key properties. For instance, the customer entity has CustomerID' as the key property. An *entity* is a single resource; it can be a customer, order, and so on. *Entity type* describes an entity (properties, keys, navigations, etc.), and *entity set* is a collection of entities. For instance, an entity set can be customers (multiple), orders, and so on.

Note
The EDM is a set of concepts that describe the structure of data, regardless of its stored form.

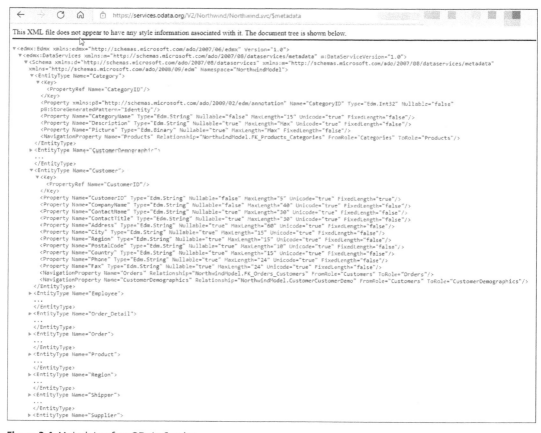

Figure 2.4 Metadata of an OData Service

- **Resource path**

  The resource path URI identifies the resources of an OData service such as customers, a single customer, or orders related to a single customer. We'll look at each of them here:

  - **Requesting resources (entity set)**

    These collections are called entity sets. Accessing each entity set will provide the data related to it. For instance, the categories entity set will return all the categories, and the customers entity set will give all the customers. In the following example, you can see the entity set *Customers* is added at the end of the URL to fetch the list of customers.

Example

To request an entity set, you need to access the URL as shown in the example at: *http://s-prs.co/v540903*.

As you can see in Figure 2.5, the response resources are in XML format because, by default, OData V2 output is in XML format. But in the case of

OData V4, the default response format will be in JSON. You can learn more about this format in Section 2.3.1.

- **Requesting an individual resource**

   If you want to get details of a single customer in the system, you pass the key property *CustomerID* in the URL (see Figure 2.6 for an example).

Example

Visit the following link to see another example of passing the key property in the URL: *http://s-prs.co/v540904*.

Alternatively, if there is only one key property in the entity, it's not required to pass the property name.

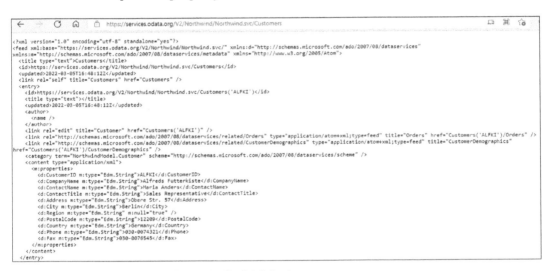

Figure 2.5 OData Customers Entity Set Output

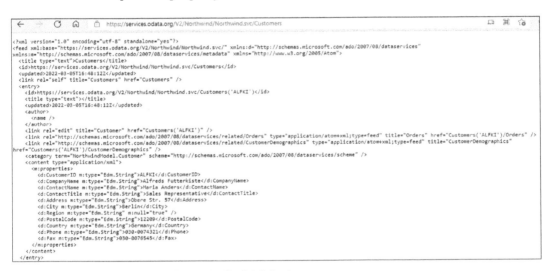

Figure 2.6 Accessing an Individual Resource

Example

You see an example of the preceding scenario at the following URL: *http://s-prs.co/ v540905.*

- **Navigation/relationships**

    You can define relationships among the resources in the OData service. Each resource (entity) can be logically connected to another entity by this concept. For instance, a customer can get the orders created by using the navigation property *Orders* (see Figure 2.7 for an example).

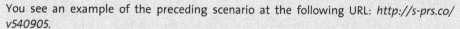

```xml
<?xml version="1.0" encoding="utf-8" standalone="yes"?>
<feed xml:base="https://services.odata.org/V2/Northwind/Northwind.svc/" xmlns:d="http://schemas.microsoft.com/ado/2007/08/dataservices"
xmlns:m="http://schemas.microsoft.com/ado/2007/08/dataservices/metadata" xmlns="http://www.w3.org/2005/Atom">
  <title type="text">Orders</title>
  <id>https://services.odata.org/V2/Northwind/Northwind.svc/Customers(%20'ALFKI')/Orders</id>
  <updated>2022-03-11T05:05:12Z</updated>
  <link rel="self" title="Orders" href="Orders" />
  <entry>
    <id>https://services.odata.org/V2/Northwind/Northwind.svc/Orders(10643)</id>
    <title type="text"></title>
    <updated>2022-03-11T05:05:12Z</updated>
    <author>
      <name />
    </author>
    <link rel="edit" title="Order" href="Orders(10643)" />
    <link rel="http://schemas.microsoft.com/ado/2007/08/dataservices/related/Customer" type="application/atom+xml;type=entry" title="Customer" href="Orders(10643)/Customer" />
    <link rel="http://schemas.microsoft.com/ado/2007/08/dataservices/related/Employee" type="application/atom+xml;type=entry" title="Employee" href="Orders(10643)/Employee" />
    <link rel="http://schemas.microsoft.com/ado/2007/08/dataservices/related/Order_Details" type="application/atom+xml;type=feed" title="Order_Details" href="Orders(10643)/Order_Details" />
    <link rel="http://schemas.microsoft.com/ado/2007/08/dataservices/related/Shipper" type="application/atom+xml;type=entry" title="Shipper" href="Orders(10643)/Shipper" />
    <category term="NorthwindModel.Order" scheme="http://schemas.microsoft.com/ado/2007/08/dataservices/scheme" />
    <content type="application/xml">
      <m:properties>
        <d:OrderID m:type="Edm.Int32">10643</d:OrderID>
        <d:CustomerID m:type="Edm.String">ALFKI</d:CustomerID>
        <d:EmployeeID m:type="Edm.Int32">6</d:EmployeeID>
        <d:OrderDate m:type="Edm.DateTime">1997-08-25T00:00:00</d:OrderDate>
        <d:RequiredDate m:type="Edm.DateTime">1997-09-22T00:00:00</d:RequiredDate>
        <d:ShippedDate m:type="Edm.DateTime">1997-09-02T00:00:00</d:ShippedDate>
        <d:ShipVia m:type="Edm.Int32">1</d:ShipVia>
        <d:Freight m:type="Edm.Decimal">29.4600</d:Freight>
        <d:ShipName m:type="Edm.String">Alfreds Futterkiste</d:ShipName>
        <d:ShipAddress m:type="Edm.String">Obere Str. 57</d:ShipAddress>
        <d:ShipCity m:type="Edm.String">Berlin</d:ShipCity>
        <d:ShipRegion m:type="Edm.String" m:null="true" />
        <d:ShipPostalCode m:type="Edm.String">12209</d:ShipPostalCode>
        <d:ShipCountry m:type="Edm.String">Germany</d:ShipCountry>
      </m:properties>
    </content>
  </entry>
  <entry>
    <id>https://services.odata.org/V2/Northwind/Northwind.svc/Orders(10692)</id>
    <title type="text"></title>
    <updated>2022-03-11T05:05:12Z</updated>
    <author>
      <name />
    </author>
    <link rel="edit" title="Order" href="Orders(10692)" />
    <link rel="http://schemas.microsoft.com/ado/2007/08/dataservices/related/Customer" type="application/atom+xml;type=entry" title="Customer" href="Orders(10692)/Customer" />
    <link rel="http://schemas.microsoft.com/ado/2007/08/dataservices/related/Employee" type="application/atom+xml;type=entry" title="Employee" href="Orders(10692)/Employee" />
    <link rel="http://schemas.microsoft.com/ado/2007/08/dataservices/related/Order_Details" type="application/atom+xml;type=feed" title="Order_Details" href="Orders(10692)/Order_Details" />
    <link rel="http://schemas.microsoft.com/ado/2007/08/dataservices/related/Shipper" type="application/atom+xml;type=entry" title="Shipper" href="Orders(10692)/Shipper" />
    <category term="NorthwindModel.Order" scheme="http://schemas.microsoft.com/ado/2007/08/dataservices/scheme" />
    <content type="application/xml">
      <m:properties>
        <d:OrderID m:type="Edm.Int32">10692</d:OrderID>
        <d:CustomerID m:type="Edm.String">ALFKI</d:CustomerID>
        <d:EmployeeID m:type="Edm.Int32">4</d:EmployeeID>
        <d:OrderDate m:type="Edm.DateTime">1997-10-03T00:00:00</d:OrderDate>
        <d:RequiredDate m:type="Edm.DateTime">1997-10-31T00:00:00</d:RequiredDate>
        <d:ShippedDate m:type="Edm.DateTime">1997-10-13T00:00:00</d:ShippedDate>
        <d:ShipVia m:type="Edm.Int32">2</d:ShipVia>
        <d:Freight m:type="Edm.Decimal">61.0200</d:Freight>
        <d:ShipName m:type="Edm.String">Alfred's Futterkiste</d:ShipName>
        <d:ShipAddress m:type="Edm.String">Obere Str. 57</d:ShipAddress>
        <d:ShipCity m:type="Edm.String">Berlin</d:ShipCity>
```

Figure 2.7 Navigation property

Example

To access the related entities via navigation, see the example at the following URL: *http:// s-prs.co/v540906.*

- **Queries**

    With the help of queries, you can filter, sort, or restrict the response fields of your OData request. These query options are added at the end of an OData service, as shown in the following illustration.

For sorting the data by ascending and descending, you can pass the orderby system query option ($orderby).

Example
You can apply sorting in the following ways:
- Ascending (see *http://s-prs.co/v540907* for an example)
- Descending (see *http://s-prs.co/v540908* for an example)

If you want to get the top three entries, then you can use the system query option $top, which gives the top *n* entries.

Example
To access the top *n* entries, add *$top* at the end of the URL. For the top two customer entries, the URL is *https://services.odata.org/V2/Northwind/Northwind.svc/Customers?$top=2*.

You can also skip the first *n* entries and get the remaining ones by using $skip.

Example
To skip the top *n* entries, add *$skip* at the end of the URL. For skipping two customer entries, the URL is *https://services.odata.org/V2/Northwind/Northwind.svc/Customers?$skip=2*.

You can combine $top and $skip to simulate pagination with OData. SAPUI5 controls such as Table and List natively support this function to simulate pagination (threshold approach). This approach is mainly used in SAP Fiori elements applications to display the data efficiently.

Example
The following URL combines *$top* and *$skip* to simulate pagination: *https://services.odata.org/V2/Northwind/Northwind.svc/Customers?$skip=2&$top=1*.

To find out the total number of entries in the collection of entries, you can use $count or query option $inlinecount that provides both entries and count. The main difference is that $inlinecount provides both the count and data in the same request, whereas $count only returns the total count of entries. SAPUI5 controls and SAP Fiori elements templates use $count to perform pagination (see Figure 2.8 for an example of $inlinecount).

Example

Visit the following URLs to see examples of the $count and $inlinecount options:

- $count: *http://s-prs.co/v540909*
- $inlinecount: *http://s-prs.co/v540910*

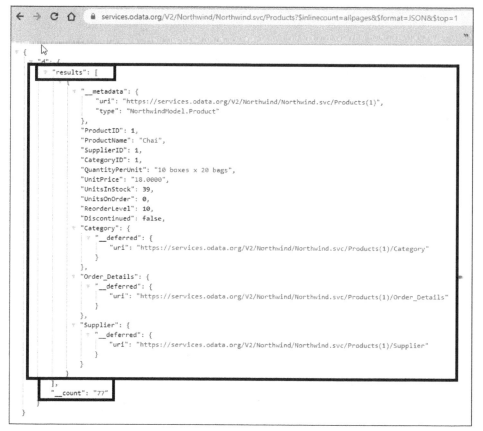

Figure 2.8 OData Inline Count

For filtering all the customers belonging to a country (e.g., Germany), you have to use the query option $filter along with the filter operator eq, as shown in Figure 2.9.

Example

Visit the following URL for an example of a query option: *http://s-prs.co/v540911*.

You can also use other filter operators to filter the entries, such as Ne (not equal), gt (greater than), or functions such as startswith, endswith, and tolower.

```
    ←    →    C    ⌂    🔒  https://services.odata.org/V2/Northwind/Northwind.svc/Customers?$filter=Country%20e...
<?xml version="1.0" encoding="utf-8" standalone="yes"?>
<feed xml:base="https://services.odata.org/V2/Northwind/Northwind.svc/" xmlns:d="http://schemas.microsoft.com/ado/2007/08/dataservices"
xmlns:m="http://schemas.microsoft.com/ado/2007/08/dataservices/metadata" xmlns="http://www.w3.org/2005/Atom">
  <title type="text">Customers</title>
  <id>https://services.odata.org/V2/Northwind/Northwind.svc/Customers</id>
  <updated>2022-03-08T15:43:11Z</updated>
  <link rel="self" title="Customers" href="Customers" />
  <entry>
    <id>https://services.odata.org/V2/Northwind/Northwind.svc/Customers('ALFKI')</id>
    <title type="text"></title>
    <updated>2022-03-08T15:43:11Z</updated>
    <author>
      <name />
    </author>
    <link rel="edit" title="Customer" href="Customers('ALFKI')" />
    <link rel="http://schemas.microsoft.com/ado/2007/08/dataservices/related/Orders" type="application/atom+xml;type=feed" title="Orders"
href="Customers('ALFKI')/Orders" />
    <link rel="http://schemas.microsoft.com/ado/2007/08/dataservices/related/CustomerDemographics" type="application/atom+xml;type=feed"
title="CustomerDemographics" href="Customers('ALFKI')/CustomerDemographics" />
    <category term="NorthwindModel.Customer" scheme="http://schemas.microsoft.com/ado/2007/08/dataservices/scheme" />
    <content type="application/xml">
      <m:properties>
        <d:CustomerID m:type="Edm.String">ALFKI</d:CustomerID>
        <d:CompanyName m:type="Edm.String">Alfreds Futterkiste</d:CompanyName>
        <d:ContactName m:type="Edm.String">Maria Anders</d:ContactName>
        <d:ContactTitle m:type="Edm.String">Sales Representative</d:ContactTitle>
        <d:Address m:type="Edm.String">Obere Str. 57</d:Address>
        <d:City m:type="Edm.String">Berlin</d:City>
        <d:Region m:type="Edm.String" m:null="true" />
        <d:PostalCode m:type="Edm.String">12209</d:PostalCode>
        <d:Country m:type="Edm.String">Germany</d:Country>
        <d:Phone m:type="Edm.String">030-0074321</d:Phone>
        <d:Fax m:type="Edm.String">030-0076545</d:Fax>
      </m:properties>
    </content>
  </entry>
  <entry>
    <id>https://services.odata.org/V2/Northwind/Northwind.svc/Customers('BLAUS')</id>
    <title type="text"></title>
    <updated>2022-03-08T15:43:11Z</updated>
    <author>
      <name />
    </author>
    <link rel="edit" title="Customer" href="Customers('BLAUS')" />
    <link rel="http://schemas.microsoft.com/ado/2007/08/dataservices/related/Orders" type="application/atom+xml;type=feed" title="Orders"
href="Customers('BLAUS')/Orders" />
    <link rel="http://schemas.microsoft.com/ado/2007/08/dataservices/related/CustomerDemographics" type="application/atom+xml;type=feed"
title="CustomerDemographics" href="Customers('BLAUS')/CustomerDemographics" />
    <category term="NorthwindModel.Customer" scheme="http://schemas.microsoft.com/ado/2007/08/dataservices/scheme" />
    <content type="application/xml">
      <m:properties>
        <d:CustomerID m:type="Edm.String">BLAUS</d:CustomerID>
        <d:CompanyName m:type="Edm.String">Blauer See Delikatessen</d:CompanyName>
        <d:ContactName m:type="Edm.String">Hanna Moos</d:ContactName>
        <d:ContactTitle m:type="Edm.String">Sales Representative</d:ContactTitle>
        <d:Address m:type="Edm.String">Forsterstr. 57</d:Address>
        <d:City m:type="Edm.String">Mannheim</d:City>
        <d:Region m:type="Edm.String" m:null="true" />
        <d:PostalCode m:type="Edm.String">68306</d:PostalCode>
        <d:Country m:type="Edm.String">Germany</d:Country>
        <d:Phone m:type="Edm.String">0621-08460</d:Phone>
        <d:Fax m:type="Edm.String">0621-08924</d:Fax>
      </m:properties>
    </content>
  </entry>
  <entry>
```

Figure 2.9 OData Filter Query Parameter

Example

Visit the following URLs for examples of filters:

- Less than filter: *http://s-prs.co/v540912*
  This URL returns the entries where freight is less than 10.
- Greater than filter: *http://s-prs.co/v540913*
  This URL returns entries with freight greater than 200.

You can use the OR operator to perform a logical OR operation on the data. The data contains Germany or Mexico as the country.

You can refer to the following documentation for other operators and functions that you can use in the filters: *http://s-prs.co/v540915*. You can also format the output as JSON instead of XML with the $format query option, as shown in Figure 2.10.

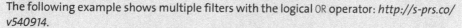

```
{
  "d": [
    {
      "__metadata": {
        "uri": "https://services.odata.org/V2/Northwind/Northwind.svc/Customers('ALFKI')",
        "type": "NorthwindModel.Customer"
      },
      "CustomerID": "ALFKI",
      "CompanyName": "Alfreds Futterkiste",
      "ContactName": "Maria Anders",
      "ContactTitle": "Sales Representative",
      "Address": "Obere Str. 57",
      "City": "Berlin",
      "Region": null,
      "PostalCode": "12209",
      "Country": "Germany",
      "Phone": "030-0074321",
      "Fax": "030-0076545",
      "Orders": {
        "__deferred": {
          "uri": "https://services.odata.org/V2/Northwind/Northwind.svc/Customers('ALFKI')/Orders"
        }
      },
      "CustomerDemographics": {
        "__deferred": {
          "uri": "https://services.odata.org/V2/Northwind/Northwind.svc/Customers('ALFKI')/CustomerDemographics"
        }
      }
    }
  ]
}
```

Figure 2.10 JSON Formatted Output

You saw earlier how to get customer relationship data using the navigation property Orders. If you use that, the service only gives the orders entries. To get data for multiple relationships simultaneously, along with the parent entity, you can use the $expand query option, as shown in Figure 2.11.

```
← → C ⌂    🔒 services.odata.org/V2/Northwind/Northwind.svc/Products?$expand=Supplier,Order_Details&$format=json&$

▼ {
  ▼ "d": {
    ▼ "results": [
      ▼ {
        ▼ "__metadata": {
            "uri": "https://services.odata.org/V2/Northwind/Northwind.svc/Products(1)",
            "type": "NorthwindModel.Product"
          },
          "ProductID": 1,
          "ProductName": "Chai",
          "SupplierID": 1,
          "CategoryID": 1,
          "QuantityPerUnit": "10 boxes x 20 bags",
          "UnitPrice": "18.0000",
          "UnitsInStock": 39,
          "UnitsOnOrder": 0,
          "ReorderLevel": 10,
          "Discontinued": false,
        ▶ "Category": { ... }, // 1 item
        ▼ "Order_Details": {
          ▶ "results": [ ... ] // 38 items
          },
        ▼ "Supplier": {
          ▶ "__metadata": { ... }, // 2 items
            "SupplierID": 1,
            "CompanyName": "Exotic Liquids",
            "ContactName": "Charlotte Cooper",
            "ContactTitle": "Purchasing Manager",
            "Address": "49 Gilbert St.",
            "City": "London",
            "Region": null,
            "PostalCode": "EC1 4SD",
            "Country": "UK",
            "Phone": "(171) 555-2222",
            "Fax": null,
            "HomePage": null,
```

Figure 2.11 OData Expand

In Figure 2.11, you can see that we're fetching the relationship data Supplier, Order_Details for the Products entity. The response also has the parent data (Products) along with the related entities.

You can use $select to specify the response entity's properties. For example, you can pass the properties ProductID and ProductName to the query option $select to fetch only those properties, as shown in Figure 2.12.

Example

See an example of how to use query option $select at the following URL: *http://s-prs.co/v540916*.

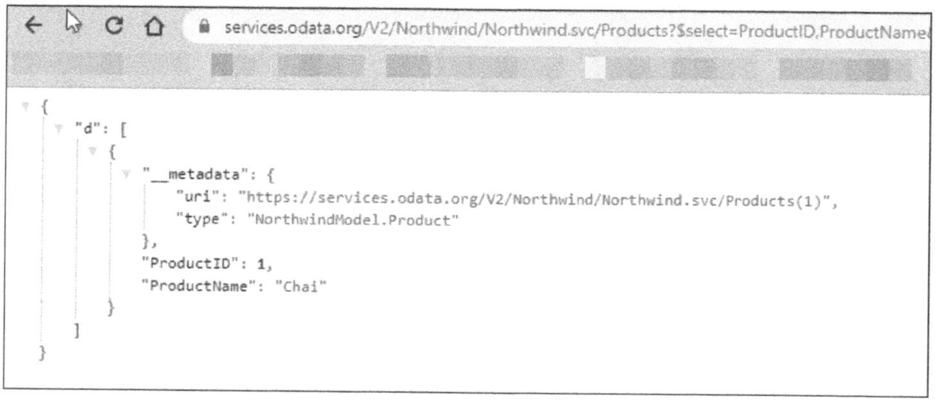

Figure 2.12 OData $select

2.3   JavaScript Object Notation and Yet Another Markup Language

JSON and YAML are two popular formats for data exchange and configuration files. They are similar in functions and features, but the difference will be in the design, which affects the scope of use. This section will provide an overview of JSON and YAML, followed by an explanation of their differences.

2.3.1   JSON

JSON is an open standard file format and data interchange format that uses human-readable text to store and transmit data objects consisting of attribute-value pairs and arrays. It's one of the common data formats used in modern web applications. Although JSON was derived from JavaScript, it's a language-independent data format. JSON files use the extension *.json*.

JSON is built on two structures:

- A collection of name-value pairs, which are called object, record, or struct in other programming languages
- An ordered list of values, which are called array, vector, or sequence in most languages.

JSON Object/Structure

An object is an unordered set of name-value pairs. It starts with a left brace ({) and ends with a right brace (}). Name-value pairs, separated by a colon (:) will be added inside these braces, and these values can be of type string, number, array, or other data types.

Example

Listing 2.1 shows an example JSON object.

```
{
  "squadName": "Super hero squad",
  "homeTown": "Metro City",
  "formed": 2016,
  "secretBase": "Super tower",
  "active": true,
  "members": [
    {
      "name": "Molecule Man",
      "age": 29,
      "secretIdentity": "Dan Jukes",
      "powers": [
        "Radiation resistance",
        "Turning tiny",
        "Radiation blast"
      ]
    }
  ]
}
```

Listing 2.1 Example JSON Object

You can notice in the preceding example that the JSON object has a mix of data types: a string, "Super hero squad"; a number, 2016; a Boolean, true; and an array.

JSON Array

An *array* is an ordered collection of objects. They begin with [(left bracket), end with] (right bracket), and have JSON objects between them.

Example

Listing 2.2 shows an example array.

```
[
  {
    "name": "Hyper Man",
    "age": 19,
    "secretIdentity": "Dan King",
    "powers": [
      "Super Strength",
      "Cold Breath",
      "Flight"
    ]
  },
  {
    "name": "Madame Tsunade",
    "age": 29,
    "secretIdentity": "Jane Tsunade",
```

```
      "powers": [
        "Million times punch",
        "Super Strength",
      ]
    }
]
```

Listing 2.2 Example Array

2.3.2   YAML

YAML is a human-friendly data serialization language. It's a superset of JSON, so JSON files are valid in YAML. The extensions of YAML files are *.yaml* or *.yml*. It's primarily used in configuration files, internet messaging, data auditing, and so on.

The YAML file is made up of name-value pairs but follows a special indentation to indicate nesting. It doesn't have braces or square brackets like JSON does.

Example

A typical YAML file looks like Listing 2.3.

```
---
# Super Hero Detail
Name: Hyper Man
Age: 19
Secret Identity: Dan King
Powers:
-    Super Strength
-    Cold Breath
-    Flight
Description1: >
     Although this text
     appears in different
     lines, it will be formatted
     to single line
```

Listing 2.3 Example YAML

From the preceding example, you can observe that name-value pairs are separated by a colon (:) and a long string, which, when specified with >, ensures that a multi-line string is formatted to a single line. A comment will have a hash (#) in the beginning. An array of values is separated by - with a single tab indentation.

Example

You can see an array in the following formats:

```
Type1:['value1', 'value2', 'value3']
Type2:
     -    value1
     -    value2
     -    value3
```

```
Type3:
    -    id: 1
         Name: franc
    -    id: 11
         Name: Tom
```

The YAML array example can also be represented in the JSON format as shown here:

```json
{
  "Type1": [
    "value1",
    "value2",
    "value3"
  ],
  "Type2": [
    "value1",
    "value2",
    "value3"
  ],
  "Type3": [
    {
      "id": 1,
      "name": "franc"
    },
    {
      "id": 11,
      "name": "Tom"
    }
  ]
}
```

2.3.3   YAML versus JSON

Although both YAML and JSON are two popular human-readable data formats, both have different priorities. Technically, YAML is a superset of JSON, so it offers more functionalities than JSON; for example, in a JSON file, you can have duplicate key values, but that can be prevented easily in YAML files. So, you can say for this specific reason, YAML is preferred in configuration files. YAML tends to be simpler to read and understand because you won't find unnecessary braces. It also has tons of better features such as comments, recursive structures, and so on. YAML also supports nonhierarchical data and doesn't need to follow the typical parent and child relationship like the JSON model.

On the other hand, JSON isn't as complex as YAML as it has simple data types and structures. It can also be parsed and generated faster than YAML. Because the JSON format is used mostly in JavaScript, it has a better developer ecosystem than YAML.

2.4   Twelve-Factor App Principles

Web applications are ubiquitous these days. As browsers become more and more powerful, desktop applications are shrinking, and delivering applications via browser is becoming increasingly common. These applications are called web applications as they are accessed using the World Wide Web (the internet).

As web applications became popular in the past two decades, many best practices and principles have emerged to develop and maintain web applications, including the twelve-factor app set of principles for building performant, scalable, and resilient web applications.

As the name suggests, twelve-factor app principles provide 12 principles for creating modern, microservice-based cloud-native web applications. It was originally introduced by Adam Wiggins in the 2011. He also happens to be the cofounder of Heroku, which was once a very popular platform-as-a-service (PaaS) for running enterprise applications.

Now, let's explore these 12 principles:

- **Codebase**

  The codebase principle states that the application resources should have a version-managed, source-code repository such as Git or Subversion. Multiple apps sharing the same code is a violation of the twelve-factor app principles. The solution here is to factor shared code into libraries that can be included through the dependency manager.

  Per the twelve-factor app methodology, a deploy is an instance of an app in the developer's system, development system, quality system, and production system, though different versions can be active in each deployment (see Figure 2.13). The codebase can be accessible to Continuous Integration/Continuous Delivery (CI/CD) as part of the software development cycle. A system's codebase can be in sync with some level of automation using CI/CD.

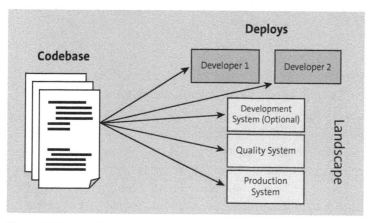

Figure 2.13 Twelve-Factor App Principle: Codebase

- **Dependencies**

  When you build an application, it's common to use other reusable repositories and tools within the application that you create. One easy way to handle dependencies is to include those dependent library codes into your application itself. However, that comes with the disadvantage of mixing the lifecycle of the application code and the dependent library code.

  This principle specifies that the dependencies should be set in your app manifest or configuration file and managed externally instead of including them directly in the source code.

  If you're using Node.js, you specify the dependencies inside a *package.json* file (see Figure 2.14). The node package manager (NPM) takes care of downloading the specified versions and installing them to make them available for the application to use. Similarly, in a Java application, you set the dependencies in a *build.gradle* file, and the Gradle dependency manager takes care of those dependencies.

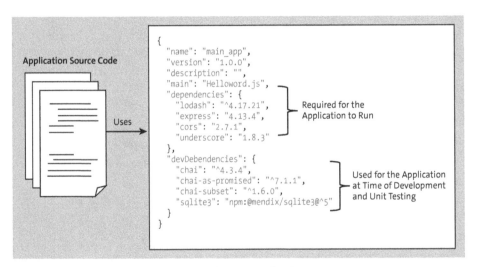

Figure 2.14 Twelve-Factor App Principle: Node.js Dependencies

- **Config**

  This principle states that configurations of an application need to be stored independently from the code itself, as environment variables, or in a configuration file.

  Examples of configuration data are hostname, port number, and credentials. These configuration data are different for each of the deployment environments where the application is going to run. By separating such configuration data, we're making it easy to run the application in different environments by just applying the independently maintained configuration data to the runtime.

  Figure 2.15 shows that when running in different landscapes, the same codebase is run, but different sets of configuration data are applied in different environments.

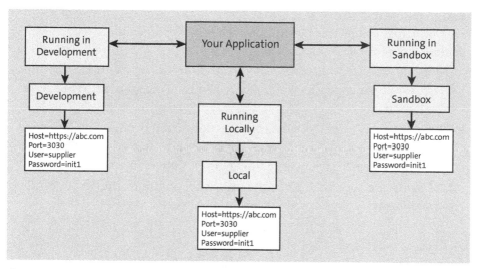

Figure 2.15 Same Application Code Running in Different Environments

- **Backing services**

  The backing service principle suggests that services such as databases, messaging systems, Simple Mail Transfer Protocol (SMTP) services, and so on, should be architected as external resources. The application consumes these backing services over the network.

  These services can be locally managed or provided by third parties such as Amazon Simple Storage Service (Amazon S3) or Google Maps. URLs, credentials, and so on should be maintained in a configuration file, and when required to replace an existing service with another one, you can easily change the details in the configuration file. Each of these backing services is referred to as a resource. In Figure 2.16, you can see an example of the SAP Cloud Application Programming Model application accessing three different resources.

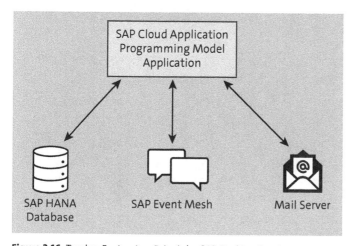

Figure 2.16 Twelve-Factor App Principle: SAP Backing Services

- **Build, release, and run**

  This principle states that there should be three independent steps in your deployment process (see Figure 2.17):

  - The *build stage* converts the code repo into an executable bundle. At this stage, all the dependencies will also be fetched and compiled into the executable bundle.

  - The *release stage* combines the configurations from configuration files and environment variables with the executable bundle. The resulting build will be an executable file ready to be run in the execution environment.

  - The *run stage* runs the app in the execution environment, which can be development, quality, or production.

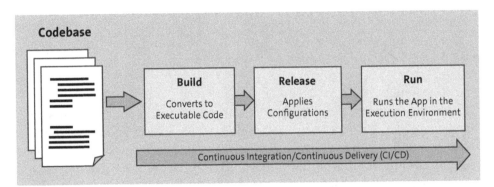

Figure 2.17 Twelve-Factor App Principle: Build, Release, Run

- **Stateless processes**

  This principle states that applications should have the provision to be served by multiple stateless, independent processes, as shown in Figure 2.18.

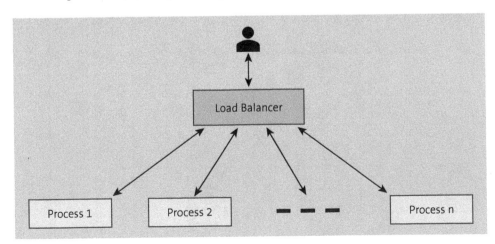

Figure 2.18 Stateless Processes Serving the Application

Consider that a user's request is served by process 1. Subsequent requests should be able to be served by process 2 or any other processes as well. There will be no session data maintained in any of the processes, and each process independently serves the request without communicating with other processes. Any data that needs to persist must use a backing service such as a database.

Following this principle makes it easy to scale the infrastructure up and down, thus making it ideal for cloud deployments.

- **Port binding**

  The twelve-factor app is a self-contained standalone app that doesn't require a web server to create a web-facing service. Instead of having a web server to handle the requests and sending to the individual services, where dependency with the web server is created, a twelve-factor app directly binds to a port and responds to incoming requests (see Figure 2.19).

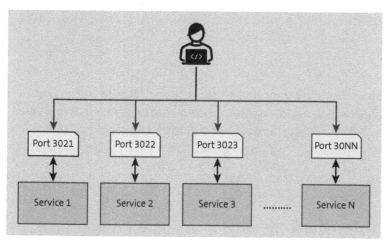

Figure 2.19 Port Binding

An individual service can act as a backing service to another app by providing the backing service URL in the configuration of the consumption app.

- **Concurrency**

  This principle states that the application needs to be broken down into multiple modules so that each of those modules can be scaled up and down independently. For instance, HTTP requests can be handled by a web process, and a worker process can take care of background jobs. Again, these individual processes can be scaled up or down to handle the increased workloads independently.

- **Disposability**

  A twelve-factor app should maximize robustness with fast startup and graceful shutdown. The processes should minimize the time to startup and ideally take a few seconds to start and receive the incoming requests; it helps while scaling up the processes. At the same time, the processes should shut down gracefully and cease to listen on the service port without allowing any incoming requests; in such cases, if there is a queuing system, the requests can be queued and processed once the processes are up.

- **DEV/PROD parity**
  The twelve-factor app methodology suggests that an app's development, staging, and production are kept as similar as possible. A twelve-factor app should be designed with the CI/CD approach by making the time gap small—where the developer writes some code and deploys it in hours or even minutes—and keeping DEV and PROD as similar as possible. This eliminates the risk of bugs in production when new changes are moved with different versions.

- **Logs**
  This rule suggests treating logs as event streams. Logs are typically time-ordered event information, or logs can be error or success messages recorded by an app. A twelve-factor app never concerns itself with storing the log information in the app, as it can die and, as a result, lose the information. Instead, the app should treat log entries as event streams and use a separate service to save them. These can be consumed by interested parties to perform analytics or for monitoring.

- **Admin processes**
  The developer often needs to perform administrative or maintenance activities for apps that need data migration, running processes, or one-time scripts. These should also be identical across different landscapes (DEV, QA, and PROD). These processes should also be shipped along with the application code to avoid synchronization issues.

2.5   Important Terminology

In this chapter, the following terminology was used:

- **Application programming interface (API)**
  APIs enable companies to securely connect their internal applications or external partners to transfer data in both directions.

- **JavaScript Object Notation (JSON)**
  JSON is an open standard file format and data interchange format that uses human-readable text to store and transmit data objects consisting of attribute-value pairs and arrays.

- **Open Data Protocol (OData)**
  OData is a REST-based protocol approved by ISO/IEC used for building and consuming RESTful APIs.

- **Representational State Transfer (REST)**
  REST is a famous web API architecture that is mainly used for lightweight web services and mobile applications.

- **Simple Object Access Protocol (SOAP)**
  SOAP is a stricter protocol with defined security rules that is standardized by the W3C and uses an XML payload to transfer the data between systems.
- **Twelve-factor app**
  A twelve-factor app defines the principles for building performant, scalable, and resilient microservice-based cloud-native web applications.
- **Yet Another Markup Language (YAML)**
  YAML is a human-friendly data serialization language. It's a superset of JSON, so JSON files are valid in YAML.

2.6   Practice Questions

1. What is an application programming interface (API)?

    ☐ **A.** Interface used for software applications to interact with each other
    ☐ **B.** Tool for creating web applications
    ☐ **C.** A software development kit of mobile applications

2. Consumers of an API need which of the following?

    ☐ **A.** Architectural design of an API
    ☐ **B.** Server details
    ☐ **C.** Database dump from the server
    ☐ **D.** Documentation of the API

3. What are the features of a RESTful API? (There are three correct answers.)

    ☐ **A.** Client-server model
    ☐ **B.** Stricter protocols
    ☐ **C.** Statelessness
    ☐ **D.** Uniform interface

4. Which of the following is valid for the OData protocol? (There are two correct answers.)

    ☐ **A.** Follow the new protocols instead of REST principles.
    ☐ **B.** Support the extensions of API without breaking the client's functionality.
    ☐ **C.** Act as a relational database.
    ☐ **D.** Follow the REST principles.

5. Where can you find the top-level feeds and Entity Data Model (EDM) of an OData service? (There are two correct answers.)

    ☐ **A.** Annotations
    ☐ **B.** Service document
    ☐ **C.** Metadata
    ☐ **D.** SOAP document

6. What can you find in the metadata document of an OData service? (There are three correct answers.)

    ☐ **A.** Entity definitions
    ☐ **B.** Relations
    ☐ **C.** Entity properties
    ☐ **D.** Entity data (entries)

7. Which of the following URIs are correct for fetching a single resource? (There are two correct answers.)

    ☐ **A.** /Customers(CustomerID = 'ALFKI')
    ☐ **B.** /Customers?$top=1
    ☐ **C.** /Customers?$select=CustomerID
    ☐ **D.** /Customers?$count

8. Which URI option will we use to fetch the parent and the associated entities together? (There are two correct answers.)

    ☐ **A.** /Customers('ALFKI')/Orders
    ☐ **B.** /Customers('ALFKI')?$expand=Orders
    ☐ **C.** /Customers?$expand=Orders
    ☐ **D.** /Customers('ALFKI')/Orders?$select=CustomerId

9. Which functionalities are used by OData to implement pagination in frontend applications?

    ☐ **A.** $top and $select
    ☐ **B.** $top, $count, and $expand
    ☐ **C.** $top, $skip, and $inlinecount
    ☐ **D.** $top, $skip, and $select

10. What is the relationship between YAML and JSON?

☐ **A.** YAML is a superset of JSON.

☐ **B.** YAML is a subset of JSON.

☐ **C.** YAML and JSON are the same.

11. For what is YAML primarily used?

☐ **A.** Creating configuration files

☐ **B.** Transferring data

☐ **C.** Storing data in the database

12. Which of the following supports nonhierarchical data?

☐ **A.** JSON

☐ **B.** YAML

☐ **C.** Both JSON and YAML

13. Which data format supports comments?

☐ **A.** YAML

☐ **B.** JSON

☐ **C.** Neither of them

14. Which of the following is true for JSON?

☐ **A.** It supports indentation.

☐ **B.** Arrays should begin with a bracket ([).

☐ **C.** YAML can be used inside JSON.

15. The codebase principle of the twelve-factor app suggests which of the following? (There are two correct answers.)

☐ **A.** Code should be shared using libraries and the dependency manager.

☐ **B.** Version/source control isn't mandatory for codebases.

☐ **C.** The CI/CD approach can be used to keep the systems codebase in sync.

16. Where can configurations such as credentials, host, or port be saved?

☐ **A.** Dependencies

☐ **B.** Code

☐ **C.** Environment variables

17. Which of the following statements are true? (There are two correct answers.)

☐ **A.** Applications should access backing services using the configuration file.

☐ **B.** A backing service is a library that can be reused in different codebases.

☐ **C.** SAP HANA database and SAP Event Mesh are called backing services.

18. What principle should be followed for deploying the codebase to a production environment?

☐ **A.** Backing services

☐ **B.** Build, release, and run

☐ **C.** Dependencies

19. The stateless principle from the twelve-factor app suggests which of the following? (There are two correct answers.)

☐ **A.** Stateless independent processes

☐ **B.** Dependent processes

☐ **C.** Use of backing services for persistency

20. Which one of the following is true in the case of a twelve-factor app?

☐ **A.** Use ports to listen to incoming requests instead of a web server directly.

☐ **B.** The application should be created from multiple modules that can be scaled up and down independently.

☐ **C.** Development, staging, and production environments should be kept similar with the help of the CI/CD approach.

☐ **D.** All of the above are true.

21. Which of the following is true for a twelve-factor app?

☐ **A.** Logs should be stored in the application.

☐ **B.** Admin processes should be similar in all the landscapes.

☐ **C.** Neither of the above are true.

2.7   Practice Question Answers and Explanations

1. Answer: **A**
APIs are used for software applications to interact with each other. An API isn't a tool for creating web applications or an SDK for developing mobile apps.

2. Answer: **D**

    While designing an API, API producers should hide the complexity of what an API does in the background and only provide the information the consumer requests. API producers will give the consumers the documentation of an API explicitly or implicitly (via metadata) to understand how the API works.

3. Answer: **A, C, and D**

    RESTful APIs follow the REST guidelines such as client-server model, cacheability, uniform interface, statelessness, and the layered system, but they don't follow any strict protocols like SOAP does.

4. Answer: **B and D**

    OData services follow the REST principles, and they should support the extension of APIs without breaking the client's functionality.

5. Answer: **B and C**

    Service documents have all the top-level feeds of an OData service, whereas the EDM can be determined from the metadata document.

6. Answer: **A, B, and C**

    You can find entity definitions, properties, key properties, and related entities (relationships) in the metadata. You need to pass the entity set name in the resource path to access the entity data.

7. Answer: **A and B**

    `/Customers(CustomerID = 'ALFKI')` returns only one record matching the key property `ALFKI` and `/Customers?$top=1` returns up to one customer entry as the `$top=1` query option is used.

8. Answer: **B and C**

    `$expand` is used to fetch the parent entity and the mentioned associated entities in `$expand`.

9. Answer: **C**

    The `$top`, `$skip`, and `$inlinecount` or `$count` query options of an OData service are used to implement pagination in frontend applications such as SAPUI5.

10. Answer: **A**

    YAML is the superset of JSON. A valid YAML file can contain JSON. You can convert JSON to YAML without any loss of information, and every JSON file is also a valid YAML file.

11. Answer: **A**

    As YAML is more human-readable than JSON, it's preferred in creating configuration files.

12. Answer: **B**

    YAML supports nonhierarchical data and doesn't need to follow the typical parent and child relationship like the JSON model.

13. Answer: **A**

    YAML supports comments by default.

14. Answer: **B**

    Arrays should begin with a bracket ([). YAML supports indentation to segregate data inside it, and JSON can be used inside YAML, but not otherwise. JSON arrays begin and end with brackets.

15. Answer: **A and C**

    Reusable code can be shared using libraries with the help of a dependency manager. Codebase should have version control such as Git to track changes and push to different landscapes. CI/CD can keep the systems in sync with the latest codebase and patches, which is the recommended approach per the twelve-factor app principles.

16. Answer: **C**

    We shouldn't save the data such as host, port, or credentials in the code; it should be saved in the environment variables.

17. Answer: **A and C**

    The application should access backing services such as SAP HANA database or SAP Event Mesh via the environment variable or configuration files. Libraries are dependencies, not backing services.

18. Answer: **B**

    The build, release, and run principle should be followed when deploying the codebase to a production environment. This principles states that there should be three independent steps in your deployment process: the build stage that converts the code repo into an executable bundle; the release stage that combines the configurations from configuration files and environment variables with the executable bundle; and the run stage that runs the app in the execution environment.

19. Answer: **A and C**

    The twelve-factor app principle suggests that stateless and independent processes should serve an application, and if there is any need for data persistency, a backing service should be used.

20. Answer: **D**

    The port binding principle suggests that instead of using a webserver to handle the requests, the application should listen to the ports to handle the incoming requests directly.

    The concurrency principle suggests that an application should be broken down into multiple modules to be scaled up and down independently based on load.

    The DEV/PROD parity principle requires all the environments to be similar and use CI/CD tools to reduce the time and have the application identical in all the environments.

21. Answer: **B**

Logs should not be stored in the application, and external services should be used to save the logs. Administrative or maintenance activities for apps such as migrations or on-time scripts should be similar in all the landscapes.

2.8   Test Takeaway

OData is a REST-based protocol for building RESTful APIs. SAP recommends using OData in its applications and frameworks, such as SAP Cloud Application Programming Model (Node.js) or RAP (ABAP), which have huge support for OData. JSON and YAML are the most popular data formats used in configuration files and while transferring the data across the web. Twelve-factor app principles are the widely endorsed principles that are recommended to be followed while designing an application with modern web capabilities.

2.9   Summary

In this chapter, you learned about important web standards such as API, REST, and OData. Then we covered YAML and JSON, two popular formats for data exchange and configuration files. We discussed how to create resilient cloud-native applications by understanding the principles of the twelve-factor app as well. In addition, we discussed the OData protocol in depth, which is a popular format used extensively in SAP applications.

In the next chapter, we'll discuss the the SAP Cloud Application Programming Model.

Chapter 3
SAP Cloud Application Programming Model

Techniques You'll Master

- Understanding SAP Business Application Studio
- Understanding the SAP Cloud Application Programming Model
- Building and deploying SAP Cloud Application Programming Model applications using Cloud Foundry command-line tools

In this chapter, we'll start with an introduction to the SAP Cloud Application Programming Model and its various features. Next, we'll cover SAP's go-to development environment: SAP Business Application Studio. We'll set up SAP Business Application Studio to develop an SAP Cloud Application Programming Model application and gradually add enterprise features to it. Next, we'll use command-line tools provided by Cloud Foundry to build and deploy the SAP Cloud Application Programming Model application to the SAP Business Technology Platform (SAP BTP), Cloud Foundry environment.

Real-World Scenario

Consider a scenario where you're in charge of the purchasing department of your organization. You're an SAP S/4HANA customer creating purchase orders for your procurement needs. Each purchase order has a delivery schedule that was agreed upon between the purchaser and the vendor. These dates are important because the manufacturing department plans its processes based on these.

Whenever these delivered schedules are missed, or if you haven't received advance shipping notifications on time, you escalate the purchase order and contact the vendor to determine the status. These communications go over a long email chain until you get a satisfactory result. Meanwhile, you need to involve several internal stakeholders throughout the process, providing them with information about the delivery status.

You're exploring whether this manual process of escalation can be digitized for better handling and follow-up, resulting in efficient delivery. Digitizing this process will provide a structured data set that can be used for reporting and later in projections.

3.1   Objectives of This Portion of the Test

This portion of the test checks your understanding of the concepts regarding the SAP Cloud Application Programming Model. It checks your ability to create and consume OData services, handle events and maintain security policies. It also checks your understanding of SAP Business Application Studio to develop SAP Cloud Application Programming Model applications. This portion also checks your familiarity with Cloud Foundry command-line tools to build and deploy SAP Cloud Application Programming Model applications.

Note
The SAP Cloud Application Programming Model topics make up more than 12% of the total exam.

3.2 SAP Business Application Studio

SAP Business Application Studio is the SAP-recommended integrated development environment (IDE) for developing business applications in the SAP landscape. It's available as a cloud software-as-a-service (SaaS) within SAP BTP. The following sections cover the technical details of SAP Business Application Studio and provide an overview of how to get started with an SAP Business Application Studio project.

3.2.1 Technical Details

SAP Business Application Studio is based on the Eclipse Theia project. Eclipse Theia is an open-source platform that allows individuals and organizations to build a desktop or a cloud IDE while building specific features (via extensions and plugins) into it. SAP used the Theia platform, built a cloud IDE from it, and named the IDE SAP Business Application Studio.

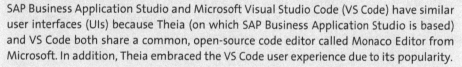

Tip

SAP Business Application Studio and Microsoft Visual Studio Code (VS Code) have similar user interfaces (UIs) because Theia (on which SAP Business Application Studio is based) and VS Code both share a common, open-source code editor called Monaco Editor from Microsoft. In addition, Theia embraced the VS Code user experience due to its popularity.

Traditionally, IDEs are installed by developers on their local machines. Though local development has many advantages, it comes with many requirements as well. A few of them are listed here:

- Installing and maintaining the right versions of all the dependencies (e.g., the correct Java version). This requirement can be an issue with new developers.
- Ensuring you have the required hardware profile (ram, disc space) for running the developed applications locally.
- Integrating with other dependent cloud services (e.g., integrating with SAP BTP services).
- Ensuring the safety of the code. For example, what happens if the local machine that has business-critical code falls into wrong hands?

Local development might still make sense when there are patchy internet speeds or a need to integrate with operating system features. SAP still supports local development with SAP Fiori tools and other technology-specific local development tools.

SAP Web IDE is the predecessor of SAP Business Application Studio. Before SAP Business Application Studio, SAP Web IDE was SAP's go-to tool for SAP Fiori and SAP HANA development. Just like SAP Business Application Studio, SAP Web IDE was a cloud-based solution, so why was a new cloud-based IDE required?

Although SAP Web IDE was built using many open-source tools, it's dependent on many SAP proprietary tools, which makes the extensibility difficult. By contrast, you can extend the capability of SAP Business Application Studio using thousands of readily available VS Code extensions. The Eclipse Theia project has created an extension library called Open VSX Registry (*https://open-vsx.org*), where you can find all the VS Code extensions (1,617 extensions as of March 2022) that are compatible with Eclipse Theia. All these extensions can be installed on SAP Business Application Studio as well.

Though SAP Web IDE supported development in multiple technologies (mobile, web, SAP HANA), the development environment was the same for all developers, thus it wasn't always optimum performance-wise. SAP Business Application Studio provides multiple predefined isolated development environments called dev spaces. Each dev space targets a specific kind of application development such as SAP Fiori, Full-Stack Cloud development, mobile development, and SAP HANA development.

Using command-line interfaces (CLIs) is a great way to control (e.g., Git integration) your development environment. SAP Web IDE didn't provide a CLI; however, because SAP Business Application Studio embraces the VS Code user experience, it provides the ability to run CLI in the local isolated environment. This also makes it easy to debug and run the app locally (local to the IDE).

3.2.2   Getting Started with SAP Business Application Studio

In the following sections, we'll explain how to get started with SAP Business Application Studio by downloading a free trial of SAP BTP. Then, we'll walk through dev spaces and steps in creating a project within SAP Business Application Studio.

Creating an SAP Business Technology Platform Trial Account

SAP Business Application Studio is available in the free trial version of SAP BTP, so you can explore and evaluate the SAP Business Application Studio without any cost. Let's explore how to get started with SAP Business Application Studio in the SAP BTP trial account.

The first step is to navigate to *www.sap.com* and register as a new user by entering your personal information. Next, you open your email inbox, open the email from SAP, and activate your SAP account. Now you're ready to access the SAP BTP trial.

Go to *https://account.hanatrial.ondemand.com*, and log in with your SAP credentials. You need to read and accept the legal disclaimer before SAP can create an SAP BTP trial account for you. You need to enter and validate a telephone number as well.

After you log in, you'll see a popup where you need to choose a region that is nearest to you and click on the **Create Account** button. Your trial account will be created in a data center in the chosen region, as shown in Figure 3.1. Your trial account will be created along with a Cloud Foundry **Org** and a **Space**. Click on the **Continue** button on the popup to see the welcome screen.

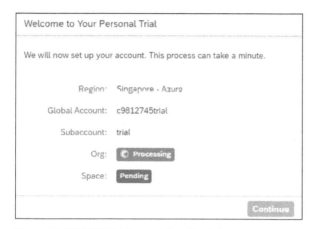

Figure 3.1 SAP BTP Trial Account Creation in Progress

Here you can click on **Enter Your Trial Account** to navigate to the global account of your SAP BTP trial that will show you the trial subaccount. Click on the trial subaccount to navigate to the SAP BTP subaccount cockpit, as shown in Figure 3.2.

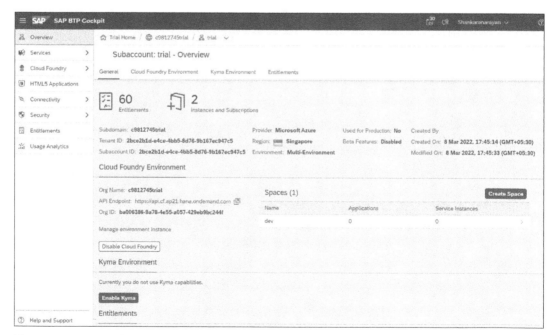

Figure 3.2 SAP BTP Trial Subaccount Cockpit

Now that you have access to the SAP BTP trial and have created a subaccount, it's time to find the SAP Business Application Studio service and subscribe to it. As

shown in Figure 3.3, go to **Service Marketplace** ❶, and search for **Business Application Studio** ❷. Once you find it, click on the menu button (three dots), and choose
Create ❸ to open a pop-up. In the pop-up, choose **Lite** as the **Plan** and click on
Create ❹ to create an instance of the SAP Business Application Studio service.
Once the subscription is created, you can click on **Instances and Subscriptions** in
the subaccount cockpit, choose the **SAP Business Application Studio** subscription,
click on the menu button, and choose **Go to Application**. This will open the homepage of SAP Business Application Studio.

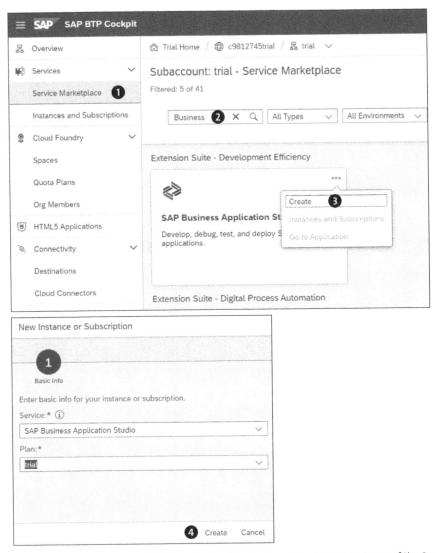

Figure 3.3 Subscribing to SAP Business Application Studio by Creating an Instance of the Service

Now you'll see the home screen of SAP Business Application Studio. Because this is
the first time you're opening SAP Business Application Studio, you'll be prompted
to create a dev space. We'll discuss dev spaces next.

Dev Spaces

Dev spaces make up a preconfigured private virtual machine environment (Kubernetes Pod) where you do your development. These virtual systems have a Ubuntu-based Linux operating system, a file system for hosting the source code you develop, command-line tools, and tools for debugging and running your applications. You'll not get root user access to this virtual system. However, you can install and execute the required modules, commands, and packages that are required for the development.

Before you do any development, you need to create at least one dev space. As of writing this book, SAP Business Application Studio provides five predefined dev space types (see Figure 3.4):

- **SAP Fiori**
  This dev space is aimed at creating SAP Fiori (both freestyle and SAP Fiori elements) applications. It has tools for code assist, code validation, visual editor, SAPUI5 templates, annotation modeling, service modeling, deployment tools, SAP Fiori tools, and other tools.

- **Full-Stack Cloud Application**
  This dev space type has tools to perform SAP Fiori development along with tools to perform development using the SAP Cloud Application Programming Model. Other tools include SAP HANA database explorer, Java tools (for SAP Cloud Application Programming Model), MTA Tools set, graphical tool to develop the Core Data Services (CDS) model, and other related tools.

- **SAP HANA Native Application**
  This dev space type has tools for native SAP HANA development. You can create SAP HANA database artifacts such as calculation views, CDS views, SQLScript procedures, and database tables. You can also create SAP HANA extended application services advanced (SAP HANA XSA) applications and deploy them to SAP HANA or SAP HANA Cloud services on SAP BTP.

- **SAP Mobile Application**
  This dev space type is suitable for creating Android and iOS enterprise apps. It has an extension that lets you use SAP's mobile development kit (MDK), connect to SAP Mobile Services, and create Android and iOS apps, along with an ability to use SAP Mobile Cards.

- **Basic**
  This is a basic version of the SAP Business Application Studio dev space type containing minimal extensions. It lets you add the available SAP extensions and create your own dev space per the development requirement.

Each of these predefined dev spaces comes with predefined SAP extensions as just explained. However, you can add features as you need from the **Additional SAP Extensions** list, as you'll see later in Section 3.4 when we create an SAP Cloud Application Programming Model project.

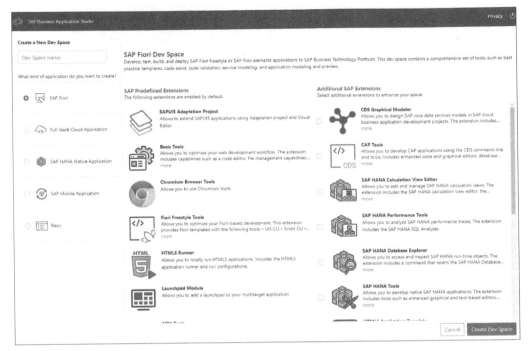

Figure 3.4 Available Types of Dev Spaces

In this step, you provide a name for your dev space, choose a predefined dev space type, add any optional extensions, and click on **Create Dev Space**. Dev space creation will take a few minutes because SAP Business Application Studio has to create and provision a virtual environment for you. You need to wait till the dev space changes its state from **Starting** to **Running**. Once that happens, you can click on the dev space to open it.

You can create up to 10 dev spaces in a licensed version. You can have two of those dev spaces running simultaneously. Every dev space will be stopped after three hours of inactivity. You can start the dev space again to get back the content within the dev space. With a trial version of SAP Business Application Studio, you can create only two dev spaces and only one of them can be running at a time.

Creating a Project

SAP Business Application Studio provides several ways to create a project:

- **Using SAP Business Application Studio templates**
  You can go to the **File** menu and choose **New Project from Template** to see all the available templates. The templates you see here are dependent on the extensions available in the current dev space type. For example, if your dev space contains the **Mobile Service App Development Tools** extension, only then will you see templates related to mobile app development. Once you choose a template, it will start a wizard and let you enter and choose various details so that it can generate a starter project for you.

- **Using CLI**

    SAP Business Application Studio comes with a Yeoman generator framework installed. Along with the framework, SAP delivers several Yeoman generators for creating applications of type SAPUI5, SAP Cloud Application Programming Model, and multi-target application (MTA). You can install more Yeoman generators as required.

    You can use the integrated CLI to install and execute any technology-specific commands to initialize the project.

- **Cloning repositories from the Git repository**

    You can clone a Git repository and use it as the starting point for your application.

Tip

SAP has a Git repository (*https://github.com/SAP-samples*) that has a huge number of sample repositories for various SAP technologies such as SAP Fiori, SAPUI5, SAP Cloud Application Programming Model, and MDK. You can use these repositories for learning as well as for the starting point of your development.

- **Importing projects**

    SAP Business Application Studio lets you import any archive folder and extract it into your SAP Business Application Studio workspace. This can be useful if you want to export it from a colleague's IDE and import it into SAP Business Application Studio to continue development.

Once you have a project, you can run the project locally within SAP Business Application Studio before you deploy it to the target environment. For backend applications such as SAP Cloud Application Programming Model, you can set breakpoints and debug the source code as well.

SAP Business Application Studio lets you deploy the developed application to multiple target environments. You can deploy the app to an on-premise ABAP system, Cloud Foundry, or SAP HANA system. Keep in mind that you can connect to different Cloud Foundry instances and deploy to a completely different Cloud Foundry instance than the instance on which SAP Business Application Studio is running.

3.3   Introduction to the SAP Cloud Application Programming Model

According to official SAP documentation, SAP Cloud Application Programming Model is a framework of languages, libraries, and tools for building enterprise-grade services and applications. When you build an enterprise application using languages such as Java or JavaScript (Node.js framework), a lot of effort is required to build it and to add enterprise qualities. SAP Cloud Application Programming

Model provides an opinionated framework that is based on industry best practices to make it easy to develop and add enterprise capabilities to your application. These features also mean that SAP Cloud Application Programming Model significantly accelerates the application development by reducing the amount of boilerplate coding (repetitive code across projects to add enterprise qualities), thus improving the quality of your application while reducing maintenance costs.

Next, we'll list and describe the various capabilities of the SAP Cloud Application Programming Model framework.

3.3.1   Capabilities of the SAP Cloud Application Programming Model

SAP Cloud Application Programming Model provides the following capabilities:

- **Object-relational mapping (ORM)-like capabilities**
  ORM libraries are specialized libraries that simplify application code's database interactions. They map real-world objects with relational database artifacts. Their main goal is to free the developers from writing complex database-specific SQL queries by providing an easy and generic way to do the following:
  - Define database schema and artifacts.
  - Query and update database records, including transaction handling (Query Builder).

  Some of the industry-standard ORMs for JavaScript are as follows:
  - Sequelize: This is the most popular ORM for Node.js.
  - Bookshelf: This uses the Knex.js Query Builder.
  - Waterline: This ORM is the default when you use the Node.js framework Sails.js.
  - Objection.js: This is built on top of the Knex.js Query Builder.

  SAP Cloud Application Programming Model provides the advantages of an ORM for the SAP HANA database. It provides an easy way to model both your database schema and service interface. The CDS Definition Language (CDL) is a set of human-readable commands in a universal modeling language that helps you model database schemas and OData schemas as well.

  For querying, creating, updating, and deleting database records, (Query Builder functionality) SAP Cloud Application Programming Model provides CDS Query Language (CQL) and Query Builder APIs. Like most other ORMs, SAP Cloud Application Programming Model aims to support multiple databases, though it officially supports only SAP HANA databases for now.

  As you consider the advantages of SAP Cloud Application Programming Model using the ORM analogy, it's important to understand that SAP Cloud Application Programming Model doesn't call itself an ORM, as it uses CQL for querying, CQL outputs are REST-like, and it doesn't use the object cache.

> **Tip**
> There is an open-source, community effort to bring SAP Cloud Application Programming Model support to the open-source database PostgreSQL. For more details, you can refer to Node.js modules cds-pg and cds-dbm.

- **Create and consume OData services**
  SAP Cloud Application Programming Model lets you define OData entities and expose an OData service. Internally, SAP Cloud Application Programming Model uses the express framework to build an OData server. As part of your extension use case, you may want to connect to SAP and non-SAP OData services to build mash-up scenarios. SAP Cloud Application Programming Model provides tools to easily consume such services and test them locally too.

- **Handle events**
  Event-driven architecture is very popular in the modern microservice-based landscape. Because SAP Cloud Application Programming Model provides support for emitting and consuming events, it also supports asynchronous communication. Using the SAP Event Mesh service in SAP BTP, you can easily subscribe to events of SAP S/4HANA and perform corresponding downstream processes.

- **Authentication and authorization**
  Authentication and authorization are basic requirements of any enterprise application. SAP Cloud Application Programming Model integrates with SAP BTP's authentication and authorization services to enable these features. SAP Cloud Application Programming Model provides several authentication strategies, including basic authentication and JSON Web Token (JWT)-based authentication strategies. It also provides a dummy authentication strategy to disable all authentication and authorization checks during local application testing.

  SAP Cloud Application Programming Model provides annotation-based capabilities for authorization. You can restrict the capabilities of services, as well as specific roles needed for performing a specific action within an OData service.

- **Extend SaaS applications**
  SaaS applications are becoming very common in enterprise landscapes. SAP Cloud Application Programming Model provides a tool to extend such SaaS applications at the tenant level (subscriber level) so that customers can extend, deploy, and consume subscriber-specific extensions.

  In addition to already explained capabilities, SAP Cloud Application Programming Model provides several capabilities:

  - Deploy projects to SAP BTP and SAP HANA XSA
  - Use language-specific texts (i18n) in domain modeling
  - Handle various media files
  - Manage data privacy by identifying private data and integrating with the SAP Personal Data Manager service in SAP BTP

3.3.2   Real-World Scenario

To better understand SAP Cloud Application Programming Model, let's consider how to get started in building the application that is described in the real-world scenario at the beginning of the chapter. Let's rephrase and expand on our requirements and the solution for clarity:

- **Requirement**
  A purchaser in the procurement division of a company issues several purchase orders for fulfilling the requirements of his manufacturing department. Each of these purchase orders has a delivery schedule that is driven by the needs of the manufacturing process. However, suppliers don't always stick to the delivery schedule, which causes delays in manufacturing.

  Currently, whenever there is a likely schedule miss, the purchaser escalates by communicating with suppliers over several emails and following up on the delivery schedule. The purchaser needs to keep his superiors informed about the communications.

- **Pain points**
  The following pain points may occur during this process:
  - At any moment, it's very cumbersome to list all the escalations that are currently under pursuit.
  - It's tedious to collect all the comments from various people on the purchase order.
  - Management has no visibility regarding the status of various escalations at any time.

- **Solution**
  Create an SAP Fiori app, where the purchaser can choose a purchase order and create an escalation against it. Escalation will be a new business object, and comments by various involved parties can be stored against it. The ability to assign statuses to each escalation can let stakeholders know the current status of the escalation. The SAP Fiori app should also list all the current escalations with the ability to search and filter based on various aspects of the escalation object.

- **Technical implementation**
  One easy solution would be to completely build the application in the backend SAP S/4HANA system. However, in that case, we're not keeping the "core clean" and would complicate the future move to an SAP S/4HANA Cloud system. So, we want to build this solution as a *side-by-side extension* while trying to minimize the footprint on the on-premise system.

  Our preferred solution to build a side-by-side extension is to use SAP BTP along with its SAP Extension Suite offering. Figure 3.5 shows this architecture. The SAP S/4HANA on-premise system would expose many APIs for external systems to consume. One of them is a purchase order API that can list purchase orders.

Next, on the SAP BTP layer, you would build a backend application that would *expose* an OData service for the SAPUI5 application to consume. This backend application would also *consume* the Purchase Order OData API from the SAP S/4HANA system and expose purchase orders via an entity set. Whenever a supplier updates the shipping information against a purchase order, the SAPUI5 app would send that to the OData API, and the backend code would capture the information and store it in an SAP HANA database via the SAP HANA Cloud service.

In this scenario, the following tasks need to be performed by the backend application developer:

– Expose the OData service for the SAPUI5 app to consume.

– Consume the OData service from external systems (SAP S/4HANA, in this case).

– Ensure that users need to be authenticated before accessing the preceding OData service.

– Ensure that the app checks the user authorization for performing the read or update.

– Create a data model (schema, tables, views) in the SAP HANA Cloud service.

– Create APIs for storing and retrieving data from the SAP HANA Cloud service in SAP BTP.

– Log errors and messages for troubleshooting.

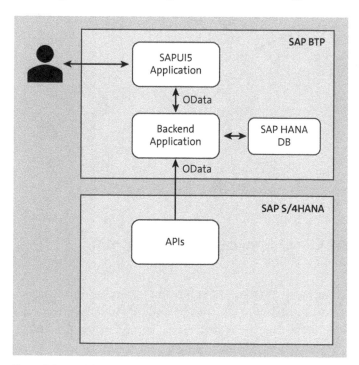

Figure 3.5 Simplified Architecture of Our Solution

3.3.3   Following the Progress in the Real-World Scenario

The real-world scenario we just specified will be developed throughout this book, across the chapters, going forward. We have a Git repository (*http://s-prs.co/ v540901*) where you can see all the code that is used in this book. However, within various lessons and stages of those lessons, you might want to see the code at that point in time. To meet this requirement, we've created multiple Git branches, as shown in Figure 3.6 ❶. The name of the branch indicates which chapter and which stage the code refers to. For example, the branch **chapter3/step4** refers to code in Chapter 3, at the fourth step. In this chapter, look for the Note boxes that will specify these steps when appropriate. The **main** branch contains the final code of the real-world scenario implementation. By clicking on **main** ❷, you can see all the branches available, and clicking on any of these branches will show the code in that branch.

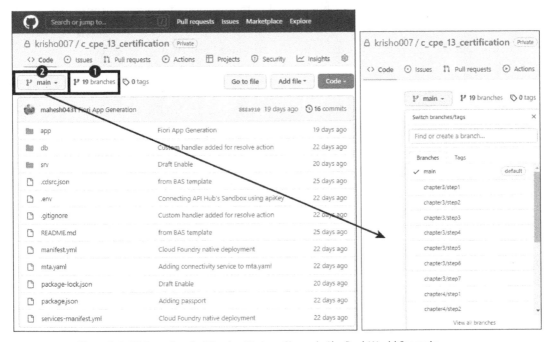

Figure 3.6 Git Branches for Viewing Various Stages in the Real-World Scenario

3.4   Creating an SAP Cloud Application Programming Model Project

In this part, let's start by creating an SAP Cloud Application Programming Model-based OData service. This SAP Cloud Application Programming Model application will serve as the backend for achieving the requirement defined in the previous section.

We'll start by creating a dev space in SAP Business Application Studio to create an SAP Cloud Application Programming Model application. Once you log in to SAP Business Application Studio, click on **Create a New Dev Space**. Provide a suitable name, and select **Full Stack Cloud Application** as the application type (see Figure 3.7), and then click on **Create**. This will trigger the process of creating the dev space, which will take a couple of minutes. Click on the dev space after it gets created to open it. This will open the **Welcome Page** within SAP Business Application Studio.

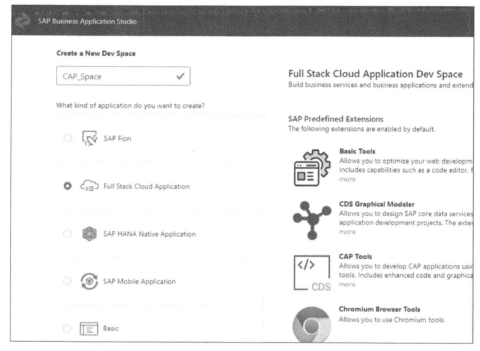

Figure 3.7 Creating a Dev Space for SAP Cloud Application Programming Model Development

To create an SAP Cloud Application Programming Model application, there are several options to choose from:

- Use the **Project Template** option in SAP Business Application Studio.
- Use command `cds init <project name>` in the terminal.
- Use a generator ecosystem such as Yeoman.
- Clone from SAP's sample repositories on GitHub.
- Import a project archive from your local file system.

Let's use the first option of creating an SAP Cloud Application Programming Model application from the SAP Business Application Studio project template. Go to **File • New Project from Template**. Select **SAP CAP Project** as your template, and click **Start**.

Provide a name for your project, and choose **Node.js** as your runtime. Note that Node.js and Java are the only two runtimes available with SAP Cloud Application

Programming Model. Click on the **Finish** button, which will create a project structure as shown in Figure 3.8. The generated project has three folders:

- *app*

  This folder is primarily used to house the static files for the JavaScript-based UI module. This folder is also used to host the AppRouter module (configurations for the AppRouter). AppRouter is the single entry point to your application and is responsible for authentication, authorization, and routing. You'll learn more details about the AppRouter module in subsequent chapters of this book.

- *db*

  This folder contains the database-specific artifacts. This folder contains at least one file in *.cds* format containing database schema definitions in the CDL. Test data also can be loaded into database tables from this folder for nonproduction test scenarios.

- *srv*

  This folder contains the application server logic. Based on your choice of runtime, this will contain either JavaScript or Java files.

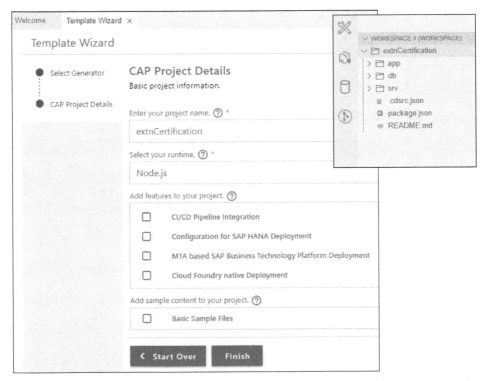

Figure 3.8 Project Template for SAP Cloud Application Programming Model and Generated Project in SAP Business Application Studio

The *package.json* file has the metadata of your SAP Cloud Application Programming Model project (Node.js environment), while the *.cdsrc.json* file has static settings for your project.

3.5   Domain Modeling

When you design an application, it's common to start with domain modeling. Domain modeling identifies various real-world entities (e.g., user, purchase order), aspects of these entities, and relationships between different entities.

The domain model should focus on the problem at hand without getting into the technical details of the implementation. It should be created with the collaboration of domain experts along with application architects and developers to better understand the problem. For domain experts, it can be a way to specify the problem, and, for developers, it can be an input to the database modeling and service modeling.

SAP Cloud Application Programming Model focuses on the domain-driven design by identifying entities in the problem space as the first step. When you start an SAP Cloud Application Programming Model project, you usually start with domain modeling in the CDL. CDL aims to make it easy and natural by using nouns, verbs, and prepositions as language constructs.

When an SAP Cloud Application Programming Model project is *built*, the SAP Cloud Application Programming Model framework creates database artifacts, or the persistence model (tables, columns, indexes, views, etc.), by interpreting the domain model. If a *service* is defined by reusing the domain model, then the domain model will also result in OData artifacts (entity sets, properties, associations, etc.), as shown in Figure 3.9.

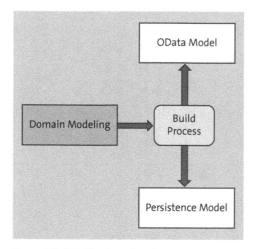

Figure 3.9 SAP Cloud Application Programming Model Interpreting the Domain Model

In this section, we'll briefly go through various artifacts that you can use while modeling the problem domain. While defining these artifacts, you use CDL, which is human readable and easy to write. When writing CDL, sometimes you'll need to query existing entities, and then you use CQL, which is an extension of SQL.

3.5.1   Entities

Entities are structured data types, containing multiple typed elements within them. They aim to represent objects in the problem domain. In Listing 3.1, we define a CDS entity representing a purchase order. The entity has a purchase order number, and its header details as its elements specified along with the data type. The purchase order number is specified as a key property.

```
entity PurchaseOrders {
        key poNumber: String(10);
        supplier: String(10);
        documentType: String(2);
        createdOn: Timestamp;
        createdBy: String(10);
}
```

Listing 3.1 A Simple Entity Declaration

CDS provides several built-in types for representing different data elements. Table 3.1 provides a list of built-in data types that can be used for element definition.

CDS Type
Universally Unique Identifier (UUID; a noninterpretable, 36-character string)
Boolean
Integer
Integer64
Decimal
Double
Date
Time
DateTime
Timestamp
String
Binary
LargeBinary
LargeString

Table 3.1 Built-in Element Types in SAP Cloud Application Programming Model

For entities, the recommended best practices are as follows:

- Provide a name in a plural form, for example, PurchaseOrders, Users, and Suppliers.
- Start the entity name with a capital letter.
- Set element names in lowercase.

3.5.2   Types

Types are common reuse artifacts that let you create new custom types that can be used within your entity, type, or view definitions. They let you keep your entity definitions succinct and consistent while reducing the development efforts.

Types can be about a single element or can contain multiple elements. You can even create a type that adds an association wherever you use it, as shown in Listing 3.2. Listing 3.3 shows how types are consumed.

```
//Single element, derived from a predefined type
type Email: String(120);


//Multiple elements within the type
type Amount {
        value: Decimal(10, 3);
        unit: String (3)
}


//Associations
type Pincode: Association to Pincodes;
```

Listing 3.2 Type Definitions

```
entity UserAddress {
        key employeeId: String(10);
        emailId: Email;
        contribution: Amount;
        pincode: Pincode;
}
```

Listing 3.3 Consuming Types

SAP provides a prebuilt model in `@sap/cds/common` that has `Country`, `Currency`, and `Language` types, which can be reused in your modeling files. For the name of a type, SAP recommends using a singular form with a capital first letter.

3.5.3   Aspects

`Aspect` lets you extend definitions (type, entity, view, etc.) by adding new elements or overriding existing elements. You can extend a predefined definition with an unnamed aspect using `extend … with` keywords. You use *extend* or *annotate* keywords for consuming a named aspect, as shown in Listing 3.4.

```
// Extend using an unnamed aspect
extend PurchaseOrders with {
        documentCategory: String(2);
}
```

```
// define a named aspect
aspect document{
      documentType: String(2);
      documentCategory: String(2);
}

// Using 'with' for using named aspects
extend PurchaseOrders with document;

// Using a named aspect during the definition of an entity
// Using the colon syntax (: shortcut)
entity PurchaseOrders: document {
key poNumber: String(10);
      supplier: String(10);
      createdOn: Timestamp;
      createdBy: String(10);
}
```

Listing 3.4 Aspect Definition and Consumption

SAP Cloud Application Programming Model provides a very handy colon syntax, which is a shortcut for consuming an aspect, as shown in Listing 3.4. Using this syntax, you can consume multiple aspects in a single line.

SAP provides the following three aspects in the @sap/cds/common package:

- **cuid**
  This aspect provides a UUID key to your entity definitions. A unique UUID gets created whenever you add an entry to such an entity. SAP recommends having technical keys in entity definitions, and using a cuid aspect is ideal in such cases.

  `entity Escalations: cuid { / * …..*/}`

- **managed**
  This aspect provides four elements to capture: createdAt, createdBy, updatedAt, and, updatedBy. In addition, whenever there is a new entry or an update entry, these four fields are automatically updated with corresponding details as well.

  Thus, using the managed aspect provides four properties to your entity definitions.

  `entity Escalations: managed { / * …..*/}`

- **temporal**
  This aspect provides two elements of the Timestamp type: validFrom and validTo. This can be used to store the validity timestamp ranges (temporal data) for a database record. SAP Cloud Application Programming Model supports out-of-the-box features for handling temporal data, for example, as-of-now and time travel queries.

  `entity WorkExperiences: temporal { / * …..*/}`

Whenever you query (direct query or via OData) an entity that uses a `temporal` aspect, only records that are valid *as-of-now* are selected.

- `sap.common.CodeList`
  These are SAP-provided code sets. We'll cover this in more detail in the next section.

3.5.4   Code List

Code list refers to a set of valid values for an element. For example, there might be fixed status codes that are valid in a domain. SAP provides code lists for countries, currencies, and languages in package `@sap/cds/common`.

Let's explore how the code list functionality is implemented as specified in Listing 3.5. Here we're creating and consuming a new type called `Status`.

```
// import the CodeList aspect from the common library
using { sap.common.CodeList as CodeList} from '@sap/cds/common';

//Code list entity consuming CodeList aspect
entity Statuses: CodeList{
    key code: String(3)
}

//Type is used for definition of element "status"
type Status : Association to Statuses;

entity Escalations: cuid, managed{
    purchaseOrder: String(10);
    status: Status;
}
```
Listing 3.5 Defining a Code List

Here are the steps involved:

1. An aspect called `CodeList` is available via the `@sap/cds/common` package. Import this package.
2. Define a new entity called `Statuses`, consuming the aspect `CodeList`.
3. Create type `Status` as an association to the preceding entity.
4. Create entity `Escalations` using the newly created type `Status`.

The aspect provides element names and descriptions to hold the content. To maintain data in these entities (code lists), you need to create custom services.

Now the newly created type can be used in any new entity definitions, as shown earlier in Listing 3.5.

3.5.5   Views and Projections

Views and projections are artifacts that aim to create new entities from existing entities. Views get data from two or more views and tables. A projection is derived from a single table or a view. Its primary aim is to expose only selected elements from the underlying entity.

To create a view, you use the syntax as select from, as shown in Listing 3.6.

```
// all elements of PurchaseOrders will be part of entity POs
entity POs as select from PurchaseOrders;

// A view using JOIN..on, and WHERE conditions
entity POs as select from PurchaseOrders JOIN DocumentTypes
          ON PurchaseOrders.documentTypeID = DocumentTypes.ID {
    poNumber, documentTypeID, DocumentTypes.name
} where supplierID = '123'

// defining a projection
entity POValues as projection on POs {
poNumber,
amount,
currency
}
```

Listing 3.6 View Definitions

Views can use all the CQL and the WHERE clauses to create complex view definitions.

If you want to expose only limited elements of an existing entity, you can do so using projection. For defining projection on an existing entity, instead of as select from syntax, you'll use as projection on syntax.

3.5.6   Associations

Associations capture relationships between entities. These associations are interpreted as foreign keys in the database.

As you see in Listing 3.7, you could write a very simple query to fetch the names of document type and supplier using the association name as the table alias. You don't need to specify the JOIN and ON keywords. SAP Cloud Application Programming Model reads it from the association definition within the entity. For this reason, associations in SAP Cloud Application Programming Model are called forward-declared (or predeclared) joins.

```
entity POs {
      key ID: string(10);
      documentType: Association to DocumentTypes on documentType.ID =
        documentType_ID;
```

```
        documentType_ID: string(2);
}
entity DocumentTypes {
        key ID: String(2);
        name: String;
}
//Query for fetching Pos along with document type name and vendor name
SELECT ID, documentType.name from POs
```
Listing 3.7 Associations Simplifying Queries

3.5.7   Unmanaged and Managed Associations

In Listing 3.7 in the previous section, in the definition of entity POs, you can see that association to DocumentTypes is done by specifying the JOIN conditions using the foreign key. Here, the join and the foreign key are fully specified and called managed associations.

In the case of one-to-one associations, you can let CDS implicitly infer the JOIN conditions and automatically add the foreign key elements (documentType_ID, and supplier_ID). Specifying the association is simple in this case, as shown in Listing 3.8. CDS lets you create one-to-many and many-to-many associations as well.

```
entity POs {
        key ID: string(10);
        documentType: Association to DocumentTypes;
        supplier: Association to Suppliers;
}
entity Suppliers {
        key ID: String(12);
        name: String;
}
entity DocumentTypes {
        key ID: string(2);
}
```
Listing 3.8 Unmanaged Associations

3.5.8   Compositions

Composition is a special type of association where the associated entity (child entity) can't exist without the parent entity. For example, consider the Items entity and PurchaseOrders entity. As items can't exist without the purchase order, this is a valid example of composition.

Listing 3.9 shows how to define compositions. The Composition of many is the key syntax in this case.

```
entity POs {
      key ID: String(10);
      Items: Composition of many Items on Items.parent = $self;
}
entity Items {
      key itemID : String(5);
      key parent : Association to POs;
      materialID: String(10);
      quantity: Integer;
}
```

Listing 3.9 Defining Compositions

3.5.9   Actions and Functions

You can create OData function imports by defining actions and functions in the service definition. Actions and functions are operations that aren't any of the create, read, update, and delete (CRUD) operations.

An action is an operation that will have a side effect; that is, it's going to update an entity or an object in the backend. Action is invoked by an HTTP POST method, whereas a function is defined for all operations that don't make any updates (i.e., not having any side effects). The function is invoked by an HTTP GET method. Within our service definition in Listing 3.10, we define action closeEscalation to close an escalation. Action definition here specifies that it takes escalationId as the input. Actions and functions can also return elements of simple types or even entity types, as shown in Listing 3.10.

```
// Action returing a predefined type
action closeEscalation(EscalationId: String) returns String;

// Function returning a single instance of an entity
function getLatestEscalation() returns Escalations;

// Function returning a collection of instances of an entity
function getTopEscalations() returns array of Escalations;
```

Listing 3.10 Defining Actions and Functions

Actions can be bound to an entity as well. *Bound* means it has been specified that the action/function will perform an action on the entity. In the following code, action retire is getting defined for entity Employees. The action returns a String as well.

```
service HumanResource {
      entity Employees as projection on db.Managers
            actions {
```

```
        action retire() returns String;
    };
}
```

To call this action, you would use URL */<service name>/Employees(id=123)/retire().*

3.5.10   Real-World Scenario: Domain Model

Now, let's use the CDS data modeling concepts you've learned so far and define the domain model for the use case at hand. In our scenario, purchase orders are coming from the backend SAP S/4HANA system, while we're going to need persistence (database tables) for data related to the escalation object.

Inside the *db* folder, create a new file with the name *schema.cds*. Let's define our simple domain model here to model the escalation object. Add the content shown in Listing 3.11 to *schema.cds*. Notice that we're not defining entities for the purchase orders because this entity will be coming from an external OData service (from an SAP S/4HANA system). We'll talk about consuming external OData services in the next chapter.

In Listing 3.11, we start with importing aspects managed, cuid, and CodeList. Then, we define an entity called Statuses using the CodeList aspect. As you learned earlier, it provides properties name and descr (for description). We also create a type Status as an association to the Statuses entity. Then, we create an entity called Comments that uses managed and cuid aspects to store comments of an escalation. In addition, we define the main CDS entity with the name Escalations that will contain all the escalations. The entity will also contain an association with Comments.

```
using { managed, cuid, sap.common.CodeList as CodeList } from '@sap/cds/
common';
namespace my.dataModel;

entity Statuses: CodeList{
    key code: String(2)
}

type Status: Association to Statuses;

entity Comments: managed, cuid{
    comment: String;
    escalation: Association to Escalations;
}

entity Escalations: managed, cuid {
    description: String (80);
    material: String(30);
    expectedDate: Date;
```

```
    status: Status;
    comments: Composition of many Comments on comments.escalation = $self;
};
```

Listing 3.11 Code in the schema.cds File, Defining a CDS Entity

> **Note**
> The preceding code can be seen in the repository at *http://s-prs.co/v540901*, branch chapter3/step1.

3.5.11   Core Data Services Language to Core Schema Notation

Core Schema Notation (CSN) is an open specification initiated by SAP to represent domain and service models. The CSN specification is based on the JSON specification but extended to represent entity-relationship models and entity extensions.

Figure 3.10 shows how a CDS model gets processed. A CDS toolset parses a CDS model (written using CDL and CQL) into a CSN schema representation.

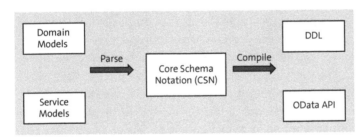

Figure 3.10 Processing CDS Models

CSN is the intermediate, target-technology-independent representation that aims to be an input to technology-specific tools. For example, for the SAP HANA database, SAP Cloud Application Programming Model provides tools that transform the CSN into SAP HANA database-specific Data Definition Language (DDL) statements. By introducing CSN, SAP hopes to make it easy to create compilers for other databases and technologies beyond SAP HANA.

Let's get the CSN for the simple domain model defined so far. This is for exploration purposes, and you don't have to do this during development.

Open a terminal in SAP Business Application Studio at the root folder of the project and run the following command:

```
cds compile db/schema.cds -2 json
```

This will provide the output as a CSN model, as shown in Figure 3.11. As you can observe, the CSN format is very readable and easy to associate with the domain model we've defined so far.

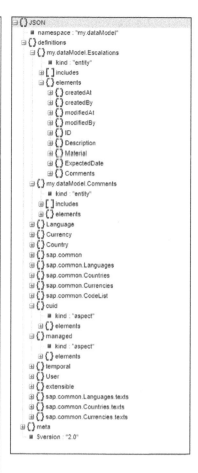

The left side shows JSON/CSN code:

```json
{
  "namespace": "my.dataModel",
  "definitions": {
    "my.dataModel.Escalations": {
      "kind": "entity",
      "includes": [
        "managed",
        "cuid"
      ],
      "elements": {
        "createdAt": {
          "@cds.on.insert": {
            "=": "$now"
          },
          "@UI.HiddenFilter": true,
          "@Core.Immutable": true,
          "@title": "{i18n>CreatedAt}",
          "@readonly": true,
          "@odata.on.insert": {
            "#": "now"
          },
          "type": "cds.Timestamp"
        },
        "createdBy": {
          "@cds.on.insert": {
            "=": "$user"
          },
          "@UI.HiddenFilter": true,
          "@Core.Immutable": true,
          "@title": "{i18n>CreatedBy}",
          "@readonly": true,
          "@odata.on.insert": {
            "#": "user"
          },
          "@description": "{i18n>UserID.Description}",
          "type": "User",
          "length": 255
        },
        "modifiedAt": {
          "@cds.on.insert": {
            "=": "$now"
          },
          "@cds.on.update": {
            "=": "$now"
          },
          "@UI.HiddenFilter": true,
          "@title": "{i18n>ChangedAt}",
          "@readonly": true,
          "@odata.on.update": {
            "#": "now"
          },
          "type": "cds.Timestamp"
        },
        "modifiedBy": {
          "@cds.on.insert": {
            "=": "$user"
          },
          "@cds.on.update": {
            "=": "$user"
          },
          "@UI.HiddenFilter": true,
          "@title": "{i18n>ChangedBy}",
          "@readonly": true,
```

The right side shows a JSON tree view:

```
JSON
  namespace : "my.dataModel"
  definitions
    my.dataModel.Escalations
      kind : "entity"
      includes
      elements
        createdAt
        createdBy
        modifiedAt
        modifiedBy
        ID
        Description
        Material
        ExpectedDate
        Comments
    my.dataModel.Comments
      kind : "entity"
      includes
      elements
    Language
    Currency
    Country
    sap.common
    sap.common.Languages
    sap.common.Countries
    sap.common.Currencies
    sap.common.CodeList
    cuid
      kind : "aspect"
      elements
    managed
      kind : "aspect"
      elements
    temporal
    User
    extensible
    sap.common.Languages.texts
    sap.common.Countries.texts
    sap.common.Currencies.texts
  meta
  $version : "2.0"
```

Figure 3.11 Generated CSN

You can also see that CSN got created for aspects managed and cuid as well.

3.5.12   Database interactions

Querying data is needed both while defining the data model and while writing server code to fetch data from database tables. Database modification operations are usually done only in the server code in custom handlers. Typically, database interactions are achieved by executing SQL queries.

SAP Cloud Application Programming Model provides two ways of writing such database queries:

- **CDS Query Language (CQL)**
  CQL is based on SQL and so looks very similar to SQL; however, it greatly enhances the SQL syntax. Listing 3.12 shows a few examples.

```
SELECT from Escalations { ID, purchaseOrder, status }
//Reading items of a Purchase order = 12345
SELECT from PurchaseOrders[12345].items
```

Listing 3.12 Examples of CQL

- **Query Builder APIs**

  SAP Cloud Application Programming Model provides APIs based on the cds.ql object. Listing 3.13 shows a few examples of CRUD operations using Query Builder APIs.

```
INSERT.into('Escalations').entries({ID:200, purchaseOrder:'123123',
  priority:'2'})
SELECT.one.from('Escalations').where({ID:100})
UPDATE('Escalations'). ).where({ID:'100'}).with({priority:'2'})
DELETE.from('Escalations') .where({ID:100})
```

Listing 3.13 Examples of Using the Query Builder API

3.6 Creating OData Services

Creating services lets you expose the functionality you build to external consumers. In this section, let's explore how to create an OData service using SAP Cloud Application Programming Model.

3.6.1 Service Modeling

An OData service (or service interface) can be defined using the service keyword. A service definition will contain a list of entities defined in the CDS language (in a *.cds* file, similar to the domain model), which will get exposed as entities within the service as shown here:

```
service demoService {
      //Entity definitions
}
```

By convention, you create service definitions in files inside the *srv* folder.

During service definition, first, you import the entities you defined in the domain model (*db/schema.cds*). If the domain model has a namespace, you can just refer to the namespace and provide an alias to it (as *db*) for ease of use.

Though you can define new entities within the service, you don't normally have to do it because the problem domain is already modeled as entities while creating the domain model. So, service definitions will usually contain projections on the entities of the domain model. Thus, services act as a facade to the domain model, deciding what gets exposed to the consumer of the service, as shown in Figure 3.12.

Entity definitions can be simple projection-based definitions, and these definitions can use complex CQL queries here to filter data records, include specific elements, and exclude specific elements of the underlying entity from the domain data.

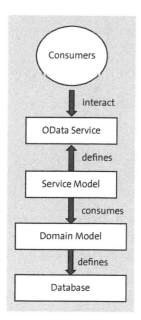

Figure 3.12 Services in SAP Cloud Application Programming Model

Once you define the domain model and service model, it's normal for developers to go on to implement the various CRUD operations on the entities. However, SAP Cloud Application Programming Model makes it easier. Both Node.js and Java runtimes provide automatic, generic implementations for CRUD operations. As soon as you define the service, you'll have CRUD functionality working for the entities defined in the domain model (and exposed via the service model). Following are a few important OData functionalities in addition to generic CRUD that are available by generic providers without writing any code:

- **Query options**
  Query with pagination, sorting, and filtering.
- **Deep Read**
  Read and query with $expand option to get the associated entities.
- **Deep insert**
  Create a new entity along with children.
- **Deep update**
  Based on the existence of child entities, child entities will be created, updated, or deleted.
- **Deep delete**
  This is useful when the association is created via composition. Whenever the entity gets deleted, all the composition entities also get deleted.

- **UUID keys**
  When an entity has UUID as the key and when a new entry is inserted into it, UUID automatically is generated and assigned to that record.
- **Search functionality**
  When you issue an OData search query, SAP Cloud Application Programming Model runtime's generic implementation will search the search string in all the text fields of the entity.
- **Input validations**
  SAP Cloud Application Programming Model automatically validates the input based on various annotations. We'll talk about these annotations in upcoming sections.
- **Automatic field updates**
  Using annotations, you can automatically fill the user name and timestamp upon insert and delete operations.
- **ETag support**
  SAP Cloud Application Programming Model runtime supports optimistic concurrency via ETags. An element of the entity needs to be marked as an ETag via annotations. This element needs to uniquely change with every update to the entity row.

3.6.2   Real-World Scenario: Create a Service

Let's create the service needed for achieving the real-world scenario. Create a new file with the name *service.cds* inside the *srv* folder. Note that the file extension is *.cds*, which indicates that the service is defined as a CDS model. Insert the content from Listing 3.14.

```
using { my.dataModel as my } from '../db/schema';
service EscalationManagementService {
    entity Escalations as projection on my.Escalations;
    entity Comments as projection on my.Comments;
    entity Statuses as projection on my.Statuses;
}
```

Listing 3.14 Service Definition Using CDS

Here, we define a service with the name `EscalationManagementService`. Within the service definition, we can define entities. In this case, we create a new entity with the name `Escalations`, which is going to be a projection of the `Escalation` entity that we defined in the domain model. Note that entities of the imported domain model are accessed via the `my` alias that we gave to the imported model with namespace `my.dataModel`. In addition, we also expose `Comments` and `Statuses` entity sets from the domain model as shown.

In Listing 3.14, we have an entity with the name Escalations. Let's create a bound action for this entity with the name resolve to close the escalation as shown here:

```
service EscalationManagementService {
    entity Escalations as projection on db.Escalations
        actions {
            action resolve();
        };
}
```

> **Note**
>
> The above code can be seen in the repository *http://s-prs.co/v540901*, branch chapter3/ step2.

3.7   Running Locally

Now that the domain model and service model are defined, let's explore how to run the application locally. We'll have simulated data to see the result of our coding so far. We'll also explore how to run the app locally while connecting to SAP HANA Cloud. In these steps, you'll learn new concepts to immediately apply to real-world scenarios.

3.7.1   Running the SAP Cloud Application Programming Model Project

As you develop the application, it's important to run the application and see if we're getting the desired outputs. To run the SAP Cloud Application Programming Model project, you can open a terminal at the root of the project and run command cds run or cds watch. This starts a CDS server and runs the current project. The cds watch command monitors the project files for any changes and restarts the server to reflect the latest changes. If you're aware of node development, you can compare the cds watch command to the nodemon command or tool.

Figure 3.13 shows the output of the cds watch command. The top portion ❶ shows that it has found CDS models in two files of our project. One is our domain model file (*schema.cds*), and the other is the service definition (*service.cds*).

As it's not practical to have an SAP HANA database run locally (in the local system or in the SAP Business Application Studio dev space), the SAP Cloud Application Programming Model framework provides an in-memory SQLite database (already installed in the SAP Business Application Studio dev space). When the app runs locally, it launches an SQLite in-memory database and deploys the models into it as the log shows ❷.

```
[cds] - model loaded from 2 file(s):          ①

  .\db\schema.cds
  .\srv\service.cds

[cds] - connect using bindings from: { registry: '~/.cds-services.json' }
[cds] - connect to db > sqlite { url: ':memory:' }
/> successfully deployed to sqlite in-memory db      ②                                         ③

[cds] - serving EscalationManagementService { at: '/escalation-management', impl: '.\\srv\\service.js' }

[cds] - server listening on { url: 'http://localhost:4004' }      ④
[cds] - launched at 22/4/2022, 5:52:22 pm, in: 734.04ms
[cds] - [ terminate with ^C ]
```

Figure 3.13 Output of the "cds watch" Command

Warning!

It's important to keep in mind that there are some edge scenarios where your application might work fine during the local run but fail during the deployment to the SAP HANA database. This is because SAP HANA can have more or different limitations and rules compared to SQLite, which is used while running locally.

In the next portion ❸, the log specifies that the service EscalationManagement-Service is running at the path '/escalation-management'. This path was auto-generated by the SAP Cloud Application Programming Model framework from the specified service name. The server is running at the address *http://localhost:4004* ❹. So you can access the service at *http://localhost:4004/escalation-management*. You can also specify a custom path to the service as follows:

```
service EscalationManagementService @(path: 'ems'){
      ...;
}
```

In the preceding code, the path annotation changes the URL of the service. The service would be available at URL *http://localhost:4004/ems*.

Note

You can't run these URLs (pointing to localhost) from your browser because the app is running on the dev space of the SAP Business Application Studio, not in your local system. You can hold the `Ctrl` key and click on the preceding URLs within the terminal output to open this URL pointing to the dev space.

3.7.2   Adding Test Data

To read collection **Escalations**, you can call URL *http://localhost:4004/ems/Escalations*. However, it won't provide any data because we haven't created any data yet in the local SQLite database. SAP Cloud Application Programming Model provides a feature to run with hard-coded data from a comma-separated values (CSV) file for testing purposes. This file needs to be present in any of the *db/data*, *db/csv*, or *db/ src/csv* folders. The name of the file has to be in the form *<namespace>-<entity name>.csv*. The SAP Cloud Application Programming Model framework lets you create this form automatically using terminal command `cds add data –for < entity name with namespace>`. Figure 3.14 shows the command, the command's output, and the generated file. The generated file will have the name of the elements (case insensitive) as headers of the CSV file data.

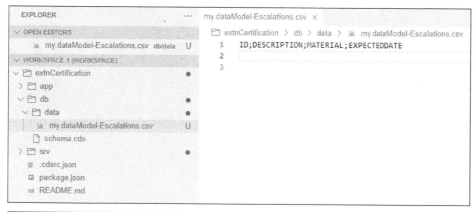

Figure 3.14 Adding File for Adding Test Data for an Entity

Let's add a couple of test records as follows:

```
ID;DESCRIPTION;MATERIAL;EXPECTEDDATE
12;For ABC project;123;1991-12-12
32;For material xyz;124;2012-12-01
```

`cds watch` will restart the server with the updated data. You can manually refresh the OData URL for the collection, which will result in the output shown in Listing 3.15.

```
{
    @odata.context: "$metadata#Escalations",
    value: [
        {
```

```
                                    ID: "12",
                                    Description: "For ABC project",
                                    Material: "123",
                                    ExpectedDate: "1991-12-12"
                                    },
                                    {
                                    ID: "32",
                                    Description: "For material xyz",
                                    Material: "124",
                                    ExpectedDate: "2012-12-01"
                                    }
                        ]
}
```

Listing 3.15 Output Showing the Test Data Added in the CSV File

Let's also add test data for the Statuses entity in the *db/data/my.dataModel-Statuses.csv* file, as shown in Listing 3.16.

```
code;name;descR
DRF;Draft;Escalation not yet sent to the vendor
INP;In Progress;Escalation sent to vendor
CMP;Resolved;Escalation is closed
```

Listing 3.16 Test Data for the Statuses Entity Set

> **Note**
> The preceding code can be seen in the repository at *http://s-prs.co/v540901*, branch chapter3/step3.

3.7.3 Connecting to SAP HANA Cloud

When you move the SAP Cloud Application Programming Model application to the server, you usually connect it to an SAP HANA Cloud service from SAP BTP as the database. However, you can still run the application locally while connecting to the SAP HANA Cloud service. Let's explore how to achieve this.

The first step is to create an instance of SAP HANA Cloud on SAP BTP:

1. Navigate to the space in your Cloud Foundry cockpit.
2. Click on **SAP HANA Cloud**, and then click on the **Create** button, as shown in Figure 3.15 ❶. This will take you to a wizard for creating the SAP HANA instance.

3. Choose the **SAP HANA Cloud, SAP HANA Database** ❷, and click on the **Next** button.

4. In the next screen (**General / Basics**), provide a name for the SAP HANA instance, and set the administrator password for the SAP HANA instance, as shown in Figure 3.16 ❸, and click on the **Next Step** button.

5. On the next screen (**SAP HANA Database**), you can leave the memory as 30 GB ❹ and click **Next**.

6. In the SAP HANA Database Advanced Settings screen, choose **Allow all IP addresses** ❺. This is required to connect to the SAP HANA instance from outside SAP BTP (e.g., from VS Code). You would usually select **Allow only BTP IP addresses** in a production instance.

7. Click on the **Create Instance** button on the current screen. This would take 10 to 15 minutes for creating an SAP HANA instance.

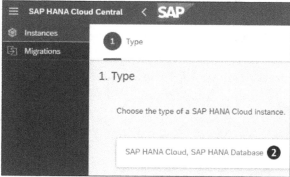

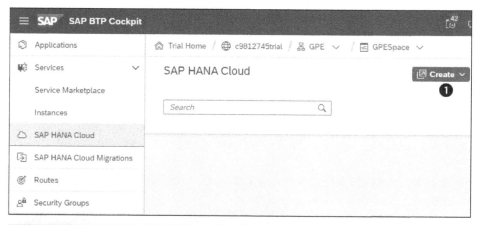

Figure 3.15 Steps for Creating an Instance of an SAP HANA Cloud Service in SAP BTP – Part 1

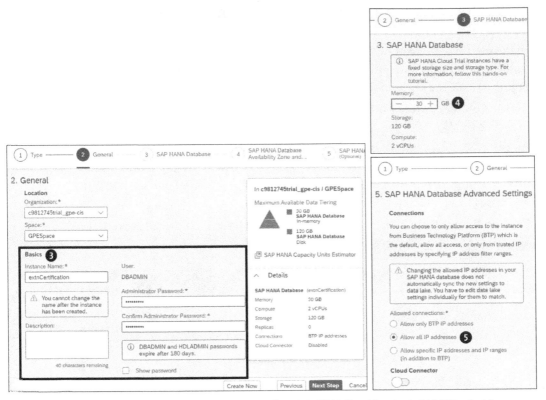

Figure 3.16 Steps for Creating an Instance of an SAP HANA Cloud Service in SAP BTP – Part 2

Now that we have the SAP HANA Cloud instance created, we need to add the required configurations to the project:

1. At the home directory, open a terminal and run command cds add hana. This command does the following:

   – Adds the hdb (SAP HANA client) node library as a dependency (within *package.json*)

   – Adds cds.requires and cds.hana parts in *package.json* as follows:

   ```
   "cds": {
     "requires": {
       "db": {
         "kind": "sql"
       }
     },
     "hana": {
       "deploy-format": "hdbtable"
     }
   }
   ```

   – Adds the SAP HANA (SAP HANA deployment infrastructure container) resource, a deployer module in the *mta.yaml* file

– Adds the SAP HANA resource as a requirement to the srv module in the *mta.yaml* file

You don't have the *mta.yaml* file yet, so you can ignore these changes for now.

Note

The preceding code can be seen in the repository at *http://s-prs.co/v540901*, branch chapter3/step4.

2. Now log in to Cloud Foundry using the command cf login, and choose the right org and space. This step is required as the next step needs to connect to Cloud Foundry and to the SAP HANA Cloud instance we created before.

3. Deploy the domain model to SAP HANA, and create local connection files to connect to the SAP HANA instance while running the app locally. SAP Cloud Application Programming Model provides a simple command to achieve all these:

```
cds deploy --to hana
```

Important parts of the output of this command include the triggering of the command (see Figure 3.17 ❶) and the step where service instance escalation-db gets created along with a service key ❷. Because we haven't deployed the app to Cloud Foundry yet, there is no HDI container available. This command creates the HDI container if not available.

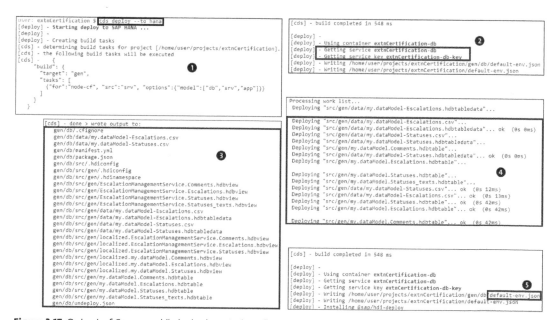

Figure 3.17 Output of Command "cds deploy --to hana"

The lower-left code portion ❸ shows the generation of SAP HANA-specific artifacts. Other portions of the code show the deployment of SAP HANA artifacts to

SAP HANA Cloud ❹ and the creation of the *default-env.json* file ❺, which contains the credentials to connect to the SAP HANA Cloud instance while testing the app locally.

4. The next step is to update the *package.json* file for the SAP Cloud Application Programming Model app to specify to use hana (from sql) as shown here:

```
"cds": {
  "requires": {
    "db": {
      "kind": "hana"
    }
  }
}
```

5. As dependencies were updated with the previous command, run command npm install on the root folder to install those dependencies.

6. Now you can run command cds watch. This will run the app locally, but it will connect to SAP HANA Cloud for the database (not from the CSV files in the */srv/db* folder). This can be very useful in bug-fixing scenarios.

3.7.4   CDS Bind Command

In the previous section, you've seen how you can test the app locally while connecting to SAP HANA Cloud. What if you need to connect to other SAP BTP services while running locally? For this purpose, SAP Cloud Application Programming Model provides command cds bind. However, the service to be connected to should be already available in SAP BTP. Let's explore how to use this command.

After the previous command, the *default-env.json* file in the root folder contains the credentials to connect. Let's delete this file and try running the app locally. You'll get an error now.

Now to connect to any cloud service, you can use the following command:

```
cds bind -2 <instance name of the service> --kind <name of the service>
```

For connecting to SAP HANA, you can run the following command:

```
cds bind -2 escalation-db --kind hana
```

Now to run the app locally by connecting to the SAP HANA service, you can run the following command:

```
cds watch --profile hybrid
```

This command can be used to connect to any service instance such as destination and xsuaa, as well as other SAP BTP services.

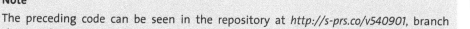

Note
The preceding code can be seen in the repository at *http://s-prs.co/v540901*, branch chapter3/step5.

3.8 Custom Handlers

Generic service providers of the SAP Cloud Application Programming Model framework provide a great deal of functionality out of the box. However, in real-world projects, generic service providers alone rarely meet the requirements. There will be customer-specific requirements that generic providers can't meet. SAP Cloud Application Programming Model provides custom handlers for this.

SAP Cloud Application Programming Model is architectured around events, meaning that events are emitted for various operations (CRUD, functions, and actions) that get triggered on the service exposed by SAP Cloud Application Programming Model. You can write event handlers (simple JavaScript functions) for these events that will help you add and override the functionality of generic service providers. Events provide event contexts, which can be used within the custom handlers to get details of the request and perform actions as required.

This section covers how to write custom handlers and what APIs to use.

3.8.1 Writing Custom Handlers

You can write your custom handlers at specific predefined locations, and the SAP Cloud Application Programming Model runtime will consider those custom handlers. There are several options:

- In a JavaScript file that has the same name as the *.cds* file of your service definition. This file has to be a sibling of your service definition file. For example, if your service is defined in *srv/service.cds*, you can write custom handlers at *srv/service.js*.
- In a *.js* file with the same name but inside either the *lib* or *handlers* folder. For example, if your service is defined in *srv/service.cds*, you can write custom handlers at *srv/lib/service.js* or *srv/handlers/service.js*.
- In any JavaScript file, and specified using @impl annotation. For example, if your service is defined in *srv/service.cds*, and the custom handlers are in the file *srv/custom/handler.js*.

Now you need to specify the @impl annotation as follows:

```
service EscalationManagementService @(impl: './custom/handler.js') { }
```

Inside the *.js* file, multiple handlers can be written inside a plain function, as shown in Listing 3.17.

```
module.exports = function () {
    //Custom handler 1
    this.on("READ", "Escalations", (req) => {
        //custom code
     });

    //Custom handler 2
    this.after("CREATE", "Escalations", (req) => {
        //custom code
    });
};
```

Listing 3.17 Custom Handler Functions inside a Function

3.8.2 Application Programming Interface for Handler Registration

Listing 3.17 in the previous section shows that you register handlers on object this. Here this is an instance of the cds.Service class. You can provide an arrow function as well, as shown in Listing 3.18. In this listing object service refers to an instance of the cds.Service class. Note that the function returned here (including the arrow function) can be by an async function so that you can use the await construct within it.

```
module.exports = (service)=>{
    //Custom handler 1
    service.on("READ", "Escalations", (req) => {
        //custom code
     });

    //Custom handler 2
    service.after("CREATE", "Escalations", (req) => {
        //custom code
    });
};
```

Listing 3.18 Using the Arrow Function for Registering Custom Handlers

3.8.3 Explicit Way of Registering Event Handlers

Instead of returning a function that implicitly registers event handlers (as in Listing 3.17 and Listing 3.18), you can explicitly subclass cds.Service class (or any of its subclasses), register handlers within the redefinition of the init method, and return this class as module.exports. This flavor of registering handlers may not be as simple as the previous methods you saw, but it provides more readability on what is happening while registering handlers. You need to ensure that you call the superclass's init method to ensure that all the event handlers specified in the superclass's init method are also considered. See Listing 3.19 for the specification.

```
const cds = require('@sap/cds');
class ExtSubClass extends cds.Service {
      async init(){
            //New event handler registrations
      this.on("READ", "Escalations", (req) => {
            //custom code
      });

      //Custom handler 2
      this.after("CREATE", "Escalations", (req) => {
      //custom code
      });
            //Ensure event registrations by parent class are considered
            await super.init();
      }
}
module.exports = ExtSubClass;
```

Listing 3.19 Event Handler Registrations via Subclass

3.8.4   Phases of Events

If you consider each operation (CRUD, functions, actions) as an event, you can consider three phases for any event. Event handlers can be attached to each of these three event phases. Here is the general scheme of attaching an event handler for a CRUD operation:

```
this.<event phase>(<event>, <entityset>, <handling function>)
```

The three phases of an event are as follows:

- **On**

  This event handler is useful for overriding the functionality provided by SAP Cloud Application Programming Model's generic service provider. Here is an example.

  ```
  module.exports = function() {
    this.on("CREATE", "Escalations", (req, next)=>{
          //Your code for custom behavior goes here
    });
  }
  ```

  This custom provider will override the generic behavior provided by the SAP Cloud Application Programming Model framework. However, if you want to go to the generic behavior in some cases, you can call the statement await next();.

  You can have multiple handlers for the on phase, but if one of the on handlers successfully executes and sets a return value, then the remaining on handlers are skipped. In the case of multiple on handlers, they are executed in the order of their registration provided the predecessor calls await next().

- **Before**
  This event handler is useful for validations and other preprocessing requirements. This is run before the on handlers. If the validation fails, you can call function req.reject or request.error and send an error (along with HTTP status **400**) back, as shown in Listing 3.20.

```
module.exports = function (){
    this.before("READ", "Escalations", async (req)=>{

        //validate the request here
        //…

        //reject the request if the request isn't valid
        req.reject(400, "Not a great request");
    });
}
```

Listing 3.20 Example of a "Before" Handler

If there are multiple before handlers, all of them will be called (in parallel) unless one of them calls the req.reject function. You should not make assumptions about the order of execution in the case of multiple handlers. In this case, req.error can be useful as it won't stop other handlers from running but will collect all the errors to be shown to the user. See Figure 3.18 for outputs in each of these cases.

Figure 3.18 "request.reject" versus "request.error"

- **After**

  This event handler is useful for postprocessing tasks such as triggering other actions and augmenting the output of generic handlers. These handlers are run after the on handler. Just like before handlers, multiple handlers for the after phase of the event are executed in parallel, and no assumptions should be done about the sequence of those handlers.

  The handler function for the after event gets the data that was returned from the on handler. In addition, the request object is also available, as you can see in Figure 3.19. The description element of the data object was overwritten with the req.path, and you can see that the output reflects that.

  Even within the after event handler, you can return an error using request. reject or return multiple errors using request.error.

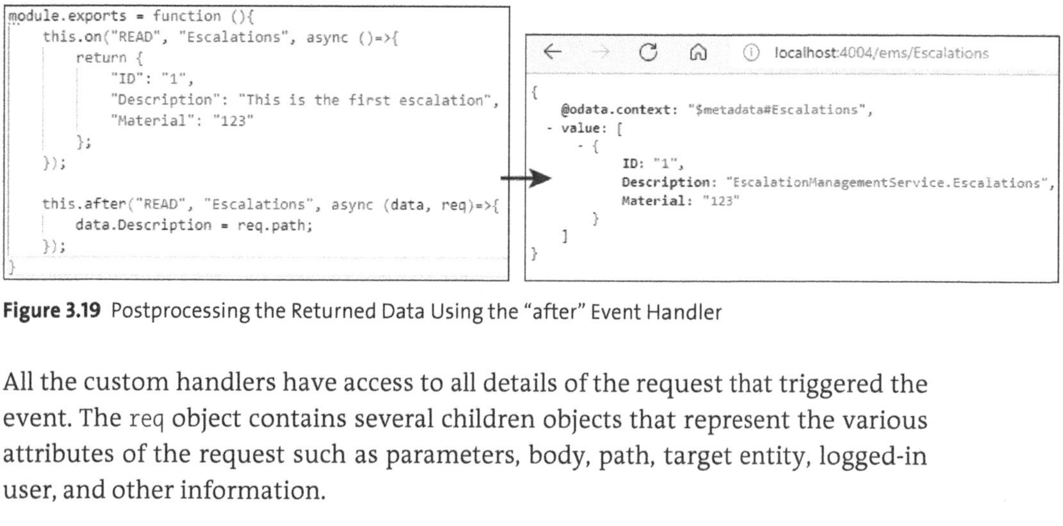

Figure 3.19 Postprocessing the Returned Data Using the "after" Event Handler

All the custom handlers have access to all details of the request that triggered the event. The req object contains several children objects that represent the various attributes of the request such as parameters, body, path, target entity, logged-in user, and other information.

3.8.5   Real-World Scenario: Creating Custom Handlers

Consider the requirement of closing escalations. In this case, you need to update the status of the escalation as CMP in the implementation of the 'resolve' action. Generic handlers of SAP Cloud Application Programming Model can take care of CRUD functionality on the Escalations entity. However, we need to explicitly code the behavior of the actions and functions. We could have done this via an UPDATE call, but we're doing this via an action for the demo purpose.

Let's create a file with the name **service.js** inside the **srv** folder. Within this service, we need to write a handler for implementing the behavior of the resolve action. As you see in Listing 3.21, whenever the action is called, an update is issued on the Escalation entity to update the status as 'CMP'.

```
const cds = require('@sap/cds');

module.exports = cds.service.impl(async function () {
```

```
this.on('resolve', async (req) => {
    const tx = cds.tx(req);
    await tx.run(
        UPDATE('Escalations')
            .set({ 'Status_code': 'CMP' })
            .where({ ID: req.params[0].ID })
    );
})
});
```

Listing 3.21 Custom Handler with Code to Implement the Action

Note

The preceding code can be seen in the repository at *http://s-prs.co/v540901*, branch chapter3/step6.

3.9   Emitting and Subscribing to Events

Publish-subscribe is an important system design pattern that is used to create resilient and efficient systems. In this architectural design, publishers emit events, and then consumers subscribe to events and perform required actions. Figure 3.20 shows a typical publish-subscribe architecture system.

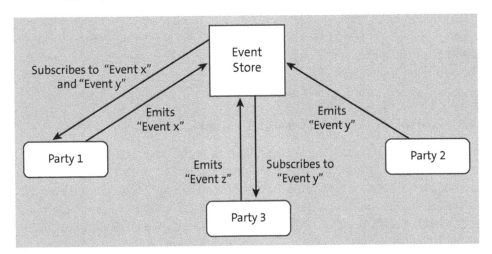

Figure 3.20 A Typical Publish-Subscribe Architecture

Tip

Within the SAP Cloud Application Programming Model framework, most of the functionality of generic providers is provided as event handlers.

The publish-subscribe design has the following advantages:

- **Resiliency due to asynchronous communication**
  In a microservices architecture, it's common to have requirements to communicate between multiple microservices. However, if these communications are synchronous, the client or the communication initiator needs the other party to be available whenever the communication happens. If the other party isn't available, the initiator won't know how to proceed, thus the initiator application will fail as well, and the whole application will go down. However, in a publish-subscribe architecture, the receivers can afford to go down without bringing down the whole application. Whenever the receiver comes back online, the event will be delivered to it. The sender will be designed to just emit the event and continue the processing without waiting for the acknowledgment from the receivers.

- **Decoupling**
  In a publish-subscribe architecture, there is no direct communication between the parties. This makes it easy to scale individual microservices independently, thus optimizing the resources. Decoupling also means that more microservices can subscribe to the event without the need for the sender to know all the receivers. This allows for dynamic targets in the communication.

Let's explore how to achieve event-based communication within an SAP Cloud Application Programming Model-based application. There are three steps involved in implementing such an application:

1. **Define events.**
   Events are defined within the service definition file. In Listing 3.22, event escalationCreated is defined. In addition to the name, the event also has a body that specifies the data that is going to accompany the event. However, this is just the definition of the event, and the SAP Cloud Application Programming Model runtime doesn't know when to trigger this event. That action is described in the next step.

```
service EscalationManagementService {
    entity Escalations as projection on db.Escalations;

    event escalationCreated : {
        escalationID : type of Escalations : ID;
        createdBy    : String;
        title        : String
    }
}
```

Listing 3.22 Definition of Event "escalationCreated"

2. **Emit events.**
   In this step, you define when the defined event should be triggered, which is after an escalation is created. To emit an event, use the *srv.emit* API, as shown in

Listing 3.23. While triggering an event, in addition to specifying the event name, you can send data that can help the receiver identify the event and take necessary actions.

```
module.exports = function() {
    this.after("CREATE", "Escalations", (req)=>{
        let { ID, createdBy, description } = req.data;
        const event = this.emit("escalationCreated", { ID, createdBy,
description });
        return event;
    })
}
```

Listing 3.23 Triggering an Event Using the srv.emit API

3. **Subscribe to events.**
   This step is done by the consumer of the event, which can be another SAP Cloud Application Programming Model-based microservice. In this microservice, you first connect to the service that is offering the event. Then you use the *srv.on* API to subscribe to the event and write a function to call whenever the subscribed event occurs. This is shown in Listing 3.24.

```
const esc = cds.connect.to('EscalationManagementService');
esc.on("escalationCreated", (data)=>{
        //Do actions to handle the event
});
```

Listing 3.24 Connecting to the Service and Subscribing to an Event

3.10   Building and Deploying

In this section, let's explore how to build the app and deploy it to the Cloud Foundry instance. We'll get started with the Cloud Foundry native deployment tool cf push to discover its challenges and then learn about the cf deploy tool. In this section, you'll work on the real-world scenario project as you learn concepts around build and deployment.

3.10.1   Cloud Foundry Native Deployment

In a native SAP BTP, Cloud Foundry environment, an application is deployed to the server via command cf push. This command requires the app to contain a set of configurations in a YAML file at the root folder with the name *manifest.yml*. You can easily create this file with command cds add cf-manifest at the root of the project. This creates *manifest.yml* and *services-manifest.yml* at the root of your application. Let's explore the generated files.

In *manifest.json*, there are two applications defined. One is for the OData service module (extnCertification-srv), while the other is a deployer module that just deploys the database artifacts (extnCertification-db-deployer) into SAP HANA Cloud. Each of them is pointing to the *srv* and *db* folders within the *gen* folder. You can also see that both these applications are dependent on the availability of a service with the name extnCertification-db. Definition of this service extnCertification-db is in the *services-manifest.json* file. As you see in Figure 3.21, it's a service instance of an SAP HANA Cloud service with plan hdi-shared.

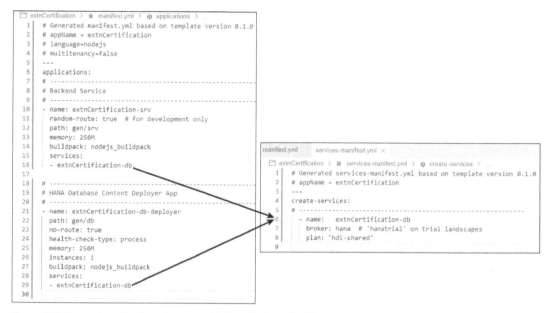

Figure 3.21 Generated Files from Command "cds add cf-manifest"

In Cloud Foundry, the command to deploy applications is cf push. If you issue this command, it will read *manifest.yaml* and push both these applications. However, these apps are dependent on extnCertification-db. In Section 3.7.3, when we ran command cds deploy -2 hana, this instance should have been created in SAP BTP. Let's assume that we didn't run that command yet and explore another way of generically creating any service instance (not just SAP HANA).

So before deploying the two applications, you need to ensure that the SAP HANA service instance extnCertification-db is created. Without this, the application deployment will fail. Creation of the service instance can be done manually in the SAP BTP cockpit; however, you can use a Cloud Foundry plug-in called Create-Service-Push to do it from the terminal itself. This plug-in provides a new command cf create-service-push, which is an extension of cf push. Command cf create-service-push reads *services-manifest.yml*, creates specified service instances there, and then does a cf push.

To install this Cloud Foundry plug-in, issue the following command:

```
cf install-plug-in Create-Service-Push
```

Before you issue command cf create-service-push, you need to ensure that the applications are *built*. To do this, issue command cds build --production. This will create content within the *gen* folder and the content for both extnCertification-srv and extnCertification-db-deployer. Figure 3.22 ❶ shows the triggering of the command, the target folder gen ❷ where the build target is stored, the two build tasks—one for the SAP HANA database and another for node module srv ❸—and the output files of the build tasks that get saved inside the gen folder ❹ and ❺.

```
user: extnCertification $ cds build --production   ❶
[cds] - determining build tasks for project [/home/user/projects/extnCertification].
[cds] - the following build tasks will be executed
[cds] -    {
             "build": {
❷            "target": "gen",
             "tasks": [
❸              {"for":"hana", "src":"db", "options":{"model":["db","srv","app"]}},
               {"for":"node-cf", "src":"srv", "options":{"model":["db","srv","app"]}}
             ]
           }
         }
```

```
[cds] - node-cf: adding node engines version to package.json >=12.18
[cds] - done > wrote output to:
  gen/db/.cfignore
  gen/db/data/my.dataModel-Escalations.csv
  gen/db/data/my.dataModel-Statuses.csv
  gen/db/manifest.yml
  gen/db/package.json
  gen/db/src/.hdiconfig                                     ❹
  gen/db/src/gen/.hdiconfig
  gen/db/src/gen/.hdinamespace
  gen/db/src/gen/EscalationManagementService.Comments.hdbview
  gen/db/src/gen/EscalationManagementService.Escalations.hdbview
  gen/db/src/gen/EscalationManagementService.Statuses.hdbview
  gen/db/src/gen/EscalationManagementService.Statuses_texts.hdbview
  gen/db/src/gen/data/my.dataModel-Escalations.csv
  gen/db/src/gen/data/my.dataModel-Escalations.hdbtabledata
  gen/db/src/gen/data/my.dataModel-Statuses.csv
  gen/db/src/gen/data/my.dataModel-Statuses.hdbtabledata
  gen/db/src/gen/localized.EscalationManagementService.Comments.hdbview
  gen/db/src/gen/localized.EscalationManagementService.Escalations.hdbview
  gen/db/src/gen/localized.EscalationManagementService.Statuses.hdbview
  gen/db/src/gen/localized.my.dataModel.Comments.hdbview
  gen/db/src/gen/localized.my.dataModel.Escalations.hdbview
  gen/db/src/gen/localized.my.dataModel.Statuses.hdbview
  gen/db/src/gen/my.dataModel.Comments.hdbtable
  gen/db/src/gen/my.dataModel.Escalations.hdbtable
  gen/db/src/gen/my.dataModel.Statuses.hdbtable
  gen/db/src/gen/my.dataModel.Statuses_texts.hdbtable
  gen/db/undeploy.json
  gen/srv/.cfignore
  gen/srv/manifest.yml
  gen/srv/package-lock.json
  gen/srv/package.json              ❺
  gen/srv/srv/_i18n/i18n.json
  gen/srv/srv/csn.json
  gen/srv/srv/service.js
[cds] - build completed in 720 ms
```

Figure 3.22 Command "cds build-production" and Its Output

Now, you can issue command cf create-service-push. From the output of the command, you'll see that the SAP HANA service gets created, and then the two applications get deployed. You'll get the URL of the OData service in the output. This URL provides the output just like the local run.

Note
The preceding code can be seen in the repository at *http://s-prs.co/v540901*, branch chapter3/step6.

3.10.2   Multi-Target Applications

In a typical enterprise application, there will be multiple *micro apps*, each with different technologies and target environments. Typically, there will be an application for the database (deploying content to the database), an application for the server (running an application server), and an application providing the UI for the users to interact with. Each of these micro apps depends on various preexisting service instances (e.g., the deployer module depends on an SAP HANA instance). Again, among the micro apps, there will be dependencies, and they need to be deployed in a particular order. In addition, these apps have a single lifecycle for development and deployment, but different build tools and target environments are used.

As you saw with the Cloud Foundry native deployment, you need all the build artifacts in various folders to deploy the apps. This may not be practical in a non-development environment. For example, in enterprise landscapes, various automated tools might be used for deployment. Sometimes even nondevelopers (e.g., admins) need to deploy the apps to systems such as testing and production. In these cases, it would be useful to have a single, distributable archive file containing all the deployment artifacts. In addition, there should be a tool to interpret the content of this archive file and deploy the content in the right sequence.

To handle these challenges, SAP came up with the concept of a multi-target application (MTA), as mentioned earlier in this chapter, along with open-source tools to build and deploy. MTA is logically a single application, containing multiple micro apps. Let's explore various parts of this concept.

mta.yaml

This file is at the root of the application, and it replaces the *manifest.yaml* file, which is used in Cloud Foundry native development and deployment. It also replaces *services-manifest.yml* that is used by the Cloud Foundry plug-in Create-Service-Push. The *mta.yaml* file defines the following items.

- **Modules**
  Defines multiple micro apps as part of the MTA. Each micro app, also called a module, specifies the source file locations, type of the app, and other settings. It also specifies the dependencies such as applications and resources.
- **Resources**
  Defines and declares various resources required to run the MTA. These resources aren't part of the application itself. Resources are usually instances of various SAP BTP services. You can refer to existing service instances or specify enough information to create those instances.
- **Configuration variables**
  Define variables statically or dynamically that can be used in application and resource definitions.

This file can be easily created by running command cds add mta in the terminal at the root of the project. The generated *mta.yaml* file will contain two modules and one resource for the SAP HANA service, as shown in Figure 3.23.

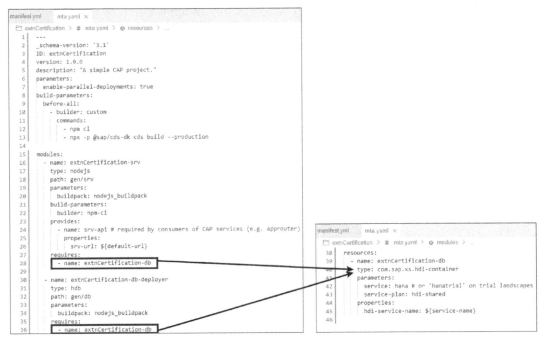

Figure 3.23 Generated mta.yaml File, Containing Modules and Resources

Note
The preceding code can be seen in the repository at *http://s-prs.co/v540901*, branch chapter3/step7.

Notice that there are two modules defined under the modules section, and this is very similar to the applications defined inside the *manifest.yaml* file, as shown earlier in Figure 3.21. Again, the SAP HANA service instance defined in *services-manifest.yaml* is defined as resources here in *mta.yaml*.

Within the *mta.yaml* file, modules and resources specify *properties* and *parameters*:

- **Properties**
  Properties are key-value pairs that are used by the (code inside) respective modules as application-specific configuration data. This means that the name of these properties is decided by the developer of the respective module. The MTA deployer usually sets this configuration data as an environment variable in the operating system where the application (module) runs. The value of the key-value pair can be dynamic and can be derived or provided by other modules and resources within the *mta.yaml* file. In the case of dynamic values, the deployer

that is interpreting *mta.yaml* will determine the value of each such property during deployment. If the deployer can't determine the value, then deployment can't succeed.

- **Parameters**

  Parameters are reserved variables that are interpreted by the tools that interpret *mta.yaml*. The most common tool is the MTA deployer. For example, when the deployer tries to deploy and run the application, it needs to know which buildpack (runtime) needs to be used for the application. This can be explicitly specified in a module definition using a parameter buildpack. Unlike properties, parameters aren't available to the application runtime.

Command "mbt build"

The Cloud MTA Build Tool (MBT) is a command-line tool that builds MTAs and creates an *.mtar* archive file ready for deployment. MBT uses *mta.yaml* as its input to build the *.mtar* file. The module type specification within the *.mtar* file drives how each module is built. You can even define custom build instructions within *mta.yaml*. In addition to SAP BTP, these *.mtar* files can be deployed to the SAP HANA XSA server as well.

Within the SAP Business Application Studio's dev space, when you selected a **Full Stack Cloud Application Dev Space**, it already includes the MTA Tools extension. This toolset, in addition to several other tools, also contains MBT, so no additional installation is required within the SAP Business Application Studio. For other IDEs, such as VS Code, you need to manually install MBT by executing the following command:

```
npm install -g mbt
```

To trigger a build of the MTA, you can run command mbt build. The build is a two-step process. First, it creates a makefile (*makefile.mta*), which defines a set of tasks to be executed as part of the build process. Next, these tasks are executed to create an *.mtar* file. The generated makefile gets deleted as part of the cleanup task. If you want to control or modify the makefile, you need to run the build process as a manual two-step (two commands) process. First, you issue command mbt init. This will generate the *makefile.mta* file, which you can edit. Once you're done updating the makefile, you can issue command make Makefile.mta, and this will generate the .mtar archive.

Let's run mbt build at the root of our project. From the output of the command, you can see that it installs all the packages, then builds each module, creates a makefile, generates the *.mtar* file at a specific location (*mta_archives* folder), and clears non-required files.

Command "cf deploy"

Now that you've created the *.mtar* archive, it's time to deploy the application to Cloud Foundry. SAP has provided an open-source Cloud Foundry plug-in called MultiApps, which is available in the Cloud Foundry Community repository. SAP Business Application Studio's Full Stack Cloud Application dev space comes installed with this plug-in. If you're in other development environments, you can install or upgrade this plug-in using the following command:

```
cf install-plug-in multiapps
```

Now you can deploy the app using command cf deploy <location of the mtar file>. This will analyze the *.mtar* archive and deploy all the modules to Cloud Foundry. It will also create service instances if specified within the *.mtar* file. Note that we had already deployed the app earlier using the Cloud Foundry native tools, so our app will be just updated (or overwritten) this time.

Note that when you use either the Cloud Foundry native tools or the Cloud Foundry MultiApps plug-in, the result will be the same. Based on your preference, you need to choose one of those.

Tip
YAML files can have either *.yaml* or *.yml* formats. They are interpreted equally by the tools processing them.

3.11   Annotations

Annotations help you add additional functionality to your models and services. These annotations are interpreted by the SAP Cloud Application Programming Model runtime and design-time library to add the required features. Let's discuss a few important annotations here:

- @cds.autoexpose
  This annotation is specified at an entity level. Whenever the targeted entity is part (via association) of an explicitly exposed entity (via projection), then the targeted entity also gets exposed in the service. However, the auto-exposed entity is read-only. This annotation is useful for modeling the value help entities as they need to be exposed but as read-only.

- @readonly and @insertonly
  When used at the entity level, this annotation ensures that the entity is read-only and that POST, PUT, and Delete operations are rejected on the target entity. You can also use this at the element or property level to ensure that the element is never altered. Following is an example of usage:

```
@readonly
entity Escalations { … }
```

As the name suggests, @insertonly allows only POST operations on the entity and restricts all other operations, including the read operations.

- **@mandatory**

  This annotation is for elements of an entity and is used for validating the inputs. Whenever an element is marked with @mandatory annotation, it's not allowed to send empty strings or null as values for those elements.

- **@cds.search**

  Whenever a search query is initiated from the OData URL, all the string elements of the entity are searched. The @cds.search annotation is useful in cases where you want to include only a set of elements to search, exclude certain elements from searching, or include associations for searching. See the following example for a sample usage, along with the effect:

```
@cds.search: {
    element1: true, // included in search
    element2, //included in search
    element4: false, //excluded from search
    element8 //association included in the search
}
entity Escalations {
    element1: String;
    element2: String;
    element3: String;
    element4: String;
    element5: String;
    element6: String;
    element7: String;
    element8 association to Category
}
```

- **@cds.on.insert and @cds.on.update**

  These two annotations can be used to auto-fill data upon insert and update operations, respectively. If the consumers of the service send data for elements with these annotations, it will be ignored. The following is a usage example:

```
entity Escalations {
    createdOn: Timestamp @cds.on.insert: $now;
    createdBy: Timestamp @cds.on.insert: $user;
    updatedOn: Timestamp @cds.on.insert: $now @cds.on.update: $now;
    updatedBy: Timestamp @cds.on.insert: $user @cds.on.update: $user;
    etagreference: UUID @cds.on.insert: $uuid @cds.on.update: $uuid;
}
```

The createdOn and updatedOn elements will be auto-filled with the current timestamp upon the insert operation. updatedOn is auto-filled with the current timestamp upon the update operation. createdBy and updatedBy elements are auto-filled by the current user's ID upon insert operation on the entity. The updatedBy element is auto-filled by the current user's ID upon update operation. Element etagreference is auto-filled with a UUID upon insert and update operations.

For auto-filling these elements, SAP Cloud Application Programming Model provides the following three pseudo-variables: $now contains the current timestamp in the UTC time zone, $user contains the current user ID, and $uuid contains a unique UUID for each operation.

- @odata.etag
  This annotation is specified at the entity's element level to identify an element that represents an ETag for the entity. ETag is an OData concept used for concurrency control using optimistic concurrency.

3.12   Important Terminology

In this chapter, the following terminology was used:

- **Custom handlers**
  The SAP Cloud Application Programming Model framework provides many functionalities, including generic implementations of CRUD operations. However, if there are additional requirements, developers can write custom (event) handlers for various events of entities.

- **Domain modeling**
  This can be considered as a requirement gathering and documenting stage. During domain modeling, each real-world entity, its elements (properties), and also the relationships among various entities are documented. When you build an SAP Cloud Application Programming Model application, you usually start with the domain modeling from which the persistence model is automatically created.

- **SAP Business Application Studio**
  This is the SAP recommended, cloud-based IDE for cloud development. It's provided as a service on the SAP BTP platform that can be subscribed to for consumption.

- **SAP Cloud Application Programming Model**
  This is a framework that is purpose-built for cloud application development within SAP BTP. It provides tools for modeling the domain, as well as providing and consuming services, events, and subscriptions. It allows developers to use either the Node.js or Java runtime.

- **SQLite**
  SQLite is an open-source database that is built-in to most computers, mobile phones, and other devices. It can also be run in memory (not from a disk file), which comes with superior performance. Whenever you run an SAP Cloud Application Programming Model application locally, it creates an in-memory database and lets you play with it. As soon as the database connection is closed, the in-memory database gets destroyed.

3.13   Practice Questions

1. Which of the following runtimes are available for creating an SAP Cloud Application Programming Model application? (There are two correct answers.)

☐ **A.** ABAP

☐ **B.** Java

☐ **C.** Python

☐ **D.** Node.js

2. What are the limitations of the trial version of SAP Business Application Studio? (There are two correct answers.)

☐ **A.** A maximum of two dev spaces can be created.

☐ **B.** All projects will be lost after 30 days.

☐ **C.** One dev space can be running at a time.

☐ **D.** There are only three predefined dev space types are available.

3. The CSN open specification is based on which of the following?

☐ **A.** OData specification

☐ **B.** JSON specification

☐ **C.** XML specification

☐ **D.** YAML specification

4. You have a requirement to increment a counter. How would you model this in your SAP Cloud Application Programming Model service?

☐ **A.** Use an update (PUT) operation on an entity.

☐ **B.** Define a function to implement the operation.

☐ **C.** Define an action to implement the operation.

☐ **D.** Use a create operation on an entity.

5. A service is defined with the following line. `service EscalationManagementSer-vice @(path: 'escalations'){..}`. What will the URL be of the generated service?

☐ **A.** *http://localhost:4004/escalation-management*

☐ **B.** *http://localhost:4004/escalationManagement*

☐ **C.** *http://localhost:4004/escalationmanagement*

☐ **D.** *http://localhost:4004/escalations*

6. How do you create a domain model in an SAP Cloud Application Programming Model project?

☐ **A.** Using Node.js or Java

☐ **B.** Using CDL (CDS Definition Language)

☐ **C.** Using CQL (CDS Query Language)

☐ **D.** Using the Query Builder API

7. Which database is used for local testing of the SAP Cloud Application Programming Model app as an in-memory database?

☐ **A.** MySQL

☐ **B.** Oracle

☐ **C.** SQLite

☐ **D.** memorySQL

8. Consider the below custom handler code. When a query is issued via a URL on an `Escalations` entity, what would it return?

```
module.exports = function () {
    this.on("READ", "Escalations", (req) => {
        return {
            ID: "4ce79175-d5fc-4d55-a98f-847bbd7a8486",
            Description: "Foo",
            Material: "bar"
        }
    });

    this.on("READ", "Escalations", (req) => {
        return {
            ID: "23a4cec1-8ea4-47b1-8af4-53ef381b397a",
            Description: "Foo1",
            Material: "bar1"
        }
    });
}
```

☐ **A.** It will return the output of the generic provider.

☐ **B.** It will return:

```
{
ID: "4ce79175-d5fc-4d55-a98f-847bbd7a8486",
Description: "Foo",
Material: "bar"
}
```

☐ **C.** It will return:

```
{
    ID: "23a4cec1-8ea4-47b1-8af4-53ef381b397a",
    Description: "Foo1",
    Material: "bar1"
}
```

☐ **D.** It will return:

```
[
    {
            ID: "4ce79175-d5fc-4d55-a98f-847bbd7a8486",
            Description: "Foo",
            Material: "bar"
    },
    {
            ID: "23a4cec1-8ea4-47b1-8af4-53ef381b397a",
            Description: "Foo1",
            Material: "bar1"
    }
]
```

9. To create an OData function import, which has side effects, you use which of the following keywords in a CDS service model?

☐ **A.** action

☐ **B.** function

☐ **C.** function-import

☐ **D.** action-import

10. Which command is used for deploying *.mtar* archives to Cloud Foundry?

☐ **A.** cf push

☐ **B.** cf pull

☐ **C.** cf send

☐ **D.** cf deploy

11. Which file is mandatory for pushing the application using Cloud Foundry native commands?

☐ **A.** *manifest.yaml*

☐ **B.** *mta.yaml*

☐ **C.** *mta.json*

☐ **D.** *manifest.json*

12. Which properties are available to the entity automatically by using aspect `sap.common.CodeList`? (There are two correct answers.)

☐ **A.** id

☐ **B.** name

☐ **C.** descr

☐ **D.** description

13. What do you use to create a domain (data) model in an SAP Cloud Application Programming Model project?

☐ **A.** *.hdbcds* file

☐ **B.** *.sql* file

☐ **C.** *.cds* file

☐ **D.** *.js* file

14. When you implement a custom handler, which class would you use (explicitly or implicitly)?

☐ **A.** cds.Request

☐ **B.** cds.Custom

☐ **C.** cds.Event

☐ **D.** cds.Service

3.14   Practice Question Answers and Explanations

1. Answer: **B and D**
   The SAP Cloud Application Programming Model provides Node.js and Java as the supported runtimes.

2. Answer: **A and C**
   In a trial account, you can create only dev spaces. Only one of them can be running at a time. If any dev space is inactive for more than 30 days, then that dev space will be deleted.

3. Answer: **B**

   JSON specification. CSN specification is an open specification based on JSON. It's used to hold OData and domain model artifacts.

4. Answer: **C**

   Incrementing a counter doesn't fit any of the CRUD operations, so an OData function import needs to be defined. To define a function import, SAP Cloud Application Programming Model provides two options. Use a *function* whenever you're going to consume the function import without updating any back-end objects. Such functions are called by an HTTP GET method. Because you need to update the backend (to increment the counter), you need to use an *action* here.

5. Answer: **D**

   Note that we have the path specified here for the service. In this case, that path will be used for the service. If the path isn't specified, then the SAP Cloud Application Programming Model framework derives the path from the name of the service itself.

6. Answer: **B**

   A data model is created in CDL. Node.js and Java are used to write the server-side logic in custom handlers. CQL and Query Builder APIs are used for querying the entities.

7. Answer: **C**

   SQLite is an open-source, widely available database that is built-in across devices. It has an ability to run in memory, making it ideal for local testing of the application with high performance.

8. Answer: **B**

   When there are multiple handlers for the on phase, if the first handler returns a value, then SAP Cloud Application Programming Model assumes that the processing is complete, and further on handlers are ignored. If you want other registered handlers to be called, ensure that you don't return any value and call await next(). If the last registered handler also calls await next(), then the generic handler of the SAP Cloud Application Programming Model framework will be called.

9. Answer: **A**

   When you want to define a function import that has a side effect, then you define an action. This means that the function import will be triggered with an HTTP POST call. Usage of the POST method informs the consumers that this results in an update in the backend. In addition, using the POST method automatically triggers additional security measures such as cross-site request forgery (CSRF) token validation.

10. Answer: **D**

    MultiApps is a Cloud Foundry CLI plug-in that provides several commands to deal with MTAs. One such command is cf deploy. You need to supply the location of the *.mtar* file along with this command. This command validates the *.mtar* file and deploys its contents to Cloud Foundry (or SAP HANA XSA server). This plug-in was originally developed by SAP but is open source.

11. Answer: **A**

    The *manifest.yaml* file contains each application to be deployed to Cloud Foundry. For each application, it contains information such as memory, location of the files, and more. However, when you use the MultiApps CLI plug-in, it looks for the *mta.yaml* file, which usually contains all the information in the *manifest.yaml* file and additional information such as dependencies.

12. Answer: **B and C**

    Aspect is a reusable artifact within the SAP Cloud Application Programming Model's CDS language. Using an aspect makes your entity definitions leaner and improves readability. A CodeList aspect provides name and descr elements or properties. It lets you maintain the name and description of a technical ID for the consuming entity.

13. Answer: **C**

    Within an SAP Cloud Application Programming Model project, CDL)= is used to create various entities and views, which get converted into database artifacts. Such definition files are written in a file with the extension *.cds*. When built with SAP HANA as the target, *.hdbcds* files will get generated from the *.cds* files.

14. Answer: **D**

    When you implement a custom handler, you can subclass the cds.Service class and define your custom event listeners inside it. Inside the subclass, you need to redefine the init() method and then define custom event handlers there. In the end, it's important to call the parent init method using the super.init() API. You can also define these custom handlers within plain functions. The SAP Cloud Application Programming Model framework automatically registers them with an instance of cds.Service.

3.15   Test Takeaway

SAP Cloud Application Programming Model is a group of tools, languages, and libraries to make it easy to develop cloud-native enterprise applications and extensions. SAP Business Application Studio is the SAP-recommended tool for developing full-stack SAP enterprise applications, including SAP Cloud Application Programming Model.

When you build an application, SAP Cloud Application Programming Model focuses on the problem domain and starts the process by creating a domain model in CDL. Services are also defined via CDL and refer to the domain model artifacts.

SAP Cloud Application Programming Model provides a generic implementation for various operations within the service. You can also write your custom implementations using the event handling functionality.

Applications can be deployed via Cloud Foundry native tools using the `cf push` command, or you can use SAP's useful extensions to Cloud Foundry apps (Multi-Apps) to easily push using command `cf deploy`.

3.16 Summary

In this chapter, we explored SAP's go-to development tool: SAP Business Application Studio. You learned how to subscribe to the SAP Business Application Studio service and how to set it up for SAP Cloud Application Programming Model development. Then we started with an introduction to SAP Cloud Application Programming Model development tools and the need for the SAP Cloud Application Programming Model framework for cloud development. Next, you learned how to get started with developing an SAP Cloud Application Programming Model application using SAP Business Application Studio.

Next, we took a deep dive into SAP Cloud Application Programming Model development by discussing domain modeling and service modeling topics. You learned how to run the projects locally for speeding up the development. We also covered the available generic handler functionalities and how to enhance them using custom handlers.

In addition, you learned the tools available for building and deploying the SAP Cloud Application Programming Model project. We ended the chapter by going over some of the most useful annotations and the features they provide.

In the next chapter, we deep dive into the SAP Cloud Application Programming Model concepts and focus on consuming an external OData service and enhancing it.

Chapter 4
Connectivity

Techniques You'll Master

- Consuming external OData service in an SAP Cloud Application Programming Model application

- Creating SAP BTP destination services

- Understanding cloud connector

- Recognizing the role of the SAP BTP connectivity service

In Chapter 3, you learned how to create an SAP Cloud Application Programming Model application. However, so far, the application works independently and doesn't connect to any external systems. In real-life scenarios, it's common to connect to external systems such as SAP ERP, SAP S/4HANA, SAP SuccessFactors, and others. In this chapter, we start by explaining how to consume OData services from external services. We use SAP API Business Hub to simulate an external system. Next, we'll explore the cloud connector, SAP BTP destination service, and SAP BTP connectivity service to figure out how to connect to an on-premise SAP S/4HANA system, replacing the SAP API Business Hub that we connected earlier.

> **Real-World Scenario**
>
> Continuing our real-world scenario from Chapter 3, we need to provide the buyer persona with the ability to create escalations against purchase order lines. However, purchase order lines (data) are located in the SAP S/4HANA system. So, in the SAP Cloud Application Programming Model application that we're building, we need to connect to an SAP S/4HANA system and expose the purchase order lines via an OData service (application programming interface [API]) so that the end user can choose the purchase order lines against which the escalation needs to be marked.

4.1   Objectives of This Portion of the Test

This portion of the test checks your understanding of connecting to external systems from SAP Cloud Application Programming Model. It also tests your knowledge about connecting to on-premise SAP products such as SAP ERP and SAP S/4HANA via the cloud connector. This portion also tests your knowledge regarding the role of SAP BTP destination service and SAP BTP connectivity service in exposing external OData services within the SAP Cloud Application Programming Model layer.

Note
Connectivity topics make up to 8% of the total exam.

4.2   Consuming External OData Services

For our use case, we need an API in our SAP S/4HANA system that can be consumed and provides details about purchase order lines. SAP API Business Hub is SAP's tool for exploring, discovering, and consuming APIs across SAP's various products. It even provides a sandbox, where it provides sample data for these APIs.

In Chapter 3, we created a data model to represent escalations per the use case. In this chapter, you'll integrate with a backend system (via an OData API) that can provide you with a list of purchase orders against which you'll create escalations. Let's use SAP API Business Hub to represent an external system and provide an OData API.

SAP API Business Hub is SAP's product to discover, explore and consume various APIs from SAP products. You can access SAP API Business Hub via *https:// api.sap.com*. If you choose SAP S/4HANA as the product, you can see that there are nearly 500 APIs available, as shown in Figure 4.1. These APIs can be of type OData (V2/V4) or Simple Object Access Protocol (SOAP). SAP keeps adding and exposing more APIs per customer needs.

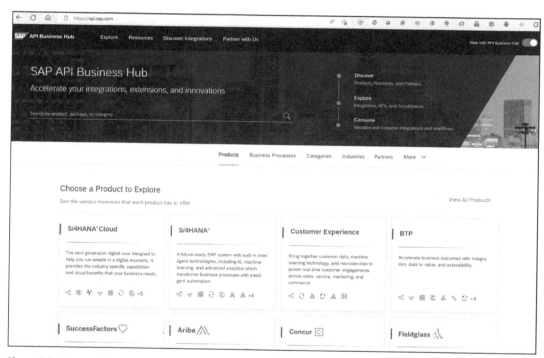

Figure 4.1 APIs Available for SAP S/4HANA Products

Within SAP API Business Hub, the URL *https://api.sap.com/api/API_PURCHASEOR-DER_PROCESS_SRV/overview* provides information about a purchase order API. This API is available both in an SAP S/4HANA and SAP S/4HANA Cloud system. At the URL, log in with your SAP credentials.

To consume an external API, follow these steps:

1. Get the external OData schema (EDMX) specification of the OData API. In this step, we download the metadata of the OData service as an EDMX file into a local folder, as shown in Figure 4.2 ❶. (Take note of the **Show API Key** button here ❷—you'll need it for a later step.)

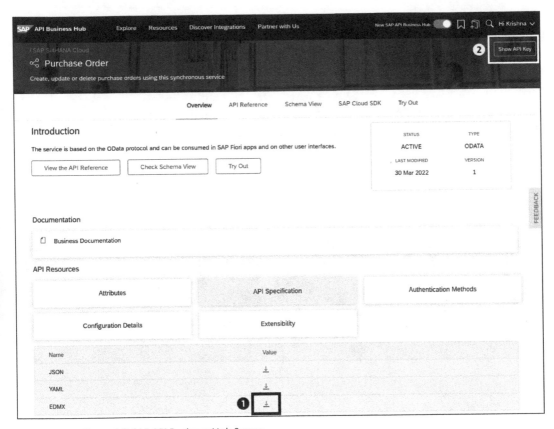

Figure 4.2 SAP API Business Hub Screen

2. Add the downloaded EDMX file into the *srv* folder, as shown in Figure 4.3 ❶.
3. In the terminal at the root of your project, enter the following command: "cds import srv/API_PURCHASEORDER_PROCESS_SRV.edmx" ❷.
4. This will create a folder called *external* within the *srv* folder along with two files in it. One is the EDMX file that we imported, and another is a Core Schema Notation (CSN) representation of it ❸.
5. The output of command ❹ also gives a sample code on how to use the imported model within the Core Data Services (CDS) files. The import functionality has also updated *package.json*'s cds.requires part ❺.

> **Note**
> The preceding code can be seen in the repository at *http://s-prs.co/v540901*, branch chapter4/step1.

Now that the import function is complete, you can get rid of the EDMX file directly added under the *srv* folder.

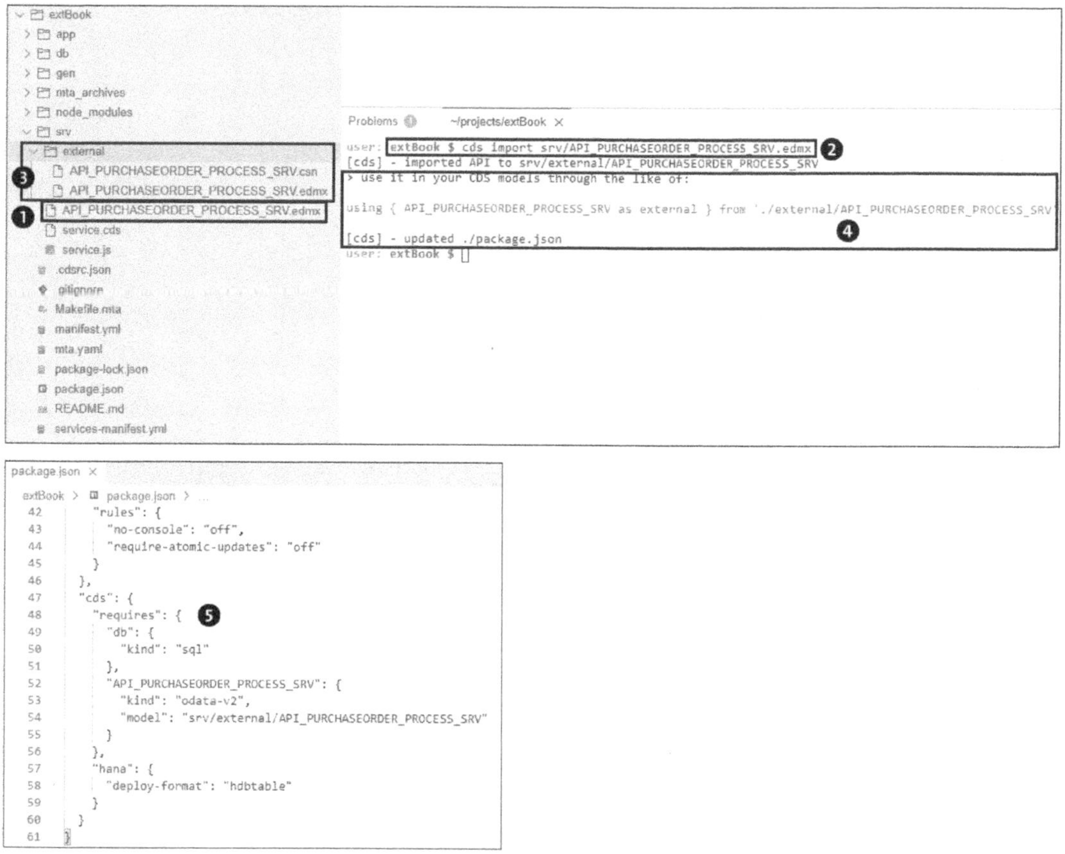

Figure 4.3 Importing an External EDMX Definition into the SAP Cloud Application Programming Model Project

Now you can enhance the data model using the imported model. In the *db/ schema.cds* file, you add a new view with the name PurchaseOrders. In addition, you enhance the Escalations entity to include a property purchase order as an association to the PurchaseOrders view, as shown in Listing 4.1.

```
using { managed, cuid, sap.common.CodeList as CodeList } from '@sap/cds/
common';
namespace my.dataModel;

using { API_PURCHASEORDER_PROCESS_SRV as external } from '../srv/external/
API_PURCHASEORDER_PROCESS_SRV.csn';

entity Statuses: CodeList{
    key code: String(3)
}
```

```
type Status : Association to Statuses;

entity Comments: managed, cuid{
    comment: String;
    escalation: Association to Escalations;
}

entity Escalations: managed, cuid {
    description     : String (80);
    material: String(30);
    purchaseOrder : Association to PurchaseOrders;
    expectedDate: Date;
    status: Status;
    comments: Composition of many Comments on comments.escalation = $self;
};

@cds.persistence.skip
view PurchaseOrders as
    select from external.A_PurchaseOrder
    {
        key PurchaseOrder as ID,
            PurchaseOrderType,
            Supplier,
            SupplierPhoneNumber
    };
```

Listing 4.1 Enhancing the Data Model with External Service

You need to enhance the service model as well to ensure that the artifacts from external services are available to the service's consumers as well.

In the *srv/service.cds* file, you need to declare the PurchaseOrders entity referring to the data model, as shown in Listing 4.2. Note that the @readonly annotation is used on the PurchaseOrders entity to ensure that the entity can't be triggered. In addition, entity A_PurchaseOrderScheduleLine is added into our service.

```
using my.dataModel as my from '../db/schema';

service EscalationManagementService {
    entity Escalations as projection on my.Escalations
    actions{
        action resolve();
    };
```

```
entity Comments as projection on my.Comments;
entity Statuses as projection on my.Statuses;

@readonly
entity PurchaseOrders as projection on my.PurchaseOrders;
}
```

Listing 4.2 Using the External Service

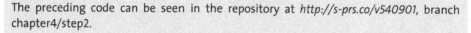

> **Note**
>
> The preceding code can be seen in the repository at *http://s-prs.co/v540901*, branch chapter4/step2.

Now that you've enhanced the data model, you need to update the SAP HANA database table as well for the local runs to work. You'll also update the test data to include the purchase order ID, as shown in Listing 4.3.

```
ID;DESCRIPTION;MATERIAL;EXPECTEDDATE;PURCHASEORDER_ID;STATUS_CODE
a43675ee-79af-44eb-826d-9c9555291c4a;For ABC project;123;1991-12-
12;4500000031;DRF
c9e78068-ddff-4f29-b71c-c4e0cf59c852;For material xyz;124;2012-12-
01;4500000033;INP
```

Listing 4.3 Purchase Order ID Added to the Sample Data

To create the new purchase order ID column and to update the preceding test data in that column, run command `cds deploy -2 hana`.

You can run command `cds watch` at the root folder, and you can see the metadata of the service, including the entity just exposed from the external service. However, you can't get the data yet, as you've neither routed the call to the external service nor specified the backend connection details.

First, let's specify the credentials to connect to the SAP API Business Hub. SAP API Business Hub provides a sandbox for SAP S/4HANA Cloud APIs so that you can play with some sample data. It requires an API key to be sent along with every request as a security feature.

In the SAP Business API Hub screen, click on **Show API Key**, as shown earlier in Figure 4.2 ❷. This will provide a key and store it in an *.env* file at the root of your project, as shown in Figure 4.4 ❶. In file *package.json* at `cds.requires.API_PUR-CHASEORDER_PROCESS_SRV.credentials`, maintain the URL of the SAP API Business Hub sandbox ❷.

Figure 4.4 Consuming an OData API from the SAP API Business Hub Sandbox

Let's now add a custom handler to route the call to an external service. The SAP API Business Hub sandbox requires you to send an API key along with every call to it. To achieve this, you create a request handler for the READ event of PurchaseOrders ❸. Within the event handler, follow these steps:

1. Connect to the external service (SAP API Business Hub sandbox) using API cds.connect.to. Here use the name that was specified previously in Figure 4.3 ❺.

2. Send a request to the external service using API srv.tx(req).send by sending the query.

3. Along with the query, you're also sending the API key from the environment variable.

Now when you run the application, you can query the entity set PurchaseOrders and get the output shown in Figure 4.4 ❹.

Note

The preceding code can be seen in the repository at *http://s-prs.co/v540901*, branch chapter4/step3.

4.3   Destination Service

SAP BTP provides a concept of *destination* that encapsulates a connection to an external system. Destinations are at the level of the SAP BTP subaccount and contain connection information such as the URL to the external system, authentication information, additional headers to be sent, and more. By externalizing the connection information from the application code, SAP BTP destinations are a great way to seamlessly connect to different systems and keep the code clean. To understand the concept of destinations, let's create an SAP BTP destination pointing to the SAP Business API Hub sandbox. Next, you'll make the SAP Cloud Application Programming Model application connect to the destination instead of connecting directly via the URL.

4.3.1   Creating a Destination

To create a destination, navigate to the subaccount cockpit (Figure 4.5 ❶), and click on **Destinations** ❷. Click on **New Destinations**, create a new destination with the name "SandboxPO" ❸, and provide the SAP API Business Hub sandbox URL as the destination's **URL** ❹.

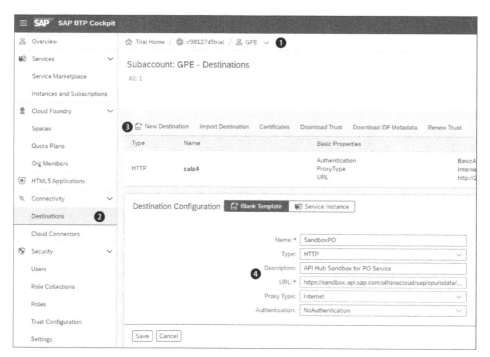

Figure 4.5 Creating a Destination in SAP BTP

To use this destination, go to the *package.json* file, and replace the URL specified under the cds.requires section, API_PURCHASEORDER_PROCESS_SRV.credentials, with the destination, as shown in Figure 4.6.

```
package.json ×
extBook  >  ▣  package.json  >  ...
  41          "cds": true
  42       },
  43       "rules": {
  44         "no-console": "off",
  45         "require-atomic-updates": "off"
  46       }
  47     },
  48     "cds": {
  49       "requires": {
  50         "db": {
  51           "kind": "sql"
  52         },
  53         "API_PURCHASEORDER_PROCESS_SRV": {
  54           "kind": "odata-v2",
  55           "model": "srv/external/API_PURCHASEORDER_PROCESS_SRV",
  56           "credentials": {
  57           | "url": "https://sandbox.api.sap.com/s4hanacloud/sap/opu/odata/sap/API_PURCHASEORDER_PROCESS_SRV"
  58           }
  59         }
  60       },
  61       "hana": {
  62         "deploy-format": "hdbtable"
  63       }
  64     }
  65  }
  66
```

```
package.json ×
extBook  >  ▣  package.json  >  {} cds  >  {} requires  >  {} API_PURCHASEORDER_PROCESS_SRV  >
  41          "cds": true
  42       },
  43       "rules": {
  44         "no-console": "off",
  45         "require-atomic-updates": "off"
  46       }
  47     },
  48     "cds": {
  49       "requires": {
  50         "db": {
  51           "kind": "sql"
  52         },
  53         "API_PURCHASEORDER_PROCESS_SRV": {
  54           "kind": "odata-v2",
  55           "model": "srv/external/API_PURCHASEORDER_PROCESS_SRV",
  56           "credentials": {
  57             "destination": "SandboxPO"
  58           }
  59         }
  60       },
  61       "hana": {
  62         "deploy-format": "hdbtable"
  63       }
  64     }
  65  }
  66
```

Figure 4.6 Using a Destination to Connect to a Backend API

However, you can't directly use the destination in your SAP Cloud Application Programming Model application because you need some way of providing the configurations done within the SAP BTP destination to the SAP Cloud Application Programming Model application. This is done via the *SAP BTP destination service*.

You need to create an instance of the SAP BTP destination service and bind it to the srv module. *Binding* is a process by which the details to access the SAP BTP destination service are available for the bound application. However, the SAP BTP destination service requires the consuming application to authenticate with a JSON Web Token (JWT). This JWT can be generated by an instance of the *SAP Authorization and Trust Management service*. This is an SAP-built service by extending Cloud Foundry's *User Account and Authorization (UAA)* service. By creating an instance of the XSUAA service and binding it to the application, you can ensure that the application gets the JWT required to access the SAP BTP destination service.

The XSUAA service requires the passport module to work. Install the passport module and save it into your project dependency by running the following command in the terminal:

```
npm install passport
```

In summary, to use the SAP BTP destinations, you need to create an instance of the SAP BTP destination service and XSUAA service and bind them to the application. Let's explore how to do this.

4.3.2   Manually Creating and Binding SAP BTP Service Instances

Let's create and bind an instance of the SAP BTP destination service. You can go to the SAP BTP cockpit, and click on the space to get into the space context (Figure 4.7 ❶), click on **Instances** ❷, and click the **Create** button ❸.

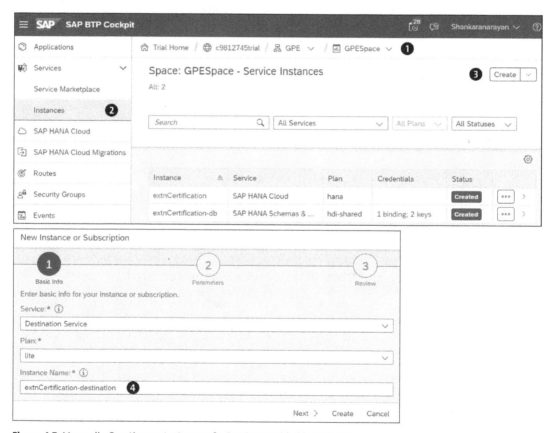

Figure 4.7 Manually Creating an Instance of a Service Provided by SAP BTP

In the newly opened popup, look for the required service, choose a plan, provide a name for the service instance ❹, and click the **Create** button. This will take a few minutes to create an instance of the chosen service.

Now that the instance is created, you need to bind this instance to your application.

Select the instance that you just created Figure 4.8 ❶, and in the context menu of this instance, choose **Create Binding** ❷. Choose the application to bind from the dropdown ❸. Click on **Create** to create the binding ❹.

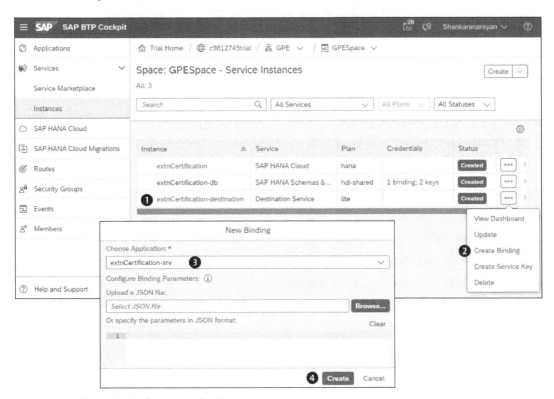

Figure 4.8 Binding an Application

4.3.3   Creating and Binding the Service via the Terminal

The creation and binding of services can be done via the terminal as well. Because the SAP BTP destination service instance requires an XSUAA instance as well, let's use the terminal to create and bind it. You can use any terminal, including the one that comes integrated with the SAP Business Application Studio. Windows Power-Shell is used here.

To create an instance, use the following command, as shown in Figure 4.9 ❶:

```
cf create-service <service name> <service plan> <a name for the new service
instance>
```

To bind an application to the newly created service instance, use the following command ❷:

```
cf bind-service <application name> <service instance name>
```

You can also see the output of these two commands showing **OK** as the output indicating the successful operation. You have an instance of the XSUAA service with the name extnCertification-xsuaa and application extnCertification-srv is bound to it.

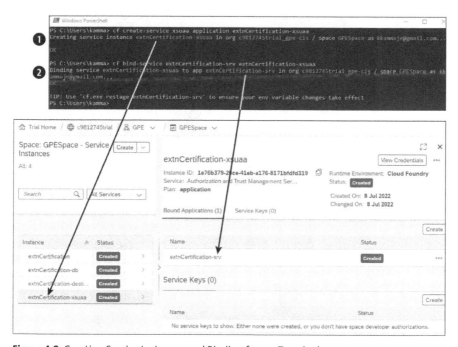

Figure 4.9 Creating Service Instances and Binding from a Terminal

4.3.4 Creating and Binding the Service via mta.yaml

Another easy way of creating a service instance and binding it to the application is by specifying the details within the *mta.yaml* file. Within *mta.yaml*, by specifying the service instances under the resources section (see Figure 4.11 ❶ and ❷, a bit later in this section), you can get those instances created as part of the application deployment process. You can see that we've specified the service name, service plan, and name of the service instance in those specifications.

For any multi-target application (MTA) module (application), under the requires section, you can specify service instances. By doing so, you can bind the specified applications to all those service instances ❷. This binding happens during deployment. In cases where service instances don't exist, the deploy command takes care of ensuring that the service instances are created (per the resources specification) before attempting the bind.

Let's delete the manually created bindings and service instances, and then deploy the application with the specified *mta.yaml*. Before that, you need to build the *.mtar* archive. Run the build using command mbt build. In Figure 4.10 ❶, you can see the triggering of the build process and the archive file that got generated as a build result ❷, ❸.

Figure 4.10 Building an MTA

Now that the archive is generated, you can deploy the application to the SAP BTP, Cloud Foundry environment, using command `cf deploy <location to the mtar archive>` (Figure 4.11 ❹). From the output of the deployment, you can see that the specified service instances are created ❶ ❷ and later bound to applications ❸.

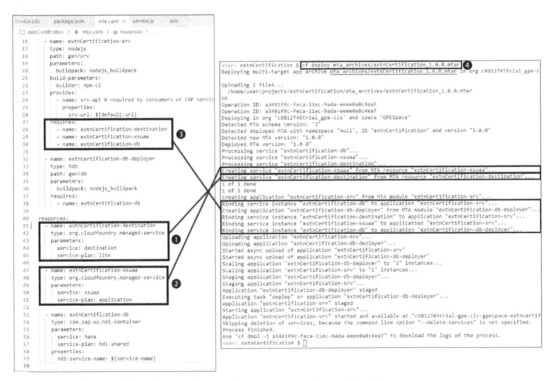

Figure 4.11 Creating and Binding Service Instances from mta.yaml

Note

The preceding code can be seen in the repository at *http://s-prs.co/v540901*, branch chapter4/step4.

4.3.5   Running the Service Locally

As you develop the application, it becomes important to run the application locally to improve the speed of development with quick feedback. Let's explore how to do that.

When you run your SAP Cloud Application Programming Model application locally, it can't access the SAP BTP service instances. To enable this, the SAP Cloud Application Programming Model framework provides a command called CDS bind. We briefly looked into this command in Chapter 3. This command connects to Cloud Foundry, verifies those service instances, and saves service details to the *.cdsrc-private.json* file. When you run the SAP Cloud Application Programming Model application locally, the SAP Cloud Application Programming Model framework reads those services from the file and connects to those service instances on SAP BTP.

It's important to have those dependent service instances running in SAP BTP so that the local application can connect with those service instances. You can create those service instances in any of the ways that we discussed earlier.

To run the application locally, follow these steps:

1. **Create service keys for service instances.**
   Service keys are credentials to be used by other clients other than the bound applications within SAP BTP. To consume these service instances from the local development environment, you need to create a service key for each service instance. To create a service key, choose **Create Service Key** from the service instance's context menu (see Figure 4.12 ❶), provide a name for the service key ❷, and click on **Create** ❸. You can easily create a service key with terminal command cf create-service-key <service instance> <name of the service key>. Create a service key for the XSUAA service instance as well in a similar way.

2. **Bind to the destination and XSUAA service.**
   At the root of the project, run the following command in a terminal:
   cds bind <service type> -2 <service instance name>:<service instance key name>.

   Figure 4.13 shows how to run these commands for destination and XSUAA service instances, as well as the resulting content of the *cdsrc-private.json*.

3. **Install the passport module.**
   The XSUAA service requires the passport node module to work, so install the passport module and save it into your project dependency by running the following command in the terminal:
   npm install passport

Now you can run the application locally using command cds watch --profile hybrid and access the remote entity set PurchaseOrders as well.

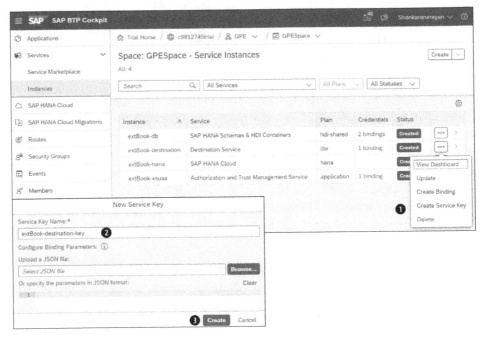

Figure 4.12 Creating Service Keys

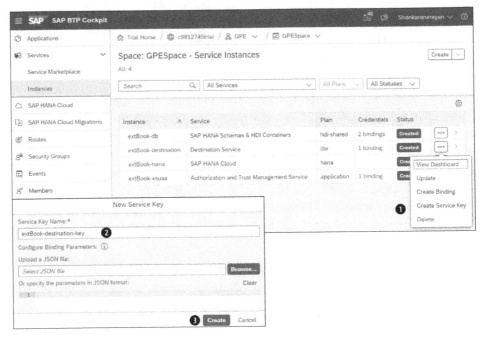

Figure 4.13 Using "cds bind" to Run the Application Locally

4.3.6   Running on SAP Business Technology Platform

When you deploy the application to Cloud Foundry and access the OData service's entity set `PurchaseOrders`, this won't work right away. This is because when you ran the application locally, the environment variable `apiKey` was read and created from the *.env* file. When the application runs on Cloud Foundry, *.env* won't be read, so you need to manually create this environment variable. Go to your development space, and click on the service (see Figure 4.14 ➊). Click on **User-Provided Variables** ➋, and select **Add Variable** ➌. Add the `apiKey` variable into the **Key** field and the actual API key into the **Value** field ➍.

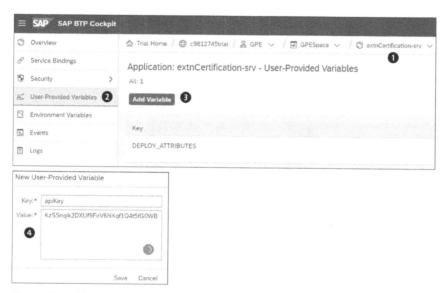

Figure 4.14 Adding an Environment Variable in Cloud Foundry for Holding the API Key

4.4   Cloud Connector

SAP has been a leader in providing on-premise enterprise applications for quite a while. As SAP and the enterprise world embrace the cloud, customers are gradually making this move. However, a complete move to the cloud is very distant, so it's common to have hybrid clouds where cloud solutions and on-premise solutions coexist and communicate. In addition, to keep the core clean, SAP recommends creating your extensions (of on-premise systems) on SAP BTP by connecting to on-premise systems.

However, on-premise backend systems are usually protected by virtual private networks and firewalls, and they aren't exposed to the internet. This is very understandable as enterprises want to protect their systems from risks such as Denial of Service (DoS) attacks posed by opening them to the internet. SAP API Business Hub is exposed to the internet and that is how SAP BTP was able to connect to it in our sample exercise earlier. So how can SAP BTP communicate with an on-premise system that isn't exposed to the internet? Enter, cloud connector!

The cloud connector is SAP proprietary software that aims to achieve communication between on-premise systems and SAP BTP by establishing a secure tunnel between them. It's installed on the on-premise network and acts as an agent to keep the connection open between SAP Cloud products and the on-premise system.

The cloud connector, as shown in Figure 4.15, initiates a connection with SAP BTP, and this step creates a Transport Layer Security (TLS) encrypted tunnel between these two systems. The tunnel is nothing but a persistent connection between two systems that don't require a firewall port to be opened. After this, the cloud connector acts as a reverse proxy; that is, connection requests coming from SAP BTP will be routed to corresponding backend systems based on routing rules set up within the cloud connector. The cloud connector also allows you to selectively expose resources of backend systems to be exposed.

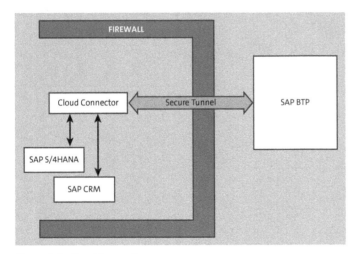

Figure 4.15 Cloud Connector

The cloud connector host itself isn't accessible from the internet, so it's safe from various internet origin attacks. However, the cloud connector needs to have access to the internet to initiate the request to SAP BTP to start a secure tunnel. Meanwhile, the cloud connector needs to connect on-premise systems as well, so it's ideal to install the cloud connector in a demilitarized zone (DMZ) network that sits in between the public internet and the private network containing on-premise installations. You can even install the cloud connector in the internal network provided it has access to the public internet and direct access to the required on-premise systems.

Tip

The cloud connector is based on the Apache Tomcat-based Java server. So, you can see as many standard configuration files within the cloud connector installation as you see in a Tomcat installation. However, you can't make any changes to them because it's not supported by SAP.

In the following sections, we'll cover details about cloud connector installation and how to configure it to expose an on-premise system.

4.4.1   Installing the Cloud Connector

The cloud connector needs to be installed in a physical system or a virtual machine where on-premise systems to be exposed to SAP BTP are accessible. This can be on a Windows, Linux, or macOS operating system. It's important to install the cloud connector in a high availability setup as it's a single point of failure and can bring down your SAP BTP-based applications.

Go to *http://s-prs.co/v540917*, and scroll down to the **Cloud Connector** subheading. For both Linux and Windows operating systems, you can choose from two options:

- **Portable version**
  This version is provided as an archive folder. You download and extract it to a suitable location and run the application from there by running a script. As there is no installation process involved, you don't need administration rights for this version. However, if the system running this version restarts, you need to manually restart the cloud connector. As you can't upgrade this version automatically, SAP doesn't recommend this version for production scenarios.

- **Installable version**
  This version is in *.msi* format for Windows and *.rpm* format for Linux operating systems. Installing this version requires administrator privileges. As the application runs as a service on Windows and as a daemon on Linux, the application will start automatically when the system restarts. You can also get it upgraded automatically without having to install the latest version. There is no macOS installer available as of writing this book.

We won't cover the step-by-step process of installation as it's out of scope for the certification exam. You can find the installation steps via the SAP Help Portal at *https://help.sap.com*.

Tip
If your local machine has access to the on-premise system, you can install the cloud connector in your local machine itself for test purposes.

4.4.2   Configuring the Cloud Connector

The first thing to do when you open the cloud connector is to establish a secure tunnel between the cloud connector and SAP BTP. As we discussed earlier, the secure tunnel is initiated by the cloud connector. As you open the cloud connector in your local machine, because there are no connections to SAP BTP yet, you'll be prompted to enter SAP BTP subaccount details, as shown in Figure 4.16: **Region ❶** and **Subaccount ID ❷** from the subaccount cockpit, **Display Name ❸**, and your SAP BTP credentials ❹.

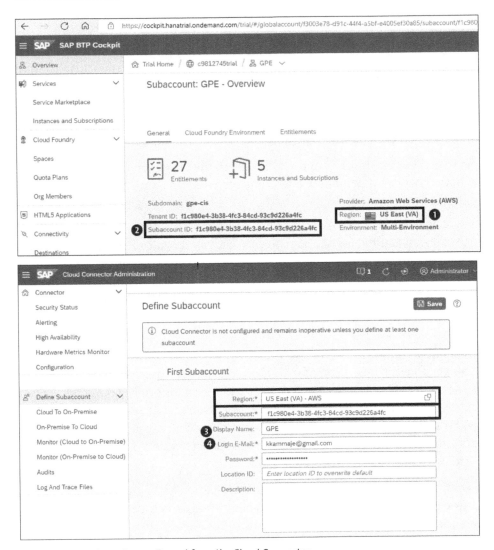

Figure 4.16 Starting a Secure Tunnel from the Cloud Connector

However, you need to ensure that this user has the **Cloud Connector Administrator** role collection. Without this role collection, the connection to SAP BTP would fail. You can click on the **Save** button after entering all the SAP BTP connection details to initiate and set up a secure tunnel between the cloud connector and SAP BTP.

Now that the secure tunnel is set up, you have to connect to an on-premise system and expose the required resources to SAP BTP. On the home screen of the cloud connector, go to **Cloud To On-Premise** (Figure 4.17 ❶), and then click on the plus icon ❷ under the **Access Control** tab.

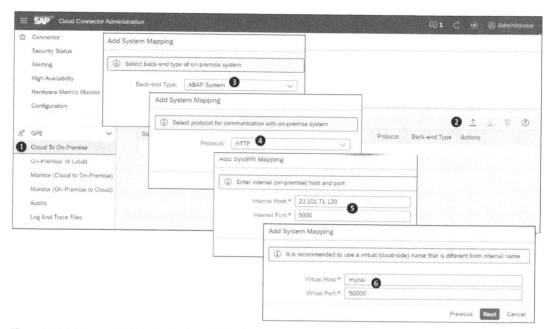

Figure 4.17 Adding an On-Premise System to the Cloud Connector

You'll go through a series of steps in a wizard now. As the SAP S/4HANA system is an ABAP server, select the **Back-end Type** as **ABAP System** ❸. Notice that there are other supported backend systems types such as SAP HANA, SAP NetWeaver Application Server for Java , and many other systems. Under **Protocol**, select **HTTP** ❹ for simplicity, as this is a connection between the systems within the firewall. You can choose HTTPS as well for additional security. Note that there are other supported protocols such as Lightweight Directory Access Protocol (LDAP), remote function call (RFC), and TCP as well based on the chosen backend type.

In the next popup screen, you need to provide the **Internal Host** and **Internal Port** ❺. This is nothing but the HTTP connection details of the SAP S/4HANA server that you're exposing. In the next screen, we need to provide the **Virtual Host** and **Virtual Port** ❻. By providing a different hostname and port here, you can hide the internal host and port of the SAP S/4HANA system. When you configure a destination within SAP BTP, you need to specify the virtual host that you're specifying in this step, and the cloud connector does the mapping of the virtual server and port to the internal host and port that you specified in the previous step.

Although you've now added the SAP S/4HANA system to the cloud connector, none of the resources of the SAP S/4HANA system are exposed to SAP BTP yet. This is because the cloud connector requires you to specify which URLs of the on-premise system are exposed. This is an additional security feature giving users fine-grain access to expose the on-premise resources. Under the exposed on-premise system, choose the plus icon under the **Resources** table, as shown in Figure 4.18 ❶. In the popup, you can specify the URL that you want to expose. You can manually add all the required URLs one by one. However, you can also choose a generic part of a URL and then select **Path And All Sub-Paths** next to **Access Policy**, so that all subpaths of the specified path are also exposed. As */sap/opu/odata* is the parent path for all OData V2 services in an ABAP system, you expose all OData V2 services by entering "/sap/opu/odata" as the **URL Path ❷** and then selecting to expose **Path And All Sub-Paths ❸**.

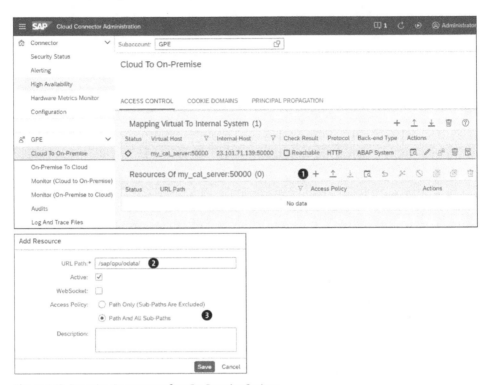

Figure 4.18 Exposing Resources of an On-Premise System

Now that you've exposed the required on-premise system to the cloud connector and established a secure tunnel to SAP BTP, you can create an SAP BTP destination pointing to the on-premise system (using the virtual host) so that you can connect to the on-premise system from the SAP BTP deployed applications.

Create a destination as specified in Figure 4.19. The **Name** refers to an identifiable destination name, and the **Description** lets you maintain useful information about the destination. Because you're going to connect to the backend via the HTTP framework, enter "HTTP" as the **Type**. In the **URL** field, specify the URL of the SAP API Business Hub API identified earlier to fetch the purchase orders. Note that the hostname and port numbers of the URL are the virtual host and virtual port values specified while exposing the on-premise system within the cloud connector. This way, the actual hostname and ports aren't exposed. In addition, choose **OnPremise** as the **Proxy Type** to tell SAP BTP that the target is an on-premise system and a secure tunnel must be used via the cloud connector to connect. For **Authentication**, choose **BasicAuthentication**, and provide the **User** and **Password** information.

You can also choose **Principal Propagation** if you want to pass the user context to the backend.

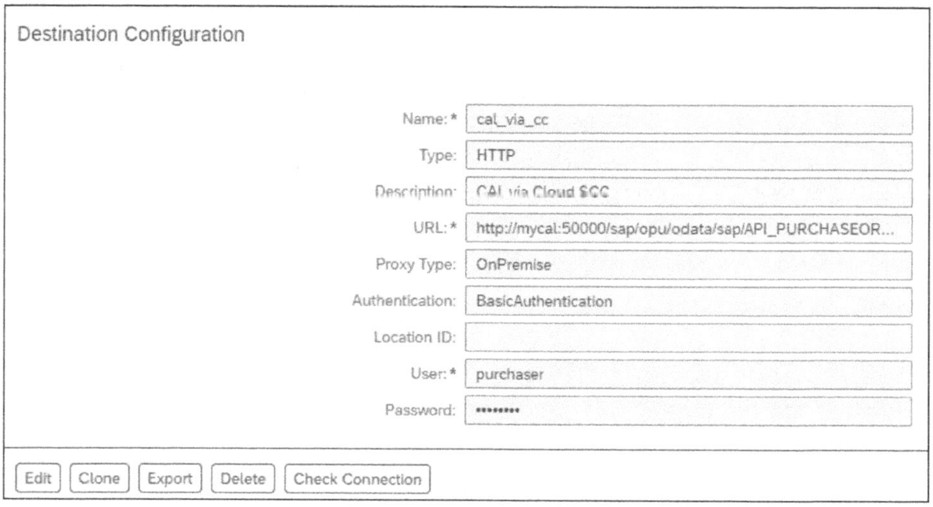

Destination Configuration

Name: *	cal_via_cc
Type:	HTTP
Description:	CAL via Cloud SCC
URL: *	http://mycal:50000/sap/opu/odata/sap/API_PURCHASEOR...
Proxy Type:	OnPremise
Authentication:	BasicAuthentication
Location ID:	
User: *	purchaser
Password:	••••••••

Edit   Clone   Export   Delete   Check Connection

Figure 4.19 Destination Pointing to Virtual Host and Virtual Port

4.5   Connectivity Service

Now that you've created the destination and ensured that the destination is set up correctly, it's time to consume the destination from the SAP Cloud Application Programming Model application. The API_PURCHASEORDER_PROCESS_SRV API consumed from the SAP API Business Hub sandbox is available from the on-premise SAP S/4HANA system as well. So to test the consumption from SAP S/4HANA, within *package.json*, under the cds.requires section and API_PURCHASEORDER_PRO-CESS_SRV.credentials section, replace destination SandboxPO with cal_via_cc.

Now, if you run the application locally and try to access the remote entity set Pur-chaseOrders, you'll see an error, as shown in Figure 4.20. The error informs the need for an SAP BTP connectivity service instance to use the new destination. This is because destination cal_via_cc points to the on-premise system via the cloud connector.

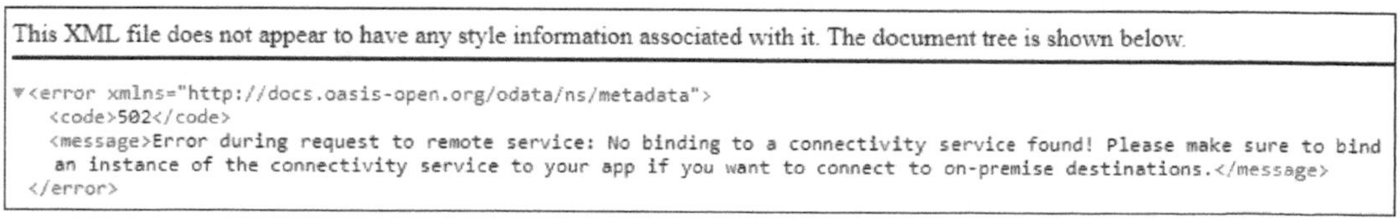

This XML file does not appear to have any style information associated with it. The document tree is shown below.

```
▼<error xmlns="http://docs.oasis-open.org/odata/ns/metadata">
    <code>502</code>
    <message>Error during request to remote service: No binding to a connectivity service found! Please make sure to bind
    an instance of the connectivity service to your app if you want to connect to on-premise destinations.</message>
  </error>
```

Figure 4.20 Error without the SAP BTP Connectivity Service

However, you can't test applications locally that use on-premise destinations via the cloud connector because only SAP BTP can communicate with the secure tunnel set up by the cloud connector (SAP Business Application Studio can't). So let's configure it in such a way that when you run from SAP Business Application Studio (locally), the application uses the SAP API Business Hub sandbox destination SandboxPO, and when deployed to SAP BTP, it uses on-premise destination cal_via_cc. To achieve this, you can specify the environment within *package.json*, as shown in Figure 4.21. Now you can run the application locally to connect to the SAP API Business Hub sandbox.

```
"cds": {
    "requires": {
        "db": {
            "kind": "sql"
        },
        "API_PURCHASEORDER_PROCESS_SRV": {
            "kind": "odata-v2",
            "model": "srv/external/API_PURCHASEORDER_PROCESS_SRV",
            "[development]": {
                "credentials": {
                    "destination": "SandboxPO"
                }
            },
            "[production]": {
                "credentials": {
                    "destination": "cal_via_cc"
                }
            }
        },
        "hana": {
            "deploy-format": "hdbtable"
        }
    },
    "sapux": [
        "app/escalationui"
    ]
}
```

Figure 4.21 Specifying Different Destinations in Different Environments

However, to resolve the error that you saw in Figure 4.20, let's update the *mta.yaml* file to create an instance of the SAP BTP connectivity service as a new resource and then bind it to the srv module. Figure 4.22 shows that extnCertification-connectivity is added as a new resource and later under the requires section of the srv module. You can now build and deploy this MTA to SAP BTP. When you access the remote entity set PurchaseOrders, you'll get data from the SAP S/4HANA system.

Note

The preceding code can be seen in the repository at *http://s-prs.co/v540901*, branch chapter4/step5.

```
🗁 extnCertification  >  ≣  mta.yaml  >  ⊚  resources  >  ...
14
15    modules:
16     - name: extnCertification-srv
17       type: nodejs
18       path: gen/srv
19       parameters:
20         buildpack: nodejs_buildpack
21       build-parameters:
22         builder: npm-ci
23       provides:
24         - name: srv-api # required by consumers of CAP serv
25           properties:
26             srv-url: ${default-url}
27       requires:
28         - name: extnCertification-destination
29         - name: extnCertification-xsuaa
30         - name: extnCertification-db
31         - name: extnCertification-connectivity
32
33     - name: extnCertification-db-deployer
34       type: hdb
35       path: gen/db
36       parameters:
37         buildpack: nodejs_buildpack
38       requires:
39         - name: extnCertification-db
40
41    resources:
42     - name: extnCertification-destination
43       type: org.cloudfoundry.managed-service
44       parameters:
45         service: destination
46         service-plan: lite
47
48     - name: extnCertification-connectivity
49       type: org.cloudfoundry.managed-service
50       parameters:
51         service: connectivity
52         service-plan: lite
53
54     - name: extnCertification-xsuaa
55       type: org.cloudfoundry.managed-service
56       parameters:
57         service: xsuaa
58         service-plan: application
59
```

Figure 4.22 Adding an SAP BTP Connectivity Service as a Resource and Dependency

4.6 Advanced Concepts

In this section, we'll go through a few advanced concepts that you need to understand while developing productive applications.

4.6.1 Sending the Application Programming Interface Key

When you make the changes and run locally, you want to connect to the SAP API Business Hub sandbox, which requires the API key. To make it easy to send the API key, switch the target development system to the URI from the destination. You can add the API key within the credentials.headers section of the *package.json* file, as shown in Listing 4.4.

```
    "API_PURCHASEORDER_PROCESS_SRV": {
      "kind": "odata-v2",
      "model": "srv/external/API_PURCHASEORDER_PROCESS_SRV",
      "[development]": {
        "credentials": {
          "url": "https://sandbox.api.sap.com/s4hanacloud/sap/opu/odata/
sap/API_PURCHASEORDER_PROCESS_SRV",
          "headers": {
            "apiKey": "API KEY HERE"
          }
        }
      },
      "[production]": {
        "credentials": {
          "destination": "cal_via_cc"
        }
      }
    }
```

Listing 4.4 Connecting to the URL and Passing an API Key for Local Testing

There can be scenarios where you want to send the API key from the destination itself. You can do this by specifying additional headers in the destination configuration.

Within the SAP BTP destination, click on **New Property**, as shown in Figure 4.23 ❶. For the property name, choose URL.headers.apiKey ❷. Click on the **Show API Key** button. This will show the apiKey in a pop-up. Specify the apiKey from here as the value of the property. With this configuration, with each request to destination **SandboxPO**, the API key will be sent as a header. Note that you can send any other header as well here just like the API key. This approach is superior to the previous approach because you don't have to store the API key within the application code.

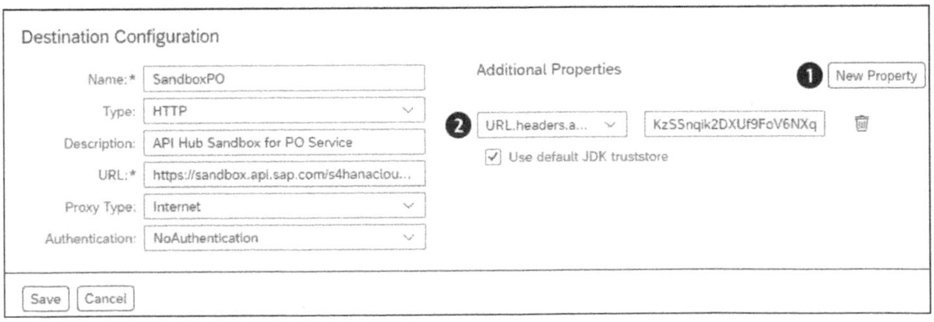

Figure 4.23 Adding API Key as a Header within a Destination

After the preceding change, you can use the destination SandboxPO for the local run as well by specifying it within the credentials.destination section, as shown in Listing 4.5.

```
"API_PURCHASEORDER_PROCESS_SRV": {
  "kind": "odata-v2",
  "model": "srv/external/API_PURCHASEORDER_PROCESS_SRV",
  "[development]": {
    "credentials": {
      "destination": "SandboxPO"
    }
  },
  "[production]": {
    "credentials": {
      "destination": "cal_via_cc"
    }
  }
}
```

Listing 4.5 Credentials Specification for Using a Destination for Both Local and Production Runs

4.6.2   Advanced Custom Handler

When we imported the external service, we enhanced the Escalations entity with a property that has an association/navigation to the PurchaseOrders entity. When you query the Escalations entity, you get the purchase order number in the property purchaseOrder_ID. However, you don't get any other details about the purchase order. To get the purchase order details along with the escalation, you need to make an $expand call. Let's explore how to write a custom handler to get a response to an $expand query.

You need to manually handle $expand queries because there is no generic handler support for external consumed entity sets. Listing 4.6 shows how this is implemented. Initially, the next() API is used to call the generic handler to get the list of escalations. Next, you need to connect to the external system and read all the relevant purchase order details. Finally, for each escalation row, set the corresponding purchase order detail and return it.

```
this.on('READ', 'Escalations', async (req, next) => {

    if (!req.query.SELECT.columns) return next();
    const expandIndex = req.query.SELECT.columns.findIndex(
        ({ expand, ref }) => expand && ref[0] === "purchaseOrder"
    );
    if (expandIndex < 0) return next();

    // Remove expand from the query
    req.query.SELECT.columns.splice(expandIndex, 1);

    // Make sure supplier_ID will be returned
    if (!req.query.SELECT.columns.indexOf('*') >= 0 &&
```

```
            !req.query.SELECT.columns.find(
                column => column.ref && column.ref.find((ref) => ref ==
"purchaseOrder_ID"))
        ) {
            req.query.SELECT.columns.push({ ref: ["purchaseOrder_ID"] });
        }

        // Use the generic handler to read the escalations
        const escalations = await next();

        const asArray = x => Array.isArray(x) ? x : [ x ];

        // Request all associated purchase orders
        const poIds = asArray(escalations).map(escalation =>
escalation.purchaseOrder_ID);
        const purchaseOrders = await po.run(SELECT.from('API_PURCHASEORDER_
PROCESS_SRV.A_PurchaseOrder').where({ PurchaseOrder: poIds }));

        // Convert in a map for easier lookup
        const purchaseOrdersMap = {};
        for (const purchaseOrder of purchaseOrders)
        purchaseOrdersMap[purchaseOrder.PurchaseOrder] = purchaseOrder;

        // Add suppliers to result
        for (const escalation of asArray(escalations)) {
            escalation.purchaseOrder = purchaseOrdersMap[note.purchaseOrder_
ID];
        }

        return escalations;
    });
```

Listing 4.6 Advanced Custom Handler to Take Care of the "$expand" Query

4.6.3   Application Details

Once you deploy the MTA to Cloud Foundry, you can see three applications at the Cloud Foundry space level, as shown in Figure 4.24. Each of these applications is identifiable by the name for the corresponding module in the *mta.yaml* file:

- extnCertification-aprouter
  This is the AppRouter application. You can see that the application is in the status **Started** as it needs to keep running to process incoming requests.

- extnCertification-db-deployer
  This is the deployer application that deploys the database artifacts into the SAP HANA Cloud service. As this application runs briefly (as soon as you deploy the app) for a couple of minutes, this app's status says **Stopped**.

- `extnCertification-srv`
  This is the SAP Cloud Application Programming Model application module. Just like the AppRouter module, this application needs to keep running and has the status **Started**.

Figure 4.24 Applications at the Space Level after Deployment

4.7   Important Terminology

In this chapter, the following terminology was used:

- **Cloud connector**
  SAP's proprietary software that is installed on SAP on-premise systems or networks to enable connectivity between the SAP on-premise system within a firewall and SAP BTP. This works by establishing a secure tunnel between the systems.

- **EDMX file**
  This is an XML file that can store an Entity Data Model (EDM). An OData metadata can be stored as an EDM and in an EDMX file. It's required to consume an external OData service within an SAP Cloud Application Programming Model application.

- **SAP BTP connectivity service**
  This is an SAP BTP service that is required to set up communication between SAP BTP and the cloud connector. Any SAP BTP application that needs to connect to an on-premise system within a firewall via the cloud connector needs to use an instance of the SAP BTP connectivity service.

- **SAP BTP destination service**
  This is one of the most widely used SAP BTP services. Whenever an SAP BTP application needs to consume SAP BTP destinations, it needs to use this instance of SAP BTP destination service. It lets the consuming applications access the configurations and credentials specified within an SAP BTP destination.

4.8   Practice Questions

1.   Which role collection is required by the user initiating a secure tunnel from the cloud connector?

☐   **A.** Subaccount Administrator
☐   **B.** Cloud Connector Administrator
☐   **C.** Cloud Connector
☐   **D.** Global Connection Administrator

2.   You want to create an SAP BTP destination pointing to an SAP S/4HANA system that you just exposed in the cloud connector. What are the hostname and the port that you'll use?

☐   **A.** Internal host and internal port
☐   **B.** Virtual host and internal port
☐   **C.** Internal host and virtual port
☐   **D.** Virtual host and virtual port

3.   SAP BTP connectivity service instance is needed for which of the following?

☐   **A.** Connecting to any SAP BTP destination
☐   **B.** Connecting to any external OData service
☐   **C.** Connecting to on-premise systems via the cloud connector
☐   **D.** Connecting to XSUAA

4.   Which command is used for consuming an external OData service into an SAP Cloud Application Programming Model application?

☐   **A.** cds input
☐   **B.** cds consume
☐   **C.** cds import
☐   **D.** cds include

5.   Consuming an SAP BTP destination requires the SAP BTP destination service. Which of the following also requires an instance of this service?

☐   **A.** SAP BTP connectivity service
☐   **B.** SaaS registry
☐   **C.** HTML5 runtime
☐   **D.** XSUAA service

6. What information does an SAP BTP destination contain? (There are two correct answers.)

☐ **A.** Technical information to connect
☐ **B.** Authorization details
☐ **C.** Cloud connector details
☐ **D.** SAP BTP connection details

7. Where can you install the cloud connector? (There are two correct answers.)

☐ **A.** Demilitarized zone (DMZ)
☐ **B.** Internal network
☐ **C.** Public internet
☐ **D.** Hybrid cloud

8. What is true about portable and installable versions of the cloud connector? (There are two correct answers.)

☐ **A.** The installable version doesn't require admin rights to the system.
☐ **B.** The portable version is provided as an archive file.
☐ **C.** The portable version is recommended for production scenarios.
☐ **D.** The installable version can be upgraded automatically.

4.9   Practice Question Answers and Explanations

1. Answer: **B**
    When you connect to SAP BTP from the cloud connector, you need to enter the user's credentials. This can be any SAP BTP user, but this user needs to be assigned a role collection cloud connector administrator.

2. Answer: **D**
    The cloud connector provides a mapping feature so that you can hide the actual hostname and port of your on-premise systems. When you create an SAP BTP destination, you use the virtual host and virtual port that you specified while exposing an on-premise system within the cloud connector. Whenever a connection request comes to the virtual host and virtual port, the cloud connector will read the mapping information and send it to the internal host and internal port.

3. Answer: **C**
    If applications need to connect to an SAP BTP destination, an instance of the SAP BTP destination service is required. However, if the destination needs to point to an on-premise system within a firewall, then you need the cloud connector installed on the on-premise network to create a secure tunnel. If

applications need to connect to such a destination, an SAP BTP connectivity service instance is required in addition to an SAP BTP destination service instance.

4. Answer: **C**
Command cds import is used for importing the OData metadata specification in EDMX format. The CDS framework adds the specified EDMX file inside the external folder (creates this folder if not existing). It also creates a CSN format of the metadata specification for later use. In addition, the *package.json* file of the project is updated with the cds.requires specification to include the external service. You can specify a destination or a URL here pointing to the external OData service.

5. Answer: **D**
Consuming an SAP BTP destination service requires an instance of the XSUAA service. An instance of the SAP BTP connectivity service is required only for scenarios involving connecting to on-premise destinations.

6. Answer: **A and B**
An SAP BTP destination aims to separate the details to connect to an external system from SAP BTP. To consume the SAP BTP destination, your SAP Cloud Application Programming Model application needs to subscribe to an SAP BTP destination service instance. The SAP Cloud Application Programming Model framework communicates with this service and gets details of the destination. An SAP BTP destination primarily contains the address and credentials to connect to the target system.

7. Answer: **A and B**
The cloud connector needs to have access to on-premise systems as well as to SAP BTP. Therefore, as long as the DMZ network or the internal network has access to these two systems, you can install a cloud connector either in the DMZ network or the internal network.

8. Answer: **B and D**
The installable version requires admin rights to the system, while the portable version doesn't have any installation process and, therefore, doesn't need admin rights. The portable version is provided as an archive file, while the installation version is provided in operating-system-specific file formats. The portable version isn't recommended for production scenarios because you can't upgrade it automatically.

4.10   Test Takeaway

Consuming an external OData service or API is one of the most common use cases in an extension scenario. You start integrating an external OData source by getting its metadata in the EDMX format and importing it into the project. This updates the *package.json* file (cds.requires section) and creates a CSN specification (inside the *srv/external* folder) for interacting with the external service. You can use an SAP BTP destination to contain all the target system details (e.g., URL, credentials, etc.) and specify this destination in the `cds.requires` section of the *package.json* file. `cds bind` is a very convenient command-line tool to connect to SAP BTP service instances and run the application locally. The cloud connector is SAP's proprietary, Java-based software that can create a secure tunnel from the on-premise network into SAP BTP.

4.11   Summary

In this chapter, you learned how to consume an external OData service in an SAP Cloud Application Programming Model application. You also saw that the application requires an SAP BTP destination service instance for consuming an SAP BTP destination. In the case of an SAP BTP destination that points to an on-premise system (within a firewall), you need an cloud connector to set up a secure tunnel through the firewall. In this case, the SAP Cloud Application Programming Model application requires an instance of the SAP BTP connectivity service to work with the secure tunnel.

Chapter 5
SAP Fiori Elements

Techniques You'll Master

- Understanding SAPUI5, SAP Fiori, and SAP Fiori elements

- Uncovering the inspiration for SAP Fiori elements

- Recognizing various floorplans and their use cases within SAP Fiori elements

- Using the draft functionality in SAP Cloud Application Programming Model applications

- Creating SAP Fiori elements apps using SAP Business Application Studio

- Using annotations to enhance the generated SAP Fiori elements app

This chapter focuses on the user interface (UI) part. We start by exploring the need for SAP Fiori and the SAPUI5 library and then move on to understand the inspiration behind the SAP Fiori elements. Then we'll deep dive and find out the steps involved in creating an SAP Fiori elements app. We'll use the real-world use case to build the application with the concepts covered in this chapter.

Real-World Scenario

Continuing our real-world scenario from Chapter 4, you need to provide a UI for the buyer persona to create and view escalations. On the home screen, the UI should list all the escalations with key information of each escalation in a table. When clicked on, an escalation row should show details of the escalation. On the home screen, there should be a button to create a new escalation. Whenever the buyer is satisfied with the actions taken by the supplier, there should also be an option to close the escalation for the buyer.

5.1   Objectives of This Portion of the Test

This portion focuses on the UI aspect, and you're expected to know the basics of SAP Fiori design principles. Your knowledge will be tested regarding SAP Fiori elements concepts and how to create these applications. The test focuses on OData annotations and how to add those annotations to the OData service created using SAP Cloud Application Programming Model. It also tests your knowledge of various floorplans available within SAP Fiori elements, their use cases, and the steps to create them.

5.2   SAPUI5

HTLM5, JavaScript, and Cascading Style Sheet (CSS) are used to create modern web applications with beautiful interfaces. But the effort you have to put into making the web pages increases with the complexity of the application. For instance, creating a simple button with a good UI (theme), as shown in Figure 5.1, takes a lot of code.

Figure 5.1 HTML CSS Button

Listing 5.1 shows the sample code for this button.

```
.button {
  display: inline-block;
  padding: 15px 25px;
  font-size: 24px;
  cursor: pointer;
  text-align: center;
  text-decoration: none;
  outline: none;
  color: white;
  background-color: #4CAF50;
  border: none;
  border-radius: 3px;
  box-shadow: 0 3px #999;
}

.button:hover {background-color: #3e8e41}
.button:active {
  background-color: #3e8e41;
  box-shadow: 0 5px #666;
  transform: translateY(4px);
}

// HTML
<button class="button">Click Me</button>
```

Listing 5.1 HTML Code for a Button

As you can see, it took more than 10 lines to create a simple button with colors, borders, and hover functionality. The complexity will be much more for creating complex controls such as tables or forms. All the controls developed manually like this example have to be updated with the company's theme. Other factors, such as data integrations (OData services), speed of application development, responsiveness across various devices, user experience (UX) consistency across different applications, and so on, must be considered while developing enterprise-grade applications. In such cases, HTML5 frameworks such as SAPUI5 can be used.

SAPUI5 is an HTML5 framework for creating enterprise-grade responsive web applications. It comes with ready-to-use controls that can be used to develop web applications rapidly. Following are the most important features that SAPUI5 delivers:

- **Consistent UX**
  SAP Fiori design can be enabled with SAPUI5 apps to deliver a consistent UX across multiple SAP solutions, products, and non-SAP solutions. This helps users use different applications seamlessly, especially as very little training is needed when a new application is assigned because the UX is consistent across all applications.

- **Use anywhere**
  Most of the SAPUI5 controls are responsive by design so you can use the applications developed for desktop in mobile by doing little to no code changes.

- **Hundreds of enterprise UI controls**
  SAPUI5 offers a rich set of UI controls/elements to build enterprise-grade web applications that support theming, security, accessibility, and so on.

- **Powerful extensions**
  You can easily extend SAP-delivered enterprise apps without code using SAPUI5's integrated adoption feature.

- **Flexible tooling**
  SAPUI5 comes with development environments such as Microsoft Visual Studio Code (VS Code) or SAP Business Application Studio, which are available in trial versions to build, test, and deploy applications.

- **Unlimited usage in SAP and non-SAP**
  You can use SAPUI5 in non-SAP stacks in the form of OpenUI5, and it's free of charge to use SAPUI5 inside SAP environments for an unlimited number of applications.

A small example of a button created using SAPUI5 is shown in Figure 5.2. The code footprint is significantly less than the pure HTML5-based button created from scratch.

```
<Button text="Click Me!!" type="Emphasized">
</Button>
```

Figure 5.2 SAPUI5 Button

SAPUI5 makes the development experience easier, right? But if we don't have rules for developing enterprise applications, every application the developer creates might look different from each other, which will spoil the UX. Let's discuss how SAP solves this by introducing the design guidelines and principles.

5.3   SAP Fiori

SAP Fiori is the design language that helps enterprises create applications with a consistent UX. Companies can use SAP Fiori guidelines and tools to simplify the application development across various SAP solutions such as SAP S/4HANA, SAP SuccessFactors, and others.

The core design principles of SAP Fiori are as follows (see Figure 5.3):

- **Role-based**
  Applications should be designed by considering the role of the user. Instead of pushing all the features in one single application for different users, SAP Fiori recommends creating applications based on the user's role.

- **Delightful**
  Application interaction should be delightful and make an emotional connection with the user. This will enrich the work experience to get the work done quickly and smoothly.

- **Coherent**
  SAP Fiori adheres to a consistent visual design across various applications. This ensures the user has an intuitive and consistent experience across different products.

- **Adaptive**
  Regardless of the user's device, applications should run seamlessly and provide a consistent UX. Instead of developing multiple versions of a single application for mobile, tablet, and desktop, the application should adapt to the user's device.

- **Simple**
  SAP Fiori enables you to get your work done quickly and efficiently. The application should have essential functions and should not complicate the UX by providing features that the user won't use.

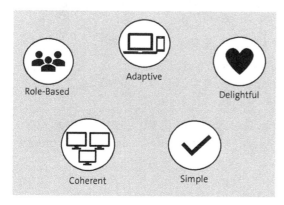

Figure 5.3 SAP Fiori: Core Design Principles

As mentioned earlier, SAP Fiori is a set of design guidelines and not a programming language. You can call an application that implements these guidelines an SAP Fiori app. For instance, SAPUI5 controls follow SAP Fiori design by default, and you can create SAP Fiori apps using the SAPUI5 framework.

Example
You can find an example of SAP Fiori UI Elements and their reference SAPUI5 controls at *http://s-prs.co/v540918*.

SAP Fiori guidelines suggest using a defined set of floorplans for creating SAP Fiori apps. list report, object page, and overview page are a few of the floorplans that are mostly used in creating enterprise-grade SAP Fiori apps. You'll use different SAPUI5 controls to create these floorplans.

SAP Fiori has evolved a lot since its inception in 2013. Let's explore the major versions as listed here:

- **SAP Fiori 1.0**
  With the introduction of SAP Fiori in 2013, SAP took the approach of a mobile-first design for its new enterprise applications. The foundation of the very core principles of SAP Fiori—role-based, responsive, coherent, delightful, and simple apps—was laid with this version. This version of SAP Fiori is available with SAPUI5 version 1.26–1.38. Floorplans such as List Report and Object Page were also introduced in this version.

- **SAP Fiori 2.0**
  After the success of the initial version of SAP Fiori, SAP Fiori 2.0 was introduced to handle much more complex scenarios with new floorplans, notifications, and chatbot features. This version of SAP Fiori received the prestigious Red Dot award in 2016. SAPUI5 version 1.42–1.70 implements this version of SAP Fiori.

- **SAP Fiori 3.0**
  In 2018, the third version, SAP Fiori 3, was introduced. It comes with a new Quartz theme, and with this version, all the product areas of SAP have committed to adopting SAP Fiori 3. This adoption ensures that UX consistency will be there across different SAP products. Along with SAPUI5 and other SAP technologies, the SAP Fiori 3 design has been extended to non-SAP technologies such as Angular, React, Vue, and web component.

Five different floorplans are available with SAP Fiori 3, based on the commonly used enterprise scenarios:

- **Worklist**
  The worklist floorplan shows a simple list of work items where the user can take action directly from the list or by navigating inside to review before performing an action, as shown in Figure 5.4:
  ❶ Optional tabs for quick filtering
  ❷ Work items and data
  ❸ Work item actions
  A typical worklist floorplan will have a table to display the work items and optional tabs to view the data in multiple views. This template should be used only if the data consists of work items or if a small set of data is needed to be shown.

Note

For more information on the worklist floorplan, visit *http://s-prs.co/v540919*.

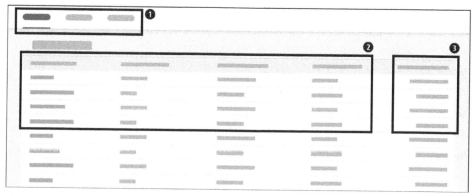

Figure 5.4 Worklist Floorplan

- **List report**

  The list report floorplan is used to display a large amount of data for the users or if the users want to sort, filter, and group the data for reporting. This floorplan is often used when users need to navigate to item/object details to display or update the data using an object page. A typical list report page will have filters to filter the data and a toolbar for the table to sort, group, or perform actions on the displayed data, as shown in Figure 5.5:

  ❶ Filters

  ❷ Toolbar for actions

  ❸ Data in table

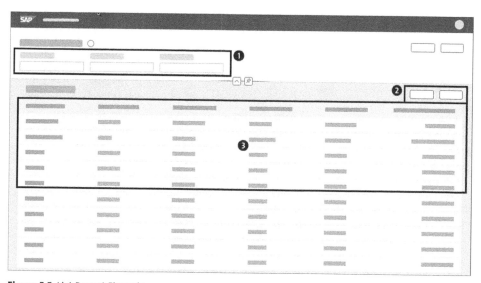

Figure 5.5 List Report Floorplan

Note

For more information on the list report floorplan, visit *http://s-prs.co/v540920*.

- **Object page**

  With an object page, users can view information about an object in different categories via tabs or edit the same, as shown in Figure 5.6:

  ❶ Object header content

  ❷ Sections

  ❸ Section – table

  ❹ Global actions

  ❺ Section – form

  Users can interact with the data by performing actions, editing, and saving or deleting the object. You can also show various charts in the object page in a read-only mode.

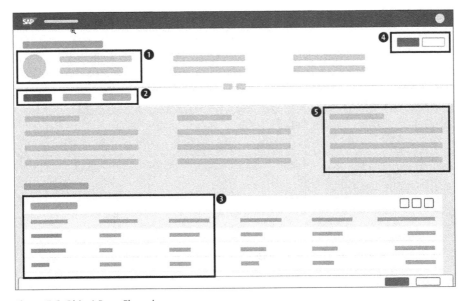

Figure 5.6 Object Page Floorplan

Note

For more information on the object page floorplan, visit *http://s-prs.co/v540921*.

- **Overview page**

  The overview page shows all the key information of a business process or a business object on a single page based on the user role, as shown in Figure 5.7. It shows them in flexible cards ❷, which come in many types, such as analytical cards, list cards, or table cards. Users can filter the cards ❶, interact with the cards, and navigate to the respective list report page or the object page to see further details.

Note

For more information on the overview page floorplan, visit *http://s-prs.co/v540922*.

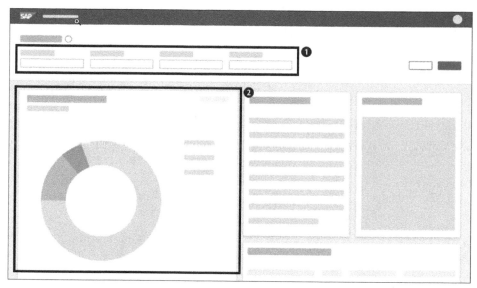

Figure 5.7 Overview Page Floorplan

- **Analytical list page**

  The analytical list page floorplan is used to visualize the analytical and transactional data using charts and tables, as shown in Figure 5.8:

  ❶ Visual filters and global key performance indicators (KPIs)

  ❷ Chart view

  ❸ Table view

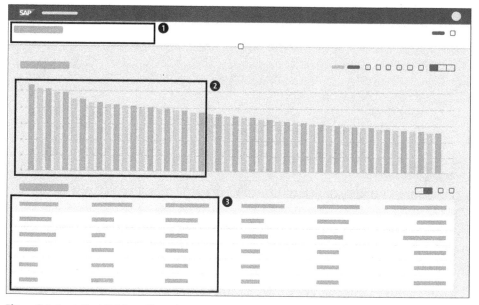

Figure 5.8 Analytical List Page Floorplan

Filters can be applied visually or by using inputs to further analyze the large data set, from which the user can navigate to a list report or an object page.

> **Note**
> For more information on the analytical list page floorplan, visit *http://s-prs.co/v540923*.

SAP introduces new design guidelines with every new version of SAP Fiori. Floorplans such as list report or object page went through many changes. Although SAPUI5 supports the latest SAP Fiori guidelines, developers should also ensure that the applications developed follow the latest SAP Fiori guidelines with every release. For instance, the list report floorplan has evolved a lot with different versions of SAP Fiori, as shown in Figure 5.9:

❶ SAP Fiori 1.0

❷ SAP Fiori 2.0

❸ SAP Fiori 3.0

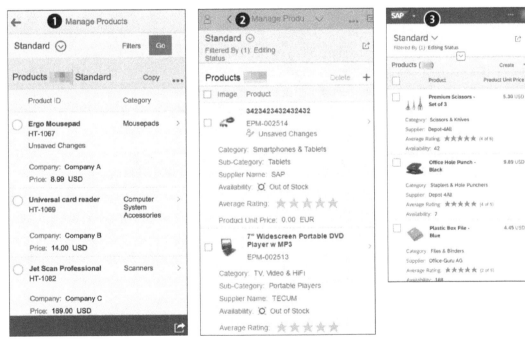

Figure 5.9 List Report Floorplan Evolution

The SAP Fiori elements framework solves this by introducing the most commonly used floorplan templates. These templates generate the UI based on metadata and annotations. You'll learn more about this in the next section.

5.4   SAP Fiori Elements

The SAP Fiori elements framework created by SAP generates the UI with low-code/no-code capabilities via the commonly used floorplan templates. These templates generate the UI on the fly based on the *metadata* and *annotations*, which offers the following flexibilities:

- Ensures UX consistency across all the applications generated with the SAP Fiori elements framework.
- Speeds up the development by reducing the frontend code required to create SAP Fiori apps, reducing maintenance costs using annotations and various available templates.
- Updates the templates automatically according to the latest SAP Fiori version, so all the applications will follow the newest SAP Fiori guidelines.

An SAP Fiori elements app uses the SAP Fiori elements template that can generate the application UI based on the SAP Fiori floorplans such as list report, analytical page, or overview page. You can use VS Code or SAP Business Application Studio to generate the SAP Fiori elements app based on the SAP Fiori floorplans. These templates are based on SAPUI5 and have minimal code. The template alone won't be sufficient to show the UI. Along with it, annotations and metadata are needed to generate the UI on the fly, as shown in Figure 5.10.

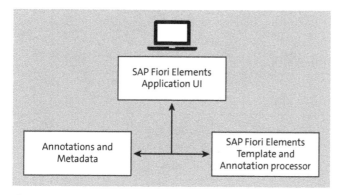

Figure 5.10 SAP Fiori Elements App: High-Level Architecture

> **Note**
> For VS Code, you should install mandatory plug-ins to create an SAP Fiori elements app, but if you use SAP Business Application Studio, all the plug-ins will be added to the dev space based on the configuration you maintain.

So, what are these annotations needed to generate the UI? Annotations help the template or client interpret the OData service's functionality to generate the UI. As the service metadata has limited information about various entities and their relationships, the annotations provide more information on how and what to show in the UI.

For instance, to show an entity's property as a column in the table, you need to provide the following annotation to the service:

```
annotate my.Escalations with @(
    UI.LineItem          : [
            {
                $Type : 'UI.DataField',
                Label : 'Description',
                Value : Description,
            }
        ]
);
```

In the coming steps, you'll learn more about these annotations while generating the SAP Fiori elements app.

5.4.1 Generating the SAP Fiori Elements Application

In the earlier chapters, we created an OData service for handling escalations using the SAP Cloud Application Programming Model. Now you'll generate a UI (list report object page) by consuming the OData service using SAP Business Application Studio.

Example
For reference, you can check the code for this project in the Git repository at *http://s-prs.co/v540901*, branch chapter5.

Follow these steps:

1. In the SAP Business Application Studio, open the dev space where you created the SAP Cloud Application Programming Model service in an earlier chapter, and open the **Welcome** page (choose **View • Find Command**, and then search for **Welcome**).
2. Click the **Start from template** tile on the **Welcome** page to create the SAP Fiori elements app, as shown in Figure 5.11.

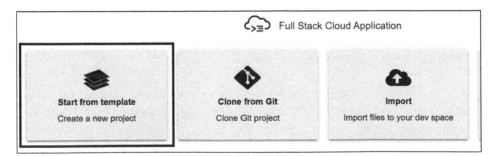

Figure 5.11 Starting a New Project

3. Select the **SAP Fiori application** template from the list of templates, and click **Start**, as shown in Figure 5.12.

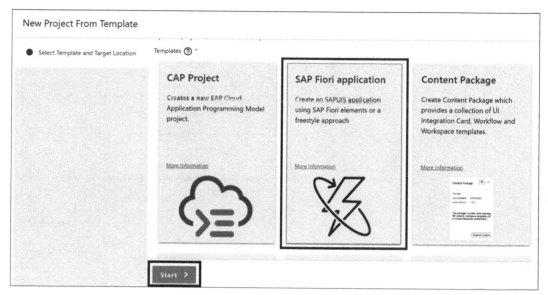

Figure 5.12 SAP Fiori App Template

4. Make sure you've selected **SAP Fiori elements** in the **Application Type** dropdown.
5. Select **List Report Object Page**, and click **Next**, as shown in Figure 5.13.

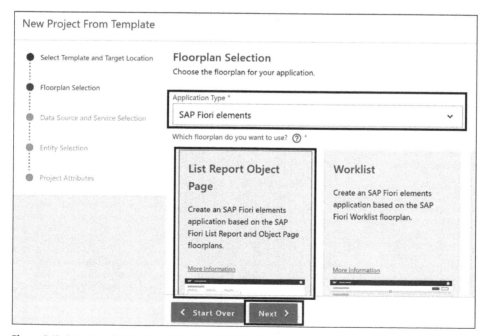

Figure 5.13 SAP Fiori Element App Selection: List Report

6. Select **Use a Local CAP Project** as the **Data source**, and click the **CAP project folder path** icon to select the existing SAP Cloud Application Programming Model project where SAP Business Application Studio will generate the SAP Fiori elements app, as shown in Figure 5.14.

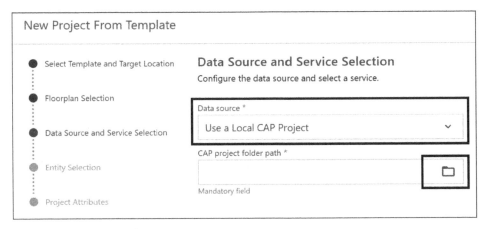

Figure 5.14 Data Source Selection

7. Select the service from the **OData service** dropdown. This is the service name from the *service.cds* file, as shown in Figure 5.15.

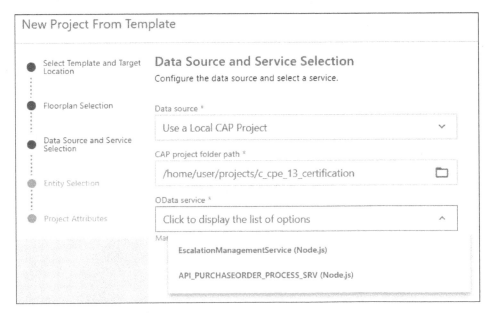

Figure 5.15 OData Service Selection

8. Select **Escalations** as the **Main entity**, which will show up as the table on the list report page, and choose **Comments** as the **Navigation entity**, which will appear on the object page as the table when you open an escalation.

9. Click the **No** radio button because you'll add the table columns and sections to the UI annotations file in the upcoming steps. Click **Next** to proceed to the next step, as shown in Figure 5.16.

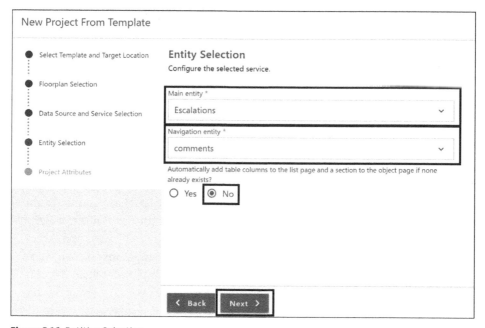

Figure 5.16 Entities Selection

10. Provide the project attributes such as **Module name** and **Application title**. You can leave all other fields as-is. Click **Next**, and on the next page, click **Finish**, as shown in Figure 5.17.

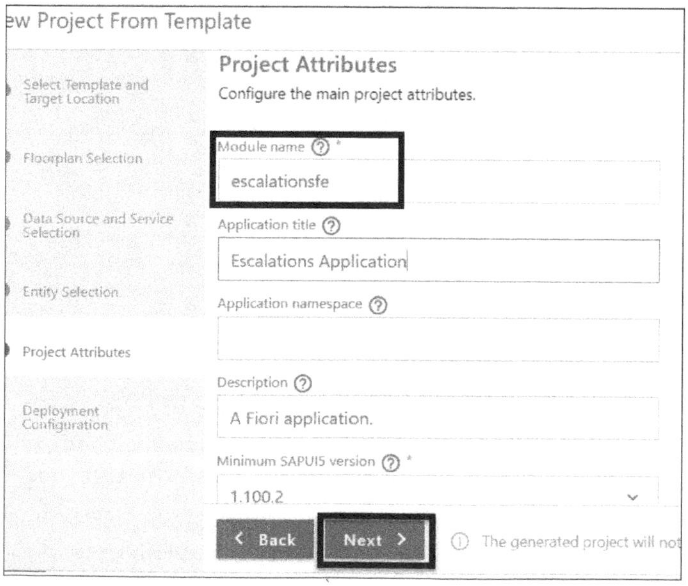

Figure 5.17 Project Attributes

Once you generate the SAP Fiori elements project, you can find it in the existing project folder, **app • escalationsfe**, as shown in Figure 5.18.

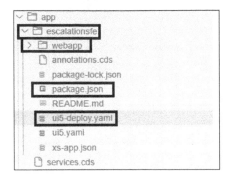

Figure 5.18 Generated SAP Fiori Elements Project

Under the *escalationfe* folder, the *webapp* folder has all the SAP Fiori elements app content, which shows the UI to create the escalation. *package.json* has the script `build:cf`, which will trigger the build process of the SAP Fiori elements app before deploying it to the SAP BTP platform, and this uses the deployment configuration from the *ui5-deploy.yaml* file that provides the path (webapp) to fetch all the content for building the application and creating a zip file with the name *escalationsfe.zip*.

Apart from these new folders and files, our project's existing *mta.yaml* file will also be updated with the configuration to deploy the SAP Fiori elements app to the Cloud Foundry, and the script `build:cf` will generate the SAP Fiori elements app *esalationsfe.zip* file, as shown in Figure 5.19.

```
43    - name: escalationsfe
44      type: html5
45      path: app/escalationsfe
46      build-parameters:
47        build-result: dist
48        builder: custom
49        commands:
50        - npm install
51        - npm run build:cf
52        supported-platforms: []
```

Figure 5.19 SAP Fiori Elements App Builder

For deploying the SAP Fiori elements app content, we use the Generic Application Content Deployer (GACD) module, which is of type `com.sap.application.content`. This module is automatically added in the *mta.yaml* file, as shown in Figure 5.20. This module searches for the *escalationsfe.zip* file generated from the module `escalationfe` and will deploy to the HTML5 application repository in SAP BTP, Cloud Foundry environment; for this, it requires the `html5-apps-repo` service to host all the application file content, which is added as a dependency using `extnCertification-repo-host`. Running this SAP Fiori elements app after deploying to SAP

BTP requires the `html5-app-runtime`, which has to be added manually and is explained in the next chapter.

```
- name: extnCertification-app-content
  type: com.sap.application.content
  path: .
  requires:
  - name: extnCertification-repo-host
    parameters:
      content-target: true
  build parameters:
    build-result: resources
    requires:
    - artifacts:
      - escalationsfe.zip
      name: escalationsfe
      target-path: resources/
```

Figure 5.20 SAP Fiori Elements App Content: mta.yaml

Now that you've generated the SAP Fiori elements project, let's test it by running the following command in the terminal Ctrl + ` .

```
CDS Watch --profile hybrid
```

Once the service is opened in the new browser tab, you can find the link to the generated SAP Fiori app at the top of the page, as shown in Figure 5.21.

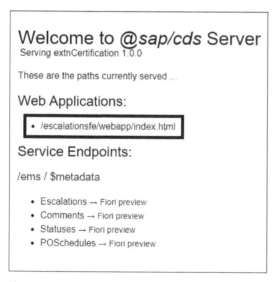

Figure 5.21 Application Links

Click on the web application link as highlighted in Figure 5.22 to open the SAP Fiori elements app.

As shown in Figure 5.22, the SAP Fiori elements app doesn't have any columns or the create option. This is because of the missing draft functionality and missing annotations. We'll discuss this in detail in the next section.

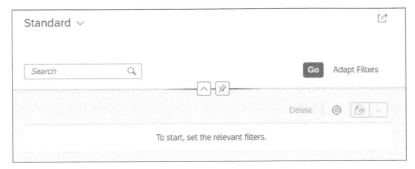

Figure 5.22 SAP Fiori Elements App

5.4.2   Enabling the Draft Functionality

Enabling the draft functionality is a more straightforward step with just one line of code, but you need to understand the draft and why it's required for transactional applications. Let's understand it in detail.

What Is a Draft?

A *draft* is an interim version of your data that isn't yet saved as an active version. This version still exists in the database but as temporary data in draft tables. If you make any changes to the data, then a draft will be saved automatically to the draft database tables, which will continuously be updated with your latest changes automatically in the background. Once you explicitly save it by clicking the **Save** button, it will be saved to the active version of the data. SAP recommends activating the draft functionality in your SAP Cloud Application Programming Model application when it needs end user data input.

Draft Functionality Uses

There are many uses for activating the draft in your application:

- **Resume and edit**
  The main functionality of the draft is to create the intermediate draft data with your changes. So let's consider a scenario where the data entry is huge, and you want to continue the work later. Because the data is saved as a draft in the background, you can close the application and open it later at another point in time to edit the draft again. Once the data entry is completed, you can submit it (actual save).

- **Data loss**
  Without the draft functionality, if your application terminates unexpectedly due to internet failure or device crash, you can't retrieve the data you entered till that time. But if you have the draft functionality activated, the data entered will be saved in the background and can be resumed later, even if your device crashes.

- **Locking**

  If two users are editing the same data simultaneously, the system should show an error message that the first user locked it. But this is difficult to achieve if the client and server are decoupled and communicate via REST services such as SAPUI5 applications. To solve this, SAP Cloud Application Programming Model uses the draft functionality to lock the data and won't allow others to edit it till you save the draft to the active version.

Further Reading

Visit the following URLs for more information on draft handling:

- *http://s-prs.co/v540924*
- *http://s-prs.co/v540925*

Activating the Draft Functionality in Your SAP Cloud Application Programming Model Application

Adding the draft functionality is just an annotation away in the SAP Cloud Application Programming Model application. Add the following annotation in the *service.cds* file:

```
service EscalationManagementService {

    …………

    annotate Escalations with @odata.draft.enabled;

    …………

}
```

After adding the annotation, you need to redeploy to the SAP HANA database as new tables related to the draft have to be generated:

```
cds deploy -2 hana
```

Rerun the app with cds.watch, and open the metadata. Now you can see new properties added to the entities, such as IsActiveEntity, HasActiveEntity, HasDraftEntity, and so on, as shown in Figure 5.23. SAP Cloud Application Programming Model framework uses these properties to handle the draft data.

When you open the application, as shown in Figure 5.24, the app will have the **Create** option enabled, but it doesn't have any columns in the table or proper filters. To show them, let's enhance the metadata data of the service by adding annotations in the coming steps.

Note

You can also observe that some fields appear by default, such as **Editing Status**, because the SAP Cloud Application Programming Model framework automatically adds the annotation to show that in the UI.

```
▼<EntityType Name="Escalations">
  ▼<Key>
    <PropertyRef Name="ID"/>
    <PropertyRef Name="IsActiveEntity"/>
  </Key>
  <Property Name="createdAt" Type="Edm.DateTimeOffset" Precision="7"/>
  <Property Name="createdBy" Type="Edm.String" MaxLength="255"/>
  <Property Name="modifiedAt" Type="Edm.DateTimeOffset" Precision="7"/>
  <Property Name="modifiedBy" Type="Edm.String" MaxLength="255"/>
  <Property Name="ID" Type="Edm.Guid" Nullable="false"/>
  <Property Name="description" Type="Edm.String" MaxLength="80"/>
  <Property Name="material" Type="Edm.String" MaxLength="30"/>
  <Property Name="expectedDate" Type="Edm.Date"/>
  ▼<NavigationProperty Name="status" Type="EscalationManagementService.Statuses">
    <ReferentialConstraint Property="status_code" ReferencedProperty="code"/>
  </NavigationProperty>
  <Property Name="status_code" Type="Edm.String" MaxLength="3"/>
  ▼<NavigationProperty Name="comments" Type="Collection(EscalationManagementService.Comments)" Partner="escalation">
    <OnDelete Action="Cascade"/>
  </NavigationProperty>
  <Property Name="IsActiveEntity" Type="Edm.Boolean" Nullable="false" DefaultValue="true"/>
  <Property Name="HasActiveEntity" Type="Edm.Boolean" Nullable="false" DefaultValue="false"/>
  <Property Name="HasDraftEntity" Type="Edm.Boolean" Nullable="false" DefaultValue="false"/>
  <NavigationProperty Name="DraftAdministrativeData" Type="EscalationManagementService.DraftAdministrativeData" Contain
  <NavigationProperty Name="SiblingEntity" Type="EscalationManagementService.Escalations"/>
</EntityType>
```

Figure 5.23 Draft-Related Properties

Standard ⌄

Editing Status:

| Search | | All | ⌄ | **Go** | Adapt Filters (1) |

Create   Delete   ⚙   ⌄

To start, set the relevant filters.

Figure 5.24 Draft-Enabled SAP Fiori Elements App without Annotations

5.4.3 Adding Annotations

Let's create a new *service_anotation.cds* file in the *srv* folder to enhance the service's metadata, as shown in Figure 5.25. This file will supply annotations to the service, which the SAP Fiori elements template will consume to generate the UI automatically.

Figure 5.25 Annotations File

To supply annotations for the service, you first need to import that service using the following code:

```
using {EscalationManagementService as my} from './service';
```

Let's now enhance the service by adding columns to the escalation table in the list report using the annotations shown in Listing 5.2.

```
annotate my.Escalations with @(
    UI: {
        LineItem  : [
            {
                $Type : 'UI.DataField',
                Label : 'Description',
                Value : description,
            },
......
            {
                $Type : 'UI.DataField',
                Value : expectedDate,
                Label : 'Expected Date',
            }
        ],
    }
);
```

Listing 5.2 Annotations for Columns

The SAP UI Vocabulary is used to represent data in UIs. The LineItem annotation, part of the SAP UI Vocabulary, represents the data collection in a table or a list. Each object in the LineItem annotation of type UI.DataField represents a column in the table. The Value property expects the entity property name, and Label expects the description of the entity property. You can find more information about the LineItem annotation in the following help links.

> **Tip**
> Visit the following URLs for help with annotations:
> - http://s-prs.co/v540926
> - http://s-prs.co/v540927

After adding the annotation, the columns from the annotations will appear in the UI, as shown in Figure 5.26.

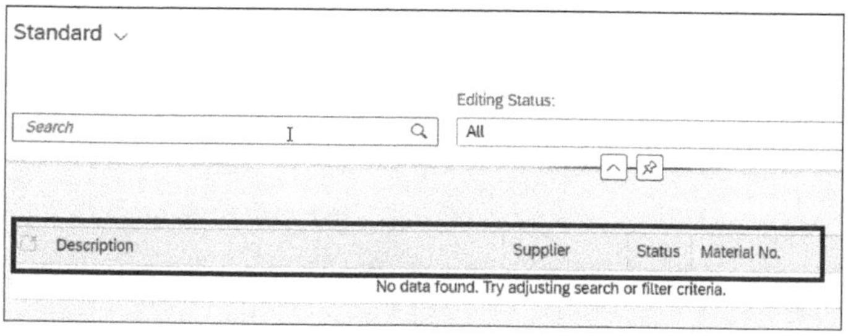

Figure 5.26 Columns in the List Report Table

You should add the SelectionFields annotation shown here, which is part of the SAP UI Vocabulary, to show the filters. You have to pass all the properties you want to display in the filter bar as an array. The added SelectionFields annotations will be reflected in the UI, as shown in Figure 5.27.

```
SelectionFields     : [
    Status_code,
    PurchaseOrder_No
],
```

Figure 5.27 Selection Fields

The list report page is ready, but there is no data. Let's show some data by creating a new escalation entry by clicking the **Create** button, as shown in Figure 5.28.

Figure 5.28 Create Button in the List Report

After clicking the **Create** button, the **New Object** screen will appear, as shown in Figure 5.29.

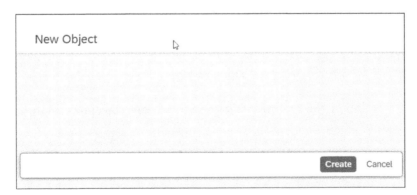

Figure 5.29 Object Page with No Annotations

There are no fields rendered in the object page, as shown in Figure 5.29. In the following steps, let's show the fields by adding annotations to the SAP Cloud Application Programming Model service.

Start by creating a *field group* to show the fields from the Escalation entity, as shown in Listing 5.3.

```
UI:    {
            ........
        FieldGroup #GenInfo : {
        $Type : 'UI.FieldGroupType',
        Data  : [
            {
                $Type : 'UI.DataField',
                Value : Description,
            },
            {
                $Type : 'UI.DataField',
                Value : PurchaseOrder_No,
            },
            {
                $Type : 'UI.DataField',
                Value : PurchaseOrder.Supplier,
                Label : 'Supplier',
            },
                    ........
        ],
    },
        ........
}
```

Listing 5.3 Field Group Annotations

As you can see in Listing 5.3, the FieldGroup annotation is also part of the SAP UI Vocabulary. #GenInfo is the name of the field group, and you have to pass the list of fields that should appear in the field group inside the Data array. When the purchase order is selected, you have to fetch the supplier associated with it and show it on the object page. For this reason, we're accessing the Supplier from the association PurchaseOrder as PurchaseOrder.Supplier.

After you refresh the UI and create a new entry again, it still won't show the field group you created. This isn't enough to show the fields on the object page. You need to add the facet annotation to show the field group, which is explained in the following steps.

Facet annotations are used to build the sections on the object page. Field groups, line items, charts, and so on can be supplied to these facets, which will be rendered inside the section (shown on the object page). Let's create a facet and add the field group created in the previous step, as shown in Listing 5.4.

```
UI:{
.......
 Facets: [
        {
            $Type: 'UI.ReferenceFacet',
            Target: '@UI.FieldGroup#GenInfo',   // Field group ID reference
            Label: 'General Information'         // Section name
        }
    ],
.......
}
```

Listing 5.4 Field Group Annotations

You need to add facet type Reference Facet, which will refer to a *thing perspective*. For instance, it refers to the LineItem annotation to show a table or to the FieldGroup annotation to show the field group. In the preceding example, the facet relates to the FieldGroup – GenInfo, the name of the field group you created in the earlier step. After adding the facet, the field group is shown on the object page (see Figure 5.30).

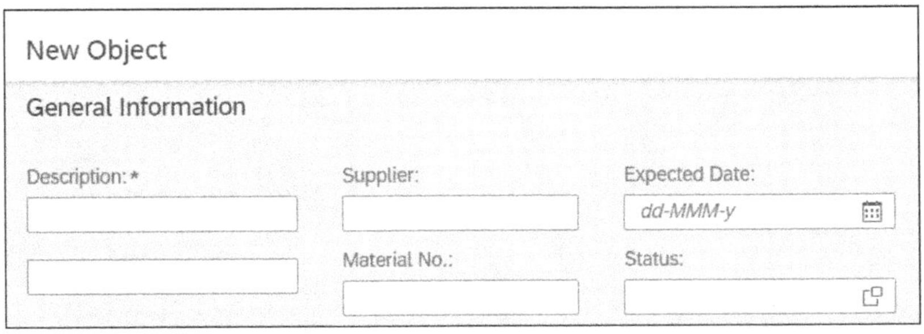

New Object
General Information

Description: * Supplier: Expected Date: dd-MMM-y

Material No.: Status:

Figure 5.30 Field Group

We only want to show the supplier details in display-only mode when the purchase order is entered. In general, we want the PurchaseOrders entity to be read-only, so add the following annotation to make the entity and all its properties display-only, as shown in Figure 5.31.

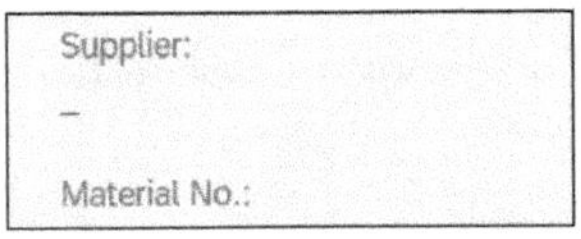

Supplier:
–
Material No.:

Figure 5.31 Supplier Read-Only

Note
The file path to do the changes is *srv/service.cds*.

```
service SupplierSBSExtSrv {
    ............

    @readonly entity PurchaseOrder as projection on my.PurchaseOrder;
}
```

We also want the **Status** field to be read-only. By default, in the create mode (draft), it should show the status as **Draft**, and when the record is created (saved) in the database, it should update to **In Progress**. You need to add the readonly annotation and add the handler methods to default the draft status.

> **Note**
> The file path to do the changes is *db/schema.cds*.

```
entity Escalations: managed, cuid {
    ........

    Status: StatusType @(Common.Label : 'Status') @readonly ;
    ........
};
```

Pass the default status as DRF (draft) in the New event handler. This event handler is triggered when a new draft is created.

> **Note**
> The file path to do the changes is *db/service.js*.

```
this.before('NEW', 'Escalations', (req) => {
    req.data.Status_code = 'INP';
});
```

After you save the record (from draft to active version), the status should be updated to INP (**In Progress**). Implement the Create event handler to default the **In Progress** status as shown in the following:

> **Note**
> The file path to do the changes is *db/service.js*.

```
this.before('CREATE', 'Escalations', (req) => {
    // After creation, update the status to 'In Progress'
    req.data.status_code = 'INP';
});
```

Discard the draft (and refresh the application), and create a new escalation again to get the default status, as shown in Figure 5.32.

Figure 5.32 Draft Default Status

But it will be difficult for an end user to understand what the status code INP or DRF means, so you should also show the status description along with the status code. To display the description for the field status_code, annotate the association Status with the common.text annotation, and pass the Text property with the association's field, where the description of the code resides.

> **Note**
> The file path to do the changes is *srv/service_annotations.cds*.

```
annotate my.Escalations with {
    Status
        @Common : {
            Text : Status.name,
        }
}
```

After adding the preceding annotation, the description of the status code will be displayed as shown in Figure 5.33.

Figure 5.33 Status Description

When you click the **Create** button to create an escalation, the SAP Fiori elements app should validate mandatory fields such as the **Escalation Description**, **Purchase Order No.**, and **Expected Date**. As shown here, these fields can be made mandatory by using the @mandatory annotation.

> **Note**
> The file path to do the changes is *srv/service_annotations.cds*.

```
annotate my.Escalations with {
    Description @mandatory;
    PurchaseOrder @mandatory
```

```
ExpectedDate @mandatory;
    ............
}
```

Our escalation application will show an error if you fill in these three fields and click the **Create** button, as shown in Figure 5.34.

Figure 5.34 Mandatory Validation

You can fill in the **Escalation Description** and **Expected Date**. But for the **Purchase Order No.**, you need to know the list of purchase orders coming from the SAP S/4HANA system via the `PurchaseOrder` entity. `Common.ValueList` should be used to show the value list to select from the list of purchase orders, as shown in Figure 5.35.

```
annotate my.Escalations with {
    ............
    ............
    PurchaseOrder @(Common : {ValueList : {
        $Type          : 'Common.ValueListType',
        CollectionPath : 'PurchaseOrder',          ─────────────►  Entity from which the purchase
        Parameters     : [                                          orders are to be fetched.
            {
                $Type             : 'Common.ValueListParameterInOut',  ─────►  When the purchase order is selected
                ValueListProperty : 'ID',                                       from the value help, $Type -
                LocalDataProperty : 'purchaseOrder_ID'                          ValueListParameterInOut tells from
            },                                                                  which field in the value help table
            {                                                                   the purchase order number should be
                $Type             : 'Common.ValueListParameterDisplayOnly',     chosen via ValueListProperty.
                ValueListProperty : 'PurchaseOrderType'                         LocalDataProperty tells where the
            },                                                                  purchase order number should be
            {                                                                   copied to.
                $Type             : 'Common.ValueListParameterDisplayOnly',
                ValueListProperty : 'Supplier'             ─────────────►  This is a display-only field
            }                                                               shown in the value help pop-up
        ]                                                                   table.
    }});
    ............
    ............
}
```

Figure 5.35 Purchase Orders Value Help

> **Note**
> The file path to do the changes is *srv/service_annotations.cds*.

After adding the annotation, the value help icon will be shown in the **Purchase Order No.** input box (see Figure 5.36), and when you click it, a popup is opened from which you can select a purchase order.

Figure 5.36 Value Help Icon

After selecting a purchase order from the value help, click **OK** to copy it to the **Purchase Order No.** input box (Figure 5.37).

Figure 5.37 Value Help Selection

After selecting the purchase order from the value help, the **Supplier** should be automatically filled in to show you who the supplier is for the purchase order. To automatically show the supplier, you need to add the side effects. So, when there is any change in the SourceProperties (PurchaseOrder_ID), a request will be sent automatically to the backend from the SAP Fiori elements app to refresh the TargetEntities (PurchaseOrder association) data.

> **Note**
> The file path to do the changes is *srv/service_annotations.cds*.

```
annotate my.Escalations with @(
    Common.SideEffects #PurchaseOrderUpdated : {
        SourceProperties : [PurchaseOrder_ID], // Property of the escalation
```

```
        TargetEntities   : [PurchaseOrder] // PurchaseOrder entity
  },
    ...........

}
```

When you select a purchase order from the value help, after adding the annotation, the **Supplier** field will be filled automatically by the framework, as shown in Figure 5.38.

New Object

General Information

Escalation Description: *

Material No.:

Purchase Order No.: *
9000000001

Expected Date: *
dd-MMM-y

Supplier:
sup_bangalore

Status:
In Process (INP)

Figure 5.38 Supplier Field Filled Automatically

Now let's show the comment section where you can provide comments on the escalation using the comments association. First, you should enhance the comments entity with the LineItem annotation to show it as a table.

> **Note**
> The file path to do the changes is *srv/service_annotations.cds*.

```
annotate my.Comments with @(UI: {
    LineItem      : [
        {Value: comment, Label: 'Comment'},
        {Value: createdAt, }
    ],
});
```

You need to add a reference facet, referencing the comments entity LineItem annotation you added previously.

> **Note**
> The file path to do the changes is *srv/service_annotations.cds*.

```
annotate my.Escalations with @(
    UI: {
    ...........
```

```
        Facets: [
    ...........
            {
                $Type   : 'UI.ReferenceFacet',
                Target : 'Comments/@UI.LineItem',
                Label   : 'Comments'
            },
        ],
    }
);
```

After adding the annotations, the comments entity will be rendered as a table on your object page, as shown in Figure 5.39

Figure 5.39 Comments Table

But when you click the **Create** button, it will open an empty page without any annotations just like in the initial steps when you tried creating a new escalation. This is because of missing object page annotations for the comments entity. You have to follow similar steps of adding the FieldGroup annotation and referencing it in the Facet annotation, as shown in Listing 5.5.

Instead of using the FieldGroup annotation, you'll now use the Identification annotation. The difference is that you can create multiple field groups using the FieldGroup annotation and show them in multiple sections, whereas the Identification annotation is just the collection of fields identifying the object and can be created one time.

Note
The file path to do the changes is *srv/service_annotations.cds*.

```
annotate my.Comments with @(UI : {
    ..........
```

```
    Identification : [
        {
            $Type : 'UI.DataField',
            Value : comment,
            Label : 'Comment',
        },
        {
            $Type : 'UI.DataField',
            Value : createdAt,
        },
    ] ,
    Facets        : [{
        $Type   : 'UI.ReferenceFacet',
        Target  : '@UI.Identification',
        Label   : 'General Information'
    }]
});
```

Listing 5.5 Comments Entity Annotations

After you add the annotation, the comments entity fields will be rendered on the object page, as shown in Figure 5.40.

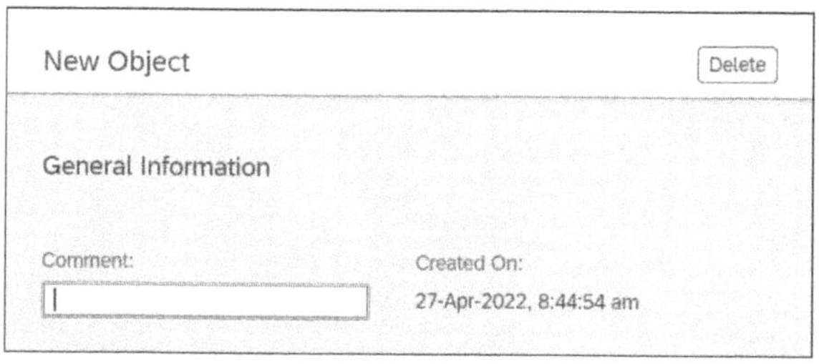

Figure 5.40 Comments Entity Fields

The status_code field is shown in the filter bar as a value help in the list report page. It makes sense to show it as a value help if there are many status codes, similar to how we showed the value help for the **Purchase Order** field. In this case, you can show it as a dropdown, which will increase the UX. You should add Common.Value-ListWithFixedValues annotations to convert it to the dropdown, as shown in Figure 5.41.

> **Note**
> The file path to do the changes is *srv/service_annotations.cds*.

```
annotate my.Escalations with {
    .........
    Status
        @Common : {
```

```
        Text : Status.name,
        ValueListWithFixedValues : true
    }
}
```

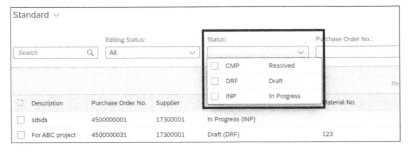

Figure 5.41 Status Dropdown

Now that the SAP Fiori elements app UI is completed. You need to provide the functionality for the administrator to resolve the escalation. This functionality can be achieved by showing the button through the annotations. To render a button, you need to add the UI.LineItem annotation, but the type will be UI.DataField-ForAction, as shown in Listing 5.6. You must also pass the action ID you created in previous chapters.

Note
The file path to do the changes is *srv/service_annotations.cds*.

```
annotate my.Escalations with @(
    UI: {

        ............
        LineItem           : [

            ............
            {
                $Type          : 'UI.DataFieldForAction',
                Action         : ' EscalationManagementService
.resolve', // Action ID
                Label          : 'Resolve'
            }
            ............

        ]
        ............

    }
);
```

Listing 5.6 Resolve Action Annotation

This will be enough to render the button. When you click the **Resolve** button, the escalation status will be updated to Completed in the backend, but the status won't be updated in the UI. You can achieve this by adding the `Common.SideEffects` annotation to the action directly in the service file, as shown in Listing 5.7.

> **Note**
> The file path to do the changes is *srv/service.cds*.

```
service EscalationManagementService{
    ...........
    entity Escalations as projection on my.Escalations actions{
        @(
            cds.odata.bindingparameter.name : '_it',
            Common.SideEffects           : {
                TargetProperties : ['_it/status_code']
            }
        )
        action resolve();
    };
    ...........
}
```

Listing 5.7 Resolve Action Side Effects

`_it` is the binding parameter name, which is of type `Escalations` entity. Using this, you can access the properties of the `escalations` entity and can be used to refresh the data of the `TargetProperties` from the `Common.SideEffects` annotation, as shown in the example code snippet. When you resolve the escalation by clicking the button, the escalation status will be updated in the backend, and the UI will be refreshed automatically, as shown in Figure 5.42.

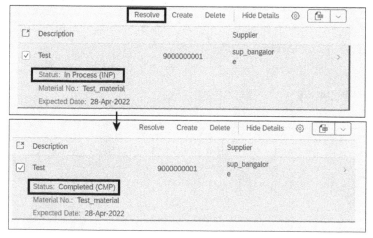

Figure 5.42 Resolve Action

Congratulations! You've now created an SAP Fiori elements app and added all necessary annotations to show the UI.

5.5   Important Terminology

In this chapter, the following terminology was used:

- **Annotations**
  Annotations help the SAP Fiori elements template interpret the OData service's functionality to generate the UI without any code.

- **Draft**
  A draft is an interim version of your data that isn't yet saved as an active version.

- **SAPUI5**
  This is an HTML5 framework for creating enterprise-grade responsive web applications developed by SAP.

- **SAP Fiori**
  The design language helps enterprises create applications with a consistent UX developed by SAP. These guidelines are implemented in SAPUI5 controls.

- **SAP Fiori elements**
  This is a framework created by SAP that generates the UI with low-code/no-code capabilities via the commonly used floorplan templates.

- **SAP Fiori floorplans**
  These are commonly used enterprise scenarios with a specific combination of UI elements, which helps to maintain the consistency of all the apps in a company.

5.6   Practice Questions

1. What are the advantages of SAPUI5 over traditional web application development?

   ☐ **A.** Speed of the application development

   ☐ **B.** Responsiveness across different devices

   ☐ **C.** OData service integration with the controls

   ☐ **D.** All of the above

2. What are some of the core design principles of SAP Fiori? (There are two correct answers.)

   ☐ **A.** Role-based

   ☐ **B.** Delightful

   ☐ **C.** Less latency

   ☐ **D.** Complex interface

3. Where can you use SAP Fiori 3?

☐ **A.** SAPUI5

☐ **B.** React

☐ **C.** Web components

☐ **D.** All of the above

4. What are the different floorplans available in SAP Fiori? (There are two correct answers.)

☐ **A.** Multipage layout

☐ **B.** List report

☐ **C.** Split app

☐ **D.** Analytical list page

5. You can develop an SAP Fiori elements app using which of the following? (There are two correct answers.)

☐ **A.** SAP GUI

☐ **B.** SAP Business Application Studio

☐ **C.** VS Code

☐ **D.** SAP Fiori launchpad

6. What kind of floorplan will you select if the data is large, and you want to sort and filter the data with the option to edit and create an item?

☐ **A.** Object page

☐ **B.** Analytical list page

☐ **C.** Overview page

☐ **D.** List report

7. Which floorplan doesn't recommend drilling down to find the root cause, doesn't allow the user to interact between different visualizations, and does show multiple sets of data for the user to interact with?

☐ **A.** Analytical list page

☐ **B.** List report

☐ **C.** Worklist

☐ **D.** Object page

8.   Is an analytical list page floorplan used to show multiple views of the same data in tabular or graphical format?

☐   **A.** True.

☐   **B.** False

9.   Why do we need to activate the draft functionality?

☐   **A.** To use for transactional applications per SAP's recommendation

☐   **B.** To provide locking of the data while multiple users are accessing it concurrently

☐   **C.** To avoid data loss when there is network outage

☐   **D.** All of the above

10.   Which annotation is used to enable the draft functionality?

☐   **A.** @odata.draft.enabled

☐   **B.** @odata.draft.on

☐   **C.** @cap.draft.enabled

11.   Which service is used to host the deployed SAP Fiori elements app content?

☐   **A.** cap-apps-repo

☐   **B.** fiori-apps-repo

☐   **C.** html5-apps-repo

12.   Which annotation is used to show the columns in a table?

☐   **A.** LineItem

☐   **B.** FieldGroup

☐   **C.** Facet

13.   Which annotation is used to show the fields in the object page?

☐   **A.** LineItem

☐   **B.** FieldGroup

☐   **C.** Facet

14.   Which annotation is used to show different groups/sections on the object page?

☐   **A.** LineItem

☐   **B.** FieldGroup

☐   **C.** Facet

5.7   Practice Question Answers and Explanations

1. Answer: **D**

   SAPUI5 speeds up the development by providing predefined controls with deeper integrations with OData service and responsive across various device types such as desktop, mobile, and tablet.

2. Answer: **A and B**

   Role-based, delightful, coherent, and simple are some of the core design principles of SAP Fiori.

3. Answer: **D**

   You can use SAP Fiori 3 in web components, SAPUI5, and Reach.

4. Answer: **B and D**

   List report, worklist, analytical list page, and overview page are some of the floorplans in SAP Fiori.

5. Answer: **B and C**

   You can develop SAP Fiori elements apps using the two SAP recommended tools: VS Code and SAP Fiori launchpad.

6. Answer: **D**

   The list report floorplan supports sorting and filtering of huge amounts of data along with the option to create and update the items with the help of the object page.

7. Answer: **D**

   Object page isn't used for scenarios where drill down is required to find the root cause or users can't interact between different visualizations.

8. Answer: **A**

   The analytical list page floorplan is used to show one set of data in different formatted views (charts and tables) for the user to interact with and analyze.

9. Answer: **D**

   SAP recommends enabling the draft functionality in transactional SAP Fiori elements apps in SAP Cloud Application Programming Model as it comes with many advantages such as data locking and data loss prevention.

10. Answer: **A**

    The `@odata.draft.enabled` annotation is used to activate the draft for an SAP Cloud Application Programming Model-based OData service.

11. Answer: **C**

    The `html5-apps-repo` service is used to host the deployed SAP Fiori elements app content.

12. Answer: **A**

    You use the `LineItem` annotation to show the columns in a table in both list report and object page.

13. Answer: **B**

    The `FieldGroup` annotation is to show group of fields on the object page.

14. Answer: **C**

    `UI.Facet` annotation is used to show multiple groups/sections on the object page.

5.8   Test Takeaway

SAPUI5 makes developing complex enterprise-grade applications easier as it provides a set of reusable libraries, controls, and themes to create modern web applications quickly and efficiently. SAP Fiori sets the rules to develop these modern web applications to enhance the UX, which is well implemented in SAPUI5. As the time to create the applications keeps increasing with the complexity level, it's crucial to have low-code/no-code tools to develop the application with SAP Fiori guidelines. That is where SAP Fiori elements helps developers use annotations and metadata to generate the UI dynamically with less effort. While developing transactional apps, SAP recommends enabling the draft in the SAP Cloud Application Programming Model-based OData service as it provides essential features such as concurrency locking and data loss protection.

5.9   Summary

We started this chapter by discussing the ease of using SAPUI5 and the need for design guidelines. Then, you learned what SAP Fiori is, along with the different versions of SAP Fiori. We talked about how SAP Fiori elements help you create enterprise-grade SAP Fiori apps without writing a lot of code with the help of annotations. Then we used SAP Business Application Studio to generate the SAP Fiori elements app using the available templates and added annotations to create the UI with minimal lines of code.

In the next chapter, you'll learn about providing authorization to the SAP Cloud Application Programming Model service.

Chapter 6
Authorization and Trust Management

Techniques You'll Master

- Understanding how to add authentication
- Exploring authorization scopes, roles, and role collections
- Using techniques to require authorizations
- Working with AppRouter and understanding its role in authentication

In Chapter 5, we added a user interface (UI) module (source files within the app folder), but we didn't deploy it to the SAP BTP, Cloud Foundry environment, yet. When you deploy it to Cloud Foundry, you need a common hostname to access both the UI as well as the OData service to conform with the cross-origin resource sharing (CORS) security policy. That is, with the same hostname (and port), based on different URL paths, you need to load the UI (route to static files) in some cases and call the OData API (route to the SAP Cloud Application Programming Model server) in other cases. SAP provides a module called AppRouter, which is a node module that can route requests based on predefined routes. We'll start this chapter by discussing and using the AppRouter module. You'll see other features of AppRouter, such as authentication, and gradually understand authorization features as well.

Real-World Scenario

In previous chapters, we've created an SAP Cloud Application Programming Model-based server for viewing current purchasing schedules and creating escalations for each of them. You want to ensure that users are required to authenticate with credentials before using the exposed service. In addition, there are business rules around authorizations that must be implemented. Only users of type purchasers and managers should be able to access the application. Both of these user types should be able to see a list of escalations, but only users of type purchasers should be able to create new escalations as only purchasers are aware of the impact of delays in materials arriving. Once created, purchasers won't update the escalations, and only managers should be able to modify the escalations to add comments and update other fields.

6.1   Objectives of This Portion of the Test

This portion of the test checks your understanding of authentication and authorization of applications deployed in SAP Business Technology Platform (SAP BTP). Authentication and authorization are basic features of enterprise applications. We're going to add authentication and authorization features to the sample application we're building. The authentication feature requires a new module in our multi-target application (MTA) application called AppRouter. We'll explore how to add and configure an AppRouter.

> **Note**
> Authorization and trust management topics make up more than 12% of the total exam.

6.2   AppRouter

AppRouter is the single entry point to your application that has multiple modules and runs on the SAP BTP, Cloud Foundry environment. It's a Node.js application that can be started along with custom configurations for routing and other features. In the following sections, we'll explore the need for AppRouter and how to add an AppRouter module to our application.

6.2.1   Challenges with the Microservices Approach

Now we'll cover the problems with the following microservices approach and how AppRouter can help you overcome them. SAP BTP applications are made up of multiple microservices. These microservices can be part of a single MTA or, in some cases, point to external microservices as well. Browsers employ a security validation where they stop an application that is loaded from origin A from accessing resources from origin B. This feature of accessing resources across origins is called cross-origin request sharing (CORS). By default, browsers block CORS as allowing it can be a security risk.

This problem with CORS can be solved by having a single point of entry to your application. Based on the path of the application, you can configure the AppRouter to route the request to various microservices as shown in Figure 6.1.

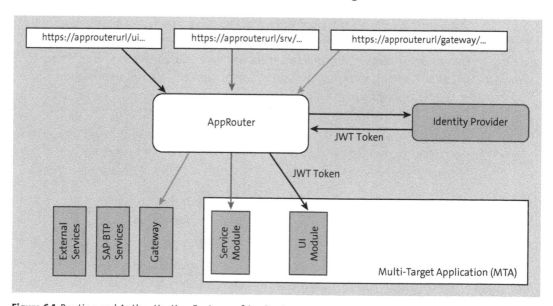

Figure 6.1 Routing and Authentication Features of AppRouter

The next challenge is authentication. Each of our enterprise microservices needs authentication to function. If you call them directly from the browser (e.g., you worked around the CORS feature), you still need to authenticate with each microservice. This won't be a nice user experience. Ideally, you want to authenticate once and use Single Sign-On (SSO) with other microservices or modules. App-Router takes care of this challenge as well. It routes the unauthenticated user to the identity provider's (IdP) login page. Once logged in, IdP provides a token to the AppRouter. Whenever AppRouter routes to any microservice, it also passes this token so that the user is logged in automatically. This is also shown in Figure 6.1.

In summary, the following lists the main features of AppRouter:

- **Routing**
  AppRouter can route the incoming requests to various services and applications running on SAP BTP. It can use SAP BTP destinations as the target of routing as well.

- **Authentication**
  Based on the configurations, if the incoming request requires authentication, the AppRouter initiates the authentication flow. Again based on configurations, it can forward the authentication to other target services and applications, thus facilitating SSO. In the case of a multitenant scenario, the AppRouter figures out the tenant and forwards the request to the SAP BTP Authorization and Trust Management service so that the user is sent to a tenant-specific IdP.

- **Authorization**
  In the AppRouter configuration, you can specify the required authorizations for the users to access a particular route.

- **Serve static files**
  The routing rules of the AppRouter can be such that it can point to a folder within the AppRouter module. You can use this to serve static content within that folder. However, in the case of serving a UI (e.g., SAP Fiori), you'll usually use the HTML5 application repository service in SAP BTP to host the static files of HTML5 applications.

- **Multitenancy scenario**
  In a multitenancy scenario, the AppRouter module fetches the tenant information from the application URL and passes it to the SAP Authorization and Trust Management service so that the user is directed to the configured IdP for the tenant.

6.2.2   Options to Add the AppRouter Module

There are two ways to add the AppRouter module to your application:

- **Using a standalone AppRouter**
  In this approach, you add a new AppRouter module to your MTA. This is called standalone as there is no dependency on any other services for this to work. On the downside, because you're running a new node application (i.e., the AppRouter module), this involves incurring additional SAP BTP costs.

- **Using a managed AppRouter**
  In this approach, you use the AppRouter functionality provided by one of the SAP BTP services. You can use this approach only if you consume any of the AppRouter-providing services, such as SAP Launchpad, SAP Work Zone, and SAP Cloud Portal.

Going forward, we'll work with a standalone AppRouter because none of the previously mentioned SAP BTP services are needed here.

Within a MTA, an AppRouter module is housed inside an app folder. This same folder is usually used to store the static UI resources as well. An AppRouter is configured using a file named *xs-app.json*. As the name suggests, the content of this file is in JavaScript Object Notation (JSON) format. We'll explore various relevant settings that are useful to achieve the example scenario.

6.2.3 Configuring AppRouter

Now let's explore various configurations that can be done on the AppRouter within the *xs-app.json* file:

- `welcomeFile`
  Whenever the AppRouter is accessed without any URL path (i.e., when the root path is accessed, then this path will be called. For example, if the AppRouter application URL *https://c9812745trial-gpe-cis-gpespace-extbook-AppRouter.cfapps.us10. hana.ondemand.com* is called, the user will be redirected to *https://c9812745trial-gpe-cis-gpespace-extbook-AppRouter.cfapps.us10.hana.ondemand.com/index.html*.

- `authenticationMethod`
  You can set this property to none to disable authentication for the AppRouter module. By default, the value route is considered, which means that the authentication is defined at each route level.

- `routes`
  This property defines an array of routes to be handled by the AppRouter. Each entry within the array can have the following properties:

  - `source`
    This is the pattern against which the AppRouter's URL path is compared. This pattern is based on regular expressions. If the source URL matches more than one route's source pattern, then only the first route is considered, and others are ignored. Therefore, the order of the routes is important within the specification of the route.

  - `target`
    This part specifies a target URL to which the source URL is rewritten. While defining the target URL, you can use specific parts of the source URL as well via the *capturing group* concept of regular expressions.

- `destination`
  This is the destination to which the incoming request is to be forwarded. All valid destinations should be available within the environment variable of the AppRouter notification. Here, the name of one such destination needs to be specified. AppRouter can also look into the SAP BTP destination service for a valid destination. If the name specified here is neither available within the environment variables nor in the destination service, an error will be thrown when you deploy the AppRouter to the SAP BTP.

- `service`
  This is the name of the SAP BTP service instance to which the incoming request is to be forwarded.

- `localDir`
  This is the name of the folder within the AppRouter module from which to fetch the static resources. It can only serve `GET` and `HEAD` requests. Note that the value for one of the `destination`, `service`, and `localDir` configurations is mandatory to be specified in the route configuration for a route.

- `authenticationType`
  This is the type of authentication required to access the specific route. It can be `none` if no authentication is required, `basic` for basic authentication, or `xsuaa` if you want the SAP Authorization and Trust Management service instance to take over the authentication.

- `scope`
  This is an array of authorization scopes the user should have to access this particular route. This is one of the declarative ways of specifying the required authorizations. AppRouter will automatically perform the validation of these scopes against the user's scopes and return an authorization error if the user doesn't have the required scopes.

Next, we'll explore a few examples of routing configurations to understand them better.

Figure 6.2 ❶ specifies `resources` as the `localDir`. Any URL path having the specified source format will look for the content from the *resources* folder. For example, calls coming to *https://approuterhost/ui/component.js* will return the file *resources/ui/component.js*.

However, URL *https://approuterhost/ui/Component.js* will return a 404, as the route configurations are case-specific. By using `matchCase: false` ❷, any variation of the URL path is also accepted.

Next, we'll use a destination in the AppRouter configuration. Consider a destination `backend` pointing to *https://scm_server.com*, as shown in the configuration ❸. A call to *https://approuterhost/app1/Escalations* will be sent to the destination `backend`. In effect, the call will be sent to *https://scm_server.com/app1/Escalations*.

In the next configuration, we have the target property as well. The target property specifies the URL path to be used instead of the matched source URL path. This concept is called *URL rewriting*. If target isn't specified, then no URL rewriting takes place, and the target URL path will be the same as the source path. Within the target path, you can specify capturing groups from the source path. The captured content is referred to as $1 and used in the target path. In this example ❹, *https:// approuterhost/app1/Escalations* is sent to the destination backend along with a URL rewrite. In effect, the call is directed to the URL *https://scm_server.com/ems/Escalations*.

The ability to capture the content from the source URL path can be used to specify a dynamic destination from the source URL path. In the next configuration ❺, there are two capture groups specified within the source URL. The captured contents can be referred to using $1 and $2 based on their order of occurrence. The captured content can be used as the value of the destination, as shown in this configuration. A call to *https://approuterhost/backend/app1/Escalations* will be sent to the destination backend (the first capture group of the source URL), and then the URL is rewritten as well. In effect, the calls are sent to *https://scm_server.com/ems/Escalations*. By changing the source URL, you can dynamically send the request to a different destination.

In the next configuration example ❻, the routing happens to an SAP BTP service instance instead of the destination. In this case, the incoming request will be sent to the specified service instead of the destination in earlier examples.

```
{                                               ❶
    "source": "^/ui/(.*)$",
    "localDir": "resources"
}
```

```
{                                               ❷
    "source": {
        "path": "^/ui/(.*)$",
        "matchCase": false
    }
    "localDir": "resources"
}
```

```
{                                               ❸
    "source": "^/app1/(.*)$",
    "destination": "backend"
}
```

```
{                                               ❹
    "source": "^/app1/(.*)$",
    "target": "/ems/$1",
    "destination": "backend"
}
```

```
{                                               ❺
    "source": "^/([^/]+)/app1/(.*)$",
    "target": "/ems/$2",
    "destination": "$1"
}
```

```
{                                               ❻
    "source": "^/app1/(.*)$",
    "target": "/new/$1/pathB",
    "service": "app-1"
}
```

Figure 6.2 Example Route Configurations of AppRouter

6.2.4   Configuring the HTML5 Application Repository Service

For storing the static resources of an SAP Fiori app (any UI application for that matter), you now know you can make use of the AppRouter module. By storing the resources within a folder inside the AppRouter and writing suitable routing rules, you can serve the required UI files. However, there are a few disadvantages when you follow that approach:

- Whenever you need to update the UI files, you need to manually restart the AppRouter after the update so that the AppRouter can start serving the updated files.
- You can't store multiple versions of the UI application simultaneously.
- Storing the static files within the AppRouter may not be the optimum solution when there is high traffic, and you might require several instances of the AppRouter module to serve the files.

The HTML5 application repository service provides a central place to store and serve all the static resources. Using this service provides several advantages when compared with storing them within the AppRouter module:

- Separating the lifecycle of the AppRouter module from the UI files lets you update the UI files without the need to restart the AppRouter.
- When there is a need, you can create multiple instances of the service instance to handle peak loads.
- You have access to earlier versions of the app.
- The UI application can be shared by multiple applications without creating any dependency on each other.
- The static files can be optimized and cached for optimum network performance.

To use the HTML5 application repository service, you need two instances of the service (technical name: `html5-apps-repo`) with plans `app-runtime` and `app-host`. Both these instances have to be bound to the AppRouter service so that the AppRouter can consume these two service instances. The service instance with `app-host` is used for hosting the HTML5 static content files. You saw this briefly in Chapter 5, Section 5.4.1. When we added the SAP Fiori UI, you also saw that the wizard in SAP Business Application Studio also added a corresponding resource in the *mta.yaml* file. The service instance with the `app-runtime` plan is used for accessing the hosted HTML5 application from the HTML5 application repository service. You need to add configurations within the *mta.yaml* file to automatically create this instance and bind it to the AppRouter service so that the AppRouter module can access HTML5 resources.

Once you deploy the UI module to the HTML5 repository service, you can use the AppRouter configuration to route any such requests to the HTML5 application repository service. In the second route definition in (shown in the next section), you can see that the requests are forwarded to the SAP BTP service `html5-apps-repo-rt`. You can refer to the application with the path */<application name>-<application version>/<resources>*. The *application name* is the name (without dots) specified in the `sap.app.id` within the *manifest.json* file of the SAPUI5 application. The application version is optional and lets you choose a specific version from the HTML5 repository service. You can omit the version to get the latest version of the SAPUI5 application.

6.2.5 Real-World Scenario: Adding an AppRouter Module

Now that you understand the AppRouter configuration and the required resources and services, let's add the configurations in *mta.yaml*, the AppRouter module, and the routing configuration for the scenario we're working toward.

Add HTML5 Rep, Runtime Instance

When we added the SAP Fiori module in Chapter 5, a resource for the HTML5 application repository service instance with the `app-host` plan was automatically created in *mta.yaml*. Now we'll add another resource of the HTML5 application repository service instance with the `app-runtime` plan, as shown in Listing 6.1.

```
- name: extnCertification-repo-runtime
  type: org.cloudfoundry.managed-service
  parameters:
    service: html5-apps-repo
    service-name: extnCertification-html5-rt
    service-plan: app-runtime
```

Listing 6.1 A New Resource for Accessing the HTML5 Static Resources

Now we need to add both the resources (`app-host` and `app-runtime`) as `required` for the AppRouter service. This ensures that the AppRouter service has the credentials to consume these services. Add the needed resources as shown in Listing 6.2.

```
modules:
- name: extnCertification-aprouter
  type: nodejs
  path: app
  requires:
    - name: extnCertification-repo-host
    - name: extnCertification-repo-runtime
    - name: extnCertification-srv
    - name: extnCertification-xsuaa
```

Listing 6.2 Adding "repo-host" and "repo-runtime" Resources as "required" for the AppRouter Module

Add the AppRouter Configuration

At the root of the application, the *app* folder is housing the UI app. It's a general practice to have UI files and AppRouter files within the *app* folder, so we're going to house our AppRouter module here as well. Create a new file in this folder with the name *xs-app.json*. This will be the AppRouter configuration file. Within the file, paste the code in Listing 6.3.

```
{
    "welcomeFile": "index.html",
    "authenticationMethod": "route",
    "routes": [
      {
        "source": "^/ems/",
        "destination": "srv_api"
      },
      {
        "source": "(.*)",
        "target": "/escalationsfe/$1",
        "service": "html5-apps-repo-rt",
        "authenticationType": "xsuaa"
      }
    ]
}
```

Listing 6.3 AppRouter Configuration File Content (xs-app.json)

As you see in , there are two routes specified here. Whenever the URL path contains the identifier ems, the request is directed to the destination srv_api. All other calls are for static UI files and therefore they are routed to the HTML5 application repository. URL rewriting is involved, where sap.app.id escalationsfe is used. You can also see that authentication type XSUAA is used to authenticate with the HTML5 repository.

When an AppRouter module consumes an XSUAA instance, it's important to specify that the XSUAA instance is created with tenant-mode configured as dedicated. By default, this property is shared in the SAP Authorization and Trust Management service, which is for multitenant scenarios. AppRouter needs more configurations in multitenant scenarios, and because we're not building a multitenant application here, we'll specify the tenant-mode as dedicated in this step. To do this, create a new file with the name *xs-security.json* at the root of the project. Within this file, maintain the content as shown here:

```
{
    "xsappname": "extnCertification",
    "tenant-mode": "dedicated"
}
```

You'll learn more about *xs-security.json* in Section 6.4.2.

In addition to creating this file, you need to specify this file within *mta.yaml* so that the XSUAA instance gets created with these settings. To do that, add the path parameter into the XSUAA resource definition as specified in the following code:

```
- name: extnCertification-xsuaa
  type: org.cloudfoundry.managed-service
  parameters:
    service: xsuaa
    service plan: application
    path: ./xs-security.json
```

Creating the Manifest File

Because the AppRouter module is a Node.js application, it requires a *package.json* file at its root. This is called the manifest file of the node application, containing dependencies, development dependencies, metadata about the module, and start and other scripts for the app.

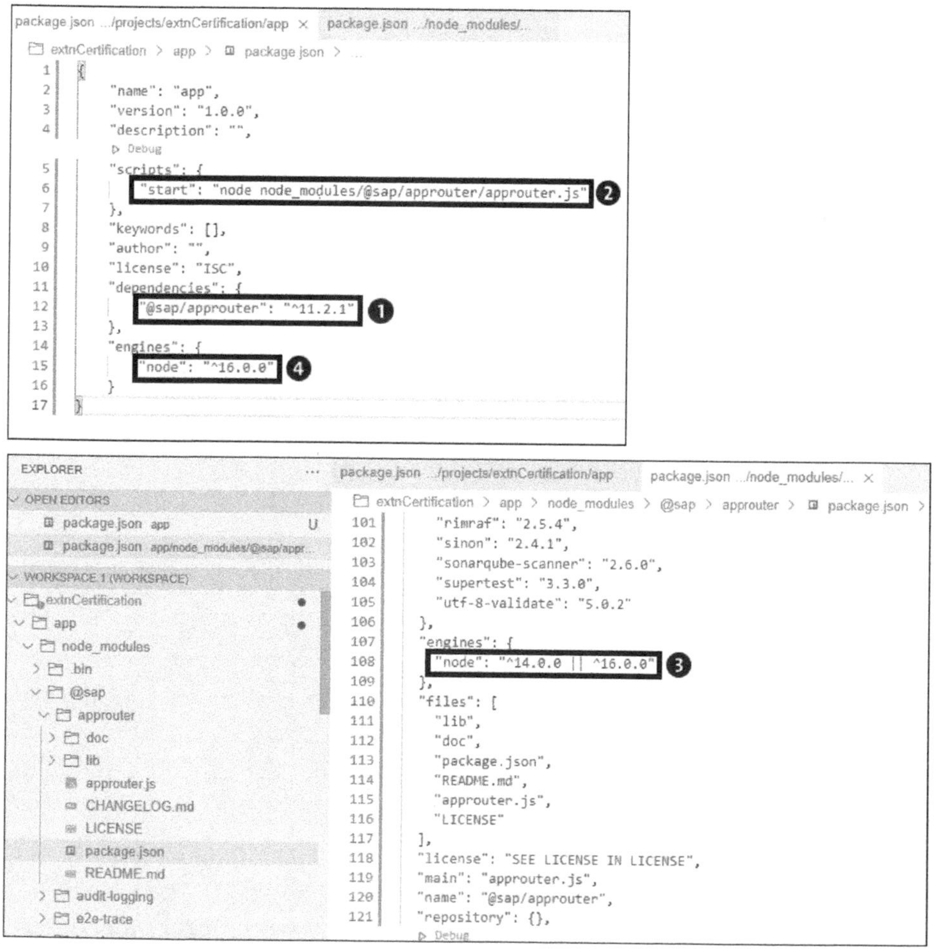

Figure 6.3 AppRouter manifest file

To create a *package.json* file of our real-world scenario, run terminal command npm init -yes at the *app* folder. Now you need to install the AppRouter node module using command npm install @sap/approuter. This command installs the AppRouter module and adds it as one of the dependencies in the *package.json* file for the application to run, as shown in Figure 6.3 ❶.

The AppRouter can be started by running command node node_modules/@sap/ approuter/approuter.js in the *app* folder of the project. Add this command as the start command of the node module ❷. In addition, remove main and other properties that aren't required.

AppRouter has specific requirements on node versions. To find out the node engine required for the just-installed AppRouter version, navigate to the App-Router node library module, and find the specified node version ❸. You can specify the suitable node version of the AppRouter module ❹.

Specify AppRouter Module inmta.yaml

Now that the AppRouter module is created, it's important to specify it within the *mta.yaml* file so that the module can be deployed to SAP BTP. Listing 6.4 shows the definition of the AppRouter module. Add the following module inside the modules specification. Here, type specifies that this is a Node.js module, and path specifies the root folder of the AppRouter module. Files *package.json* and *xs-app.json* should be available at this location.

```
- name: extnCertification-aprouter
  type: nodejs
  path: app
  requires:
    - name: extnCertification-repo-runtime
    - name: extnCertification-xsuaa
    - name: srv-api
      group: destinations
      properties:
        # defining a destination with the name srv_api for the AppRouter to use
        name: srv_api
        url: '~{srv-url}'
        forwardAuthToken: true
```

Listing 6.4 A New Module within mta.yaml for the AppRouter

The requires section specifies all the required resources for the AppRouter module to work, including the following:

- Resource srv-api (provided by module extnCertification-srv) provides a destination srv_api for consumption by the AppRouter module.
- Resource extnCertification-repo-runtime is required because the AppRouter needs to connect to the HTML5 repository to access the deployed UI module.

- Resource `extnCertification-xsuaa` is the XSUAA instance that is required for handling authentication to the HTML5 application repository service.

Let's deploy the MTA now.

> **Note**
> The preceding code can be seen in the Git repository at *http://s-prs.co/v540901*, branch chapter6/step1.

6.3   Authentication and Trust Management

Before we deep dive into authentication and authorization, we'll briefly talk about the difference between them. *Authentication* refers to validating the user's identity according to what the user claims to be. The server that has the required resources is called a *resource server*. A resource server usually delegates the authentication to a trusted external server called the identity provider IdP, as we've mentioned earlier. Once the IdP authenticates the user, it communicates with the resource server securely to inform about the user. This process of using external IdP is called *identity federation*.

Authorization refers to validating if the user is allowed to perform actions that he set out for. There are several authorization objects and levels that facilitate this validation. User's authorizations are usually stored within the resource server itself.

In the following sections, we'll explore specifying an IdP at the subaccount level, authentication strategies, the SAP Authorization and Trust Management service service, relevance of the JSON Web Token (JWT), and the types of users in SAP BTP.

6.3.1   Identity Provider at the Subaccount Level

When you receive access to SAP BTP from SAP, you get SAP IDs to log in and access SAP BTP. However, for all other users of SAP BTP within your organization, you may not want to create all those users within SAP BTP. For this use case, SAP BTP supports identity federation, where you can configure your organization's IdP as the supported IdP for logging in to the SAP BTP cockpit and applications deployed within it.

By default, SAP ID provider is set up as the default IdP for your subaccount. This is the reason you can log in to SAP BTP using the ID provided by SAP. To enable your organization's user base to log in to SAP BTP applications, a trust needs to be established between the SAP BTP tenant and your organization's IdP.

Figure 6.4 ❷ shows that SAP ID is set as the **Default identity provider** for all subaccounts. If you need to set a new IdP, you can navigate to **Trust Configuration** ❶, and click on the **New Trust Configuration** button ❸.

The Identity Authentication service is an SAP BTP service to simplify authentication configuration for SAP BTP applications. It acts as a hub for various IdPs you need to utilize. Within SAP BTP, you just need to configure IAS. Within IAS, you can configure your various IdPs and thus enable authentication with your IdPs. You can specify conditions and the corresponding IdPs to use in those conditions. In Figure 6.5, you can see that there is a trust configuration between SAP BTP and IAS. Whenever a user tries to access the SAP BTP deployed applications, he will be redirected to IAS, which delegates the user to one of the configured IdPs. Upon successful authentication, Security Assertion Markup Language (SAML) assertion reaches the SAP IAS and the user gets access to the application.

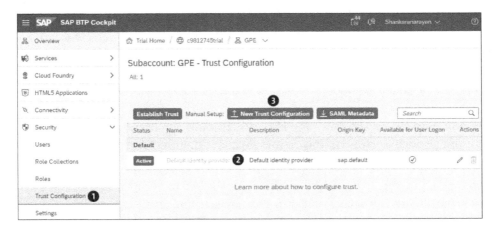

Figure 6.4 SAP ID set as the Default IdP for a Subaccount along with the Trust

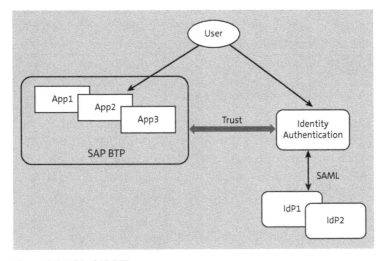

Figure 6.5 IAS in SAP BTP

6.3.2   Authentication Strategies

In this section, we explore how to authenticate the users making incoming HTTP requests to the SAP Cloud Application Programming Model server. So far, by accessing the SAP Cloud Application Programming Model-based OData services, we've seen that there is no authentication involved, and the services are open.

To enable authentication at the service level, you need to annotate the service with @requires: 'authenticated-user'. This annotation specifies that the logged-in user should have the role authenticated-user. This is a dummy role that gets added to every logged-in user. The authentication process validates the credentials and later sets the req.user object with an instance of cds.User, so that within your handler functions you can use core data services (CDS), user properties, and application programming interfaces (APIs) for validation.

cds.User has the following properties and APIs:

- **id**
  This provides the unique string to identify the user. Within your handler, you can use req.user.id to access this user ID.

- **attr.<attribute name>**
  This property lets you access various attributes that get set from the SAML assertion. If company_code is the name of the attribute, you can access it using req.user.attr.company_code.

- **Method user.is**
  This method lets you check if the user has a particular role. req.user.is("manager") will return Boolean true if the user has a role called "manager"; it will return false otherwise.

Authentication strategies perform authentication and set the req.user attribute. SAP Cloud Application Programming Model comes with four prebuilt authentication strategies for your use:

- **Dummy authentication**
  The dummy authentication strategy disables authorization checks when you run the application locally. As the name suggests, this is never used in a production scenario. Listing 6.5 shows how to specify the dummy authentication in the *package.json* file of the MTA.

```
"cds": {
  "requires": {
    "auth": {
      "kind": "dummy-auth"
    }
  }
}
```

Listing 6.5 Specifying Dummy Authentication

- **Basic Authentication**
  A Basic Authentication strategy is also used during testing the application locally. This lets you use different mock users along with arbitrary passwords

for testing. When you enable Basic Authentication, you can also specify mock users and the corresponding roles when you use these users. Unlike dummy authentication, Basic Authentication can be used to test the roles locally. Listing 6.6 shows how to specify Basic Authentication as the authentication strategy. In addition, you can also see that the specification specifies two mock users "vipin" and "krishna". When you log in with "vipin", then the user will have the manager role, and when you log in with "krishna", then the user will have both developer and admin roles.

```
"cds": {
  "requires": {
    "auth": {
      "kind": "basic-auth",
      "users": {
        "vipin": { "roles": ["manager"] },
        "krishna": { "roles": ["developer", "admin"] }
  }
    }
  }
}
```

Listing 6.6 Specifying Basic Authentication, along with Mock Users and Roles

In addition to the specified mock users, the CDS framework also provides the user configuration (see Listing 6.7) that will get merged with the developer-specified configuration as shown in Listing 6.6. This means that you get two additional mock users, "alice" and "bob," along with the specified roles. Also note that "*": true allows you to log in with any user but without any roles.

```
"users": {
    "alice": { "roles": ["admin"] },
    "bob": { "roles": ["builder"] },
    "*": true
}
```

Listing 6.7 Default User Configuration That Comes with CDS

Note that you can use any password in these cases. There is no validation of the entered password.

- **JWT-based Authentication**
  In production, the SAP Cloud Application Programming Model application can use this authentication strategy. This strategy uses a JWT-based authentication token to store a user's identity, attributes, and roles. A user account and authentication service (SAP Authorization and Trust Management service in the case of SAP BTP) creates this JWT and provides the AppRouter and browser for reuse. Listing 6.8 specifies this authentication strategy.

```
"cds": {
  "requires": {
```

```
    "auth": { "kind": "jwt-auth" }
  }
}
```

Listing 6.8 Specifying the JWT-Based Authentication Strategy

In addition, you need to install node modules `passport` and `@sap/xssec` for this authentication strategy to work.

■ **SAP Authorization and Trust Management service-based authentication**
The SAP Authorization and Trust Management service-based authentication strategy is the one recommended by SAP to be used in production. This is very similar to the JWT-based authentication, but it provides additional access to the SAML attributes in the event handlers. You can use the object `req.user.attr.<attribute name>` to access the SAML attributes. The configuration in Listing 6.9 specifies this authentication strategy.

```
"cds": {
  "requires": {
    "auth": { "kind": "xsuaa" }
  }
}
```

Listing 6.9 Specifying the SAP Authorization and Trust Management service Authentication Strategy

6.3.3 SAP Authorization and Trust Management Service

The SAP Authorization and Trust Management service is responsible for authorization flow and SSO within SAP BTP. This service acts as an OAuth server in the entire authorization flow. The AppRouter of the MTA acts as the OAuth client. We'll now discuss the authorization flow in a typical OAuth flow involving SAP BTP and SAP Authorization and Trust Management service.

When a user tries to access an application (see Figure 6.6 ❶), the AppRouter checks if the request contains an authorization token. If there is no authorization token present, or if the token is invalid, then the AppRouter accesses the SAP Authorization and Trust Management service ❷. The AppRouter needs to be bound to an instance of the SAP Authorization and Trust Management service so that credentials to contact the SAP Authorization and Trust Management service are available for the AppRouter. The SAP Authorization and Trust Management service server figures out the configured IdP and sends the user to authenticate on the IdP's login page ❸. Once the user successfully authenticates, the IdP sends the user's attributes (e.g., user ID, first name, last name, email) to the SAP Authorization and Trust Management service server as a SAML assertion. The SAP Authorization and Trust Management service server creates the authorization token and sends it back to the AppRouter for use. The SAP Authorization and Trust Management service looks into its configuration table, where it fetches all role collections for the logged-in user. For each role collection, it goes to roles and then fetches all the application-specific scopes. All this authorization information is added to the authorization token.

This token is sent back to the user and gets stored as a cookie in the browser for reusing later. AppRouter uses, validates, and sends this token to other microservices when accessing them ❹. Microservices (e.g., SAP Cloud Application Programming Model application) connect to the SAP Authorization and Trust Management service and validate the JWT ❺. Microservices are also bound to an instance of the SAP Authorization and Trust Management service server so that it has credentials to connect to the SAP Authorization and Trust Management service server.

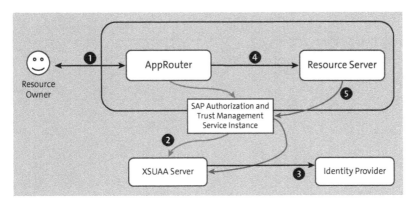

Figure 6.6 OAuth flow for SAP BTP Applications

6.3.4   JSON Web Token

In the preceding OAuth authorization flow, we mentioned the authentication token. When the user is authenticated and his scopes are determined, SAP Authorization and Trust Management service creates this token and sends it to the AppRouter, as shown in Figure 6.7.

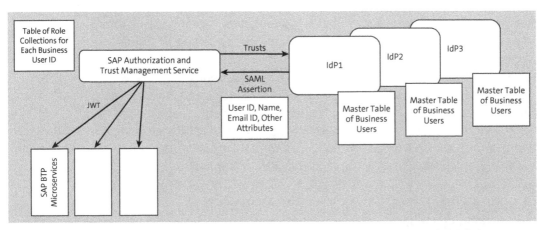

Figure 6.7 Interaction between SAP Authorization and Trust Management service and IdP

Later, the AppRouter needs to pass on this information to other microservices whenever the AppRouter forwards requests to them, but in what format? JWT is one such industry-accepted, open-standard format that can be used. SAP Authorization and Trust Management service and SAP BTP-based services are designed to deal with JWT.

JWT is an open standard for securely transferring information between multiple entities. A JWT can be digitally signed using public/private keys, thus making it secure. As the name suggests, a JWT has its content in the form of a JSON object.

A JWT has three parts: header, payload, and signature. All three parts are separated by a period (.). Figure 6.8 ➊ shows an encoded token.

Figure 6.8 Encoded JWT

The three parts of the decoded token are described here (see Figure 6.9):

- **Header**
  The header is the first part of the JWT and contains two pieces of information: the type of token, which is always JWT, and the algorithm used for signing the JWT. This JSON information is Base64 URL encoded. You can see an example header in ➋. According to the header it uses the algorithm RS256.

- **Payload**
  The second part of the JWT is called the payload, and it contains the main information of the JWT. Figure 6.8 shows a sample payload of a JWT. As we discussed earlier, this information contains the user ID and attributes ➌, the issuer of the JWT ➍, and the relevant authorization scopes and role collections ➎, ➏.

- **Signature**
  The signature part of the JWT is used to verify that the JWT wasn't altered manually after it was issued by the issuer. A signature hash is created by using an

algorithm such as HS256. The header and payload are used as the input for the hashing algorithm, and a secret similar to a private key is used. The pseudocode for generating the signature looks like the following:

```
Signature = algorithm(base64Url encoded header + "." + base64Url encoded
payload, signing secret)
```

PAYLOAD: DATA

```
{
  "jti": "8954e6a9accc48ec93c098b0bc862885",
  "ext_attr": {
    "enhancer": "XSUAA",
    "subaccountid": "ca3b1239-2b0d-419d-857d-
473916b7a04d",
    "zdn": "cis-development"
  },
  "xs.system.attributes": {
    "xs.rolecollections": [
      "GPE_ProcessDesigner_RC",
      "~eh1new2_ZS:CIS_BTP_MANAGER",
      "Subscription Management",
      "~eh1new_ZS:CIS_BTP_EMPLOYEE",
      "Subaccount Administrator"
    ]
  },
  "given_name": "Krishna",
  "xs.user.attributes": {},
  "family_name": "Kammaje",
  "sub": "b5945501-0eb6-488f-8298-55f0f220519b",
  "scope": [
    "gpe!t37704.Manage",
    "openid"
  ],
  "client_id": "sb-gpe!t37704",
  "cid": "sb-gpe!t37704",
  "azp": "sb-gpe!t37704",
  "grant_type": "authorization_code",
  "user_id": "b5945501-0eb6-488f-8298-55f0f220519b",
  "origin": "httpscisiastest.accounts.ondemand.co",
  "user_name": "KKammaje@convergentis.com",
  "email": "KKammaje@convergentis.com",
  "auth_time": 1655982894,
  "rev_sig": "e148a500",
  "iat": 1655982895,
  "exp": 1656026095,
  "iss": "https://cis-
development.authentication.us10.hana.ondemand.com/oauth
/token",
  "zid": "ca3b1239-2b0d-419d-857d-473916b7a04d",
  "aud": [
    "gpe!t37704",
    "openid",
    "sb-gpe!t37704"
  ]
}
```

HEADER: ALGORITHM & TOKEN TYPE

```
{
  "alg": "RS256",
  "jku": "https://cis-
development.authentication.us10.hana.ondemand.com/token
_keys",
  "kid": "default-jwt-key--168595078",
  "typ": "JWT"
}
```

Figure 6.9 Decoded JWT

6.3.5   Types of Users

In SAP BTP, there are two types of users:

- **Platform users**
  These are the users that develop applications, administrate functionality, and manage the security of SAP BTP. By default, platform users use the SAP ID

service as the IdP to log in to SAP BTP. SAP BTP feature set A allows you to configure other IdPs for platform users (via IAS). However, feature set B doesn't support third-party IdPs for platform users. In feature set A, you need to use the SAP BTP cockpit to maintain these platform users. In feature set B, you make a user a platform user by assigning a specific role collection. This can be done using command-line interface (CLI) tools as well.

- **Business users**
  These are the users that use business applications deployed on SAP BTP. You can use any third-party IdP for business users. Business users get authorizations by getting assigned suitable role collections against the relevant IdPs.

6.3.6 Real-World Scenario Adding Authentication

We'll continue to use the SAP ID provider when we run our application in SAP BTP. However, we want to disable the authentication when we run locally. In the *package.json* file at the root of the application, you can specify this setting as shown in Listing 6.10, where dummy-auth is specified for local development, and xsuaa is used when running from SAP BTP.

```
"cds": {
        "requires": {
            "auth": {
                "[development]": {
                    "kind": "dummy-auth"
                },
                "kind": "xsuaa"
            }
        }
}
```

Listing 6.10 Authentication Strategies for Local Run and SAP BTP

As you've learned so far, AppRouter and srv modules need to communicate with the SAP Authorization and Trust Management service to perform authentication and receive and validate authentication tokens. Communicating with SAP Authorization and Trust Management service requires credentials, which can be delivered to these modules by binding an XSUAA instance. You can manually perform these bindings in the SAP BTP cockpit or can specify these bindings in the *mta.yaml* file so that these bindings happen automatically.

Figure 6.10 shows the content of the mta.yaml file. Under resources, you need to specify an XSUAA instance that will create an instance of the SAP Authorization and Trust Management service (during the first deployment) for your MTA. This instance needs to be specified under the requires section of the AppRouter and srv modules so that binding happens.

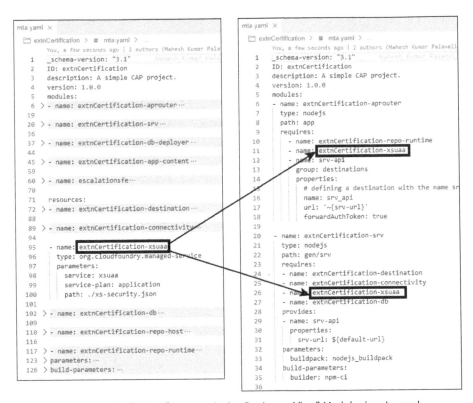

Figure 6.10 Binding the "XSUAA" Instance to AppRouter and "srv" Modules in mta.yaml

If you run command cds watch at the root of the application, it will run without the need of authentication because we're running locally. Once you create the .*mtar* archive and deploy it to SAP BTP, open the AppRouter URL. You can see that it will ask for the SAP ID credentials.

Figure 6.11 shows that the XSUAA instance is bound to the AppRouter and srv modules, after deployment.

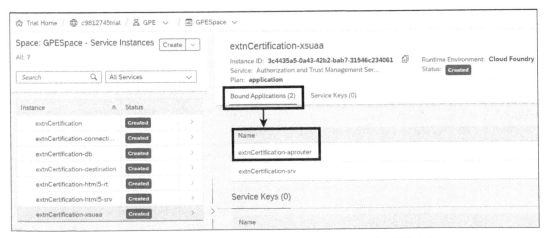

Figure 6.11 Deployed "XSUAA" Instance Bound to AppRouter and "srv" Modules

> **Note**
> The preceding code can be seen in the Git repository at *http://s-prs.co/v540901*, branch
> chapter6/step2.

6.4   Authorization

In this section, we'll discuss various authorization related artifacts within SAP BTP. The SAP Cloud Application Programming Model framework provides several tools for handling authorizations. During CDS modeling, you can specify annotations to declaratively define authorization requirements. Within the event handler, SAP Cloud Application Programming Model provides APIs to programmatically check authorization requirements as well.

We'll also discuss how to create these artifacts manually as well as using a descriptor file called the authorization descriptor. Next, you'll see how to assign authorizations to the user. On the application side, you'll see how to specify and verify if the current user has the right authorizations.

While working on authorization, it's important to understand that authentication is a prerequisite to authorization. Authentication verifies a user's identity and establishes his privileges. Without authentication, there is no way to figure out a user's privileges. Once a user is authenticated, the following information is available to the application:

- User ID that uniquely identifies the user
- User's privileges
- User's attributes (company code, cost center, etc.)
- Tenant in case of multitenant applications

In the following sections, we'll explore the authorization concepts, including specifying, verifying, and assigning authorizations.

6.4.1   Role Collections, Roles, Scopes, Attributes

In this section, you'll learn about the various authorization artifacts relevant within SAP BTP, as follows:

- **Scope**
  A scope is an arbitrary object that specifies a functional authorization. You can specify this scope against one or more of the create, read, update, delete (CRUD) operations of an entity, to be checked during runtime. Scope names need to be prefixed with xsappname, which is a unique identifier within an XSUAA instance. A scope is the smallest unit of authorization in SAP BTP.

  A scope is never manually created, but rather specified in the security descriptor to be created. Security descriptors will be covered later in this section.

- **Role**
  Roles hold one or more scopes. An individual scope can be put into multiple roles as well. A scope can be assigned to a role by declaratively assigning privileges to that role.

- **Attribute**
  Attributes are used for data-based (context data) authorizations. When a user gets authenticated, his attributes are also received from the IdP.

- **Pseudo role**
  These are used like roles to verify access conditions that aren't application-specific. In the authentication section of this chapter, to make the service require authentication, we used annotation `@require: authenticated-user`. Here, `authenticated-user` refers to a pseudo role, which is predelivered by SAP. Every user who is authenticated by providing valid credentials is assigned this role. This role is called as "pseudo" because this role is automatically assigned to the user rather than manually assigned.

  If a technical user (unnamed) accesses the application, then you can use the `system-user` role. You can use this pseudo role to identify such an unnamed user. As the `system-user` passes credentials to authenticate, such a system user is an `authenticated-user` as well.

  The any pseudo role is assigned to all user contexts, including when the application is open and doesn't have any authentication.

- **Role template**
  When you model a role for your application using *xs-security.json* (explained in the next section), it's called a role template. If your role specification contains attributes, those are left out in a role template (or a default value can be specified). When you create a role, you specify those attributes and create an instance of the role template. There might be scenarios where you can create multiple roles from a single role template with each role for a different value of an attribute.

- **Role collection**
  As the name suggests, a role collection is a collection of one or more roles. Only a role collection can be assigned to a business user.

6.4.2   Application Security Descriptor: xs-security.json

An application security descriptor is a JSON file that defines the scopes, attributes, roles, and role collections required for the application to function. That is, it declares the security artifacts of your application. However, it doesn't enforce them. The authorization objects defined in this file get created in SAP BTP upon deployment (i.e., upon creation of the XSUAA instance).

Important parts of the security descriptor are listed here:

- xsappname

  This is the name of the application that is going to be created within the XSUAA instance. All scopes in your application are going to be created with this name as the prefix.

- tenant-mode

  You choose this as **Shared** if you create a multitenant application. Otherwise, you choose **Dedicated**.

- scopes

  An array of scopes will be created within the XSUAA instance. Scope names have to be prefixed with variable $XSAPPNAME so that scopes are created specifically for the application.

- role-templates

  This is a list of models of roles to be created in the XSUAA instance.

- role-collections

  This is a list of role collections to be created. You can specify role templates to specify the roles to be part of this role collection.

You can automatically populate this file from various authorizations declaratively specified within the CDS view declarations by running the following command at the root of the application:

```
cds compile srv/ --to xsuaa >xs-security.json
```

6.4.3 Assigning and Enforcing Authorizations

Now that you understand the hierarchies of authorizations in SAP BTP, we'll determine how to assign and enforce authorizations both declaratively and programmatically.

Declarative Authorization Enforcement

SAP Cloud Application Programming Model provides annotations to specify the required authorizations for accessing entities and performing actions. The annotations declaratively specified in the CDS definition are automatically enforced in the generic handlers. We'll explore the following annotations:

- @requires

  The @requires annotation lets you specify one or more roles (including pseudo roles) as a prerequisite for the logged-in user to access resources. @requires annotation can be at the service level or the entity level.

  We'll define a business rule that our application is available only to a purchaser or to a manager. Because this is at the application level, it makes sense to set this annotation at the service level as shown here:

```
@requires: ['manager', 'purchaser']
service EscalationManagementService
```

Now we'll run the command `cds compile srv/ --to xsuaa >xs-security.json` to generate the security descriptor. Running this command creates the content specified in Listing 6.11 within the *xs-security.json* file. Because we've specified two roles (manager and purchaser) in our CDS annotation, the generated file content also specifies two scopes and two role templates with the same name. However, both the scope and role names are the same here; that is, the name of the role used in the CDS definitions is used for creating a scope and a role with the same name in SAP Authorization and Trust Management service. However, if you manually create an *xs-security.json* file, you can create scopes and roles with separate names.

For differentiating between roles and scopes, we'll rename the scopes in the generated file by adding a `scope` suffix, as shown in Listing 6.11. This will help you better understand the concepts in later sections.

```json
{
  "scopes": [
    {
      "name": "$XSAPPNAME.manager_scope",
      "description": "manager"
    },
    {
      "name": "$XSAPPNAME.purchaser_scope",
      "description": "purchaser"
    }
  ],
  "attributes": [],
  "role-templates": [
    {
      "name": "manager",
      "description": "generated",
      "scope-references": [
        "$XSAPPNAME.manager_scope"
      ],
      "attribute-references": []
    },
    {
      "name": "purchaser",
      "description": "generated",
      "scope-references": [
        "$XSAPPNAME.purchaser_scope"
      ],
      "attribute-references": []
    }
```

```
    ]
}
```

Listing 6.11 Generated xs-security.json Security Descriptor, along with Renamed Scopes

@requires uses/validates scopes not roles. As we've renamed scopes, you need to update the require annotation as well as follows:

```
@requires: ['manager_scope', 'purchaser_scope']
service EscalationManagementService
```

■ **@restrict**

Using the @requires annotation, you can just specify the scopes that are required for the user for performing actions. If you specify the @requires annotation on an entity, it means that the specified scope is required for performing any operation on the entity. However, if you want to specify fine-grained authorizations such as "specific operations on specific entities are allowed for specific roles/scopes," then you need to choose the annotation @restrict.

For the application we're building, let's define an authorization rule that only allows the user with scope purchaser_scope to create escalations:

```
entity Escalations @(restrict : [
    { grant: ['CREATE'], to: ['purchaser_scope'] }
]) as projection on db.Escalations;
```

Here, grant refers to a list of events or operations that are allowed. It can have values CREATE, READ, UPDATE, and DELETE. A single value WRITE can be used to replace CREATE, UPDATE, and DELETE. You can even have an asterisk (*) to refer to all the events.

The to property refers to a list of scopes that are allowed to perform the events (grant). In addition, you can also specify a where condition, which specifies a condition to be evaluated to be true for the event on the entity to happen. Consider a scenario where you want the update privilege to be granted only to the author who created the escalation. The following code declares this authorization rule:

```
entity Escalations @(restrict : [
    { grant: ['CREATE'], to: ['purchaser_scope'] },
    { grant: ['UPDATE'], where: 'CreatedBy = $user' }
]) as projection on db.Escalations;
```

You can even refer to the user's attributes in the where condition. In the following code, the user's attribute company_code is used to limit the user's authorization to update only records of that company code:

```
entity Escalations @(restrict : [
  { grant: ['CREATE'], to: ['purchaser_scope'] },
  { grant: ['UPDATE'], to: ['purchaser_scope'], where: 'company =
$user.company_code' }
]) as projection on db.Escalations;
```

In the following definition, a user with the purchaser role (scope `purchaser_scope` to be specific) can only update escalations in the status `PURCHASER_REVIEW`:

```
entity Escalations @(restrict : [
  { grant: ['UPDATE'], to: ['purchaser_scope'], where: 'status =
'PURCHASER_REVIEW'' }
]) as projection on db.Escalations;
```

- **Other restriction annotations**

  There are other annotations available that are applicable at the entity level:

  - `@readonly`: This annotation ensures that the entity is read-only, and none of the create, update, and delete events are allowed. This restriction applies to all users.

  - `@insertonly`: This annotation ensures that the only insert operation is allowed for all the users. The below code shows how to specify these annotations:

    ```
    @readonly entity Escalations { …. }
    @insertonly entity Escalations { …. }
    ```

  - `@capabilities`: This OData annotation allows you to restrict any of the create, delete, update, and delete operations on an entity. The following code snippet shows this annotation, where the entity record is readable, updateable, and deletable, but not insertable:

    ```
    @Capabilities : {
        Readable,
        Insertable: false,
        Updatable,
        Deletable,
    }
    entity POScheduleLines as projection on external.A_
    PurchaseOrderScheduleLine;
    ```

- **Specification at the AppRouter**

  You can declaratively specify the authorization scopes in the *xs-app.json* file of the AppRouter module. You can specify one or more scopes in a route, as shown in Listing 6.12. For the first route, you can see that scopes `buyer_scope` and `manager_scope` are specified. AppRouter checks the authorization token (JWT) to see if the authenticated user has at least one of the specified scopes. Otherwise, the user will see a 403 error.

  ```
  {
      "welcomeFile": "index.html",
      "authenticationMethod": "route",
      "routes": [
          {
              "source": "^/ems/",
              "destination": "srv_api",
  ```

```
                "scope": ["buyer_scope", "manager_scope"]
        },
        {
            "source": "(.*)",
            "target": "/extbookescalationui/$1",
            "service": "html5-apps-repo-rt",
            "authenticationType": "xsuaa"
        }
    ]
}
```

Listing 6.12 Declaratively Specifying Scopes within the Routes

Programmatic Authorization Enforcement

SAP Cloud Application Programming Model provides APIs to programmatically check the scopes assigned to a user. Let's remove the declarative authorization annotation entered in the CDS models as we'll check the authorization programmatically now. Just retain the authenticated-user, as shown in Listing 6.13, to ensure that the OData service requires authentication.

```
using {my.dataModel as db} from '../db/schema';
using {API_PURCHASEORDER_PROCESS_SRV as external} from './external/API_
PURCHASEORDER_PROCESS_SRV';

@path: 'ems'
service EscalationManagementService @(requires: 'authenticated-user'){

    entity Escalations as projection on db.Escalations;
    entity POScheduleLines as projection on external.A_
PurchaseOrderScheduleLine;

    // Function returing a predefined type
    action    closeEscalation(EscalationId : String) returns String;

    // Action returning a single instance of an entity
    function getLatestEscalation()                    returns Escalations;

    // Action returning a collection of instances of an entity
    function getTopEscalations()                      returns array of Escalati
ons;

}
```

Listing 6.13 CDS Definition with Only "authenticated-user"

You can use API req.user to programmatically check authorizations. For example, when you query for the Escalations entity, let's say the requirement is to ensure that the user has the `manager_scope` scope. This can be coded in a `before` custom handler, as shown in Listing 6.14.

```
const cds = require("@sap/cds")

module.exports = function() {
    this.before("GET", "Escalations", (req)=>{
        if (!req.user.is("purchaser_scope")){
            req.reject(403, "User does not have the 'purchaser' role");
        }
    })
}
```

Listing 6.14 Custom Handler to Verify That the User Has the Purchaser Role

Accessing the `Escalations` entity would give an error as follows:

```
<error xmlns="http://docs.oasis-open.org/odata/ns/metadata">
        <code>403</code>
        <message>User does not have purchaser role</message>
        <annotation term="Common.numericSeverity" type="Edm.Decimal">4</
annotation>
</error>
```

As we know, scope `purchaser_scope` is contained within the purchaser role. You can create a new role collection and assign the purchaser role to it. By assigning this role collection to the user, you can indirectly give scope `purchaser_scope` to the user so that the user can access the escalation collection.

> **Tip**
> You may not have access to the SAP BTP subaccount cockpit to view the authorizations assigned to your user. If you want to know all the authorization scopes that you have access to, go to *https://<Subdomain>.authentication.<Region ID>.hana.ondemand.com/config?action=who*.

Assigning Authorizations

In Listing 6.11 earlier, you saw the generated security descriptor. Let's now build the project and deploy it to SAP BTP to create the roles and role templates in SAP BTP.

Go to the SAP BTP subaccount cockpit, click on **Roles** (see Figure 6.12 ❶), and search for string "ext" ❷. You can see that entries under **Role Template** ❸ and **Role Name** ❹ are generated from the *xs-security.json* file.

If you run the AppRouter URL in a browser and navigate to the **Escalations** collection, as shown in Figure 6.13 ❶, you'll get a 403 error, which is an authorization error. You need to assign the user manager or purchaser role to the current user (so that the user gets the corresponding `manager_scope` and `purchaser_scope` scopes). However, roles can't be assigned directly, so you'll create a role collection. In the subaccount cockpit, go to **Role Collections**, and click on the **Create** button ❷. In the popup, enter a name for the role collection ❸ and click **Create**.

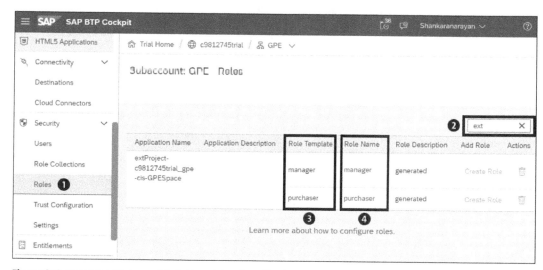

Figure 6.12 Generated Roles and Role Templates from the Security Descriptor

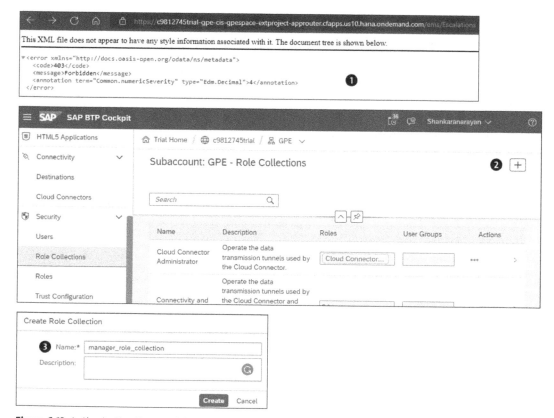

Figure 6.13 Authorization Error and Steps to Create a Role Collection

Now you need to assign the role to the role collection and then assign the role collection to the user. Open the newly created role collection by clicking on it (Figure 6.14 ❶). Click on **Edit**, add the manager role ❷ and the user **ID** ❸, and click on **Save**.

Now you can sign out and sign in again, and you should be able to access the escalation collection successfully.

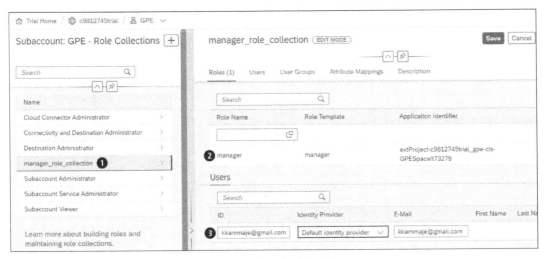

Figure 6.14 Assigning Role and User to the Role Collection

6.4.4   Real-world Scenario: Adding Authorizations

Let's continue to develop our application by adding authorization-related coding and configurations.

Specify Required Authorizations

Within our escalation application, let's define a business rule that the application is available only to a purchaser or to a manager. Because this is at the application level, it makes sense to set this annotation at the service level as shown here:

```
@requires: ['manager_scope', 'purchaser_scope']
@path: 'ems'
service EscalationManagementService
```

Generate the Security Manifest

At the root of your application, run command `cds compile srv/ --to xsuaa >xs-security.json` to generate the security descriptor. This will overwrite the current *xs-security.json* file. Within the generated file, add the `xsappname` and `tenant-mode`, as shown in Figure 6.15 ❶. In addition, rename the generated role names by removing the `_scope` suffix ❷. Thus, you can clearly differentiate a role from a scope.

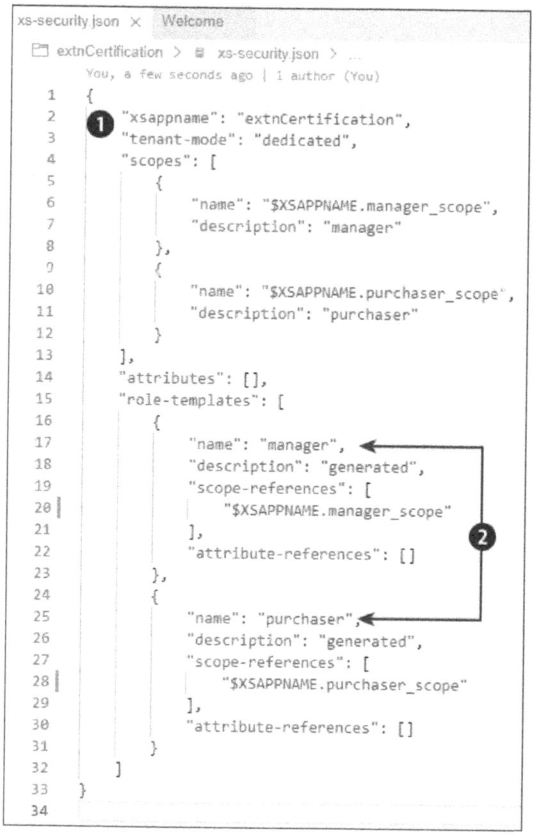

Figure 6.15 Generated xs-security.json along with Modifications

Build and Deploy

At the root of the application, run command mbt build to build the application and cf deploy <path to generated mtar file> to deploy the application to SAP BTP. After the deployment, the roles specified in *xs-security.json* get created in SAP BTP, as shown in Figure 6.16 ❶. Now you need to access the application via the AppRouter URL. To get the AppRouter URL, navigate to the space, as shown in Figure 6.16. **Under Space: GPESpace - Applications**, click on the AppRouter application ❷, and then click on the specified AppRouter URL ❸.

The preceding URL will throw an error. You can open the browser's developer tools and see that the metadata URL failed with error code 403, which denotes an authorization error.

As we've specified that the service needs any one of the manager or the purchaser roles, let's create a role collection containing one of these roles and then assign it to the user.

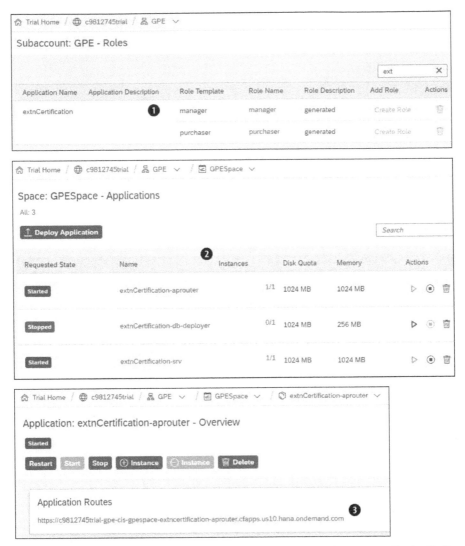

Figure 6.16 After Deployment: Generated Roles and the AppRouter URL to Access the Application

Create and Assign a Role Collection

Create two new role collections with the name manager_role_collection to contain the role manager and purchaser_role_collection to contain the role purchaser. Steps to do this were shown earlier in Figure 6.13 and Figure 6.14. Next, assign the role collection purchaser_role_collection to your own user ID.

Fine-Grained Authorization Specification

Now let's limit who can create and modify an escalation via the following business rules:

- Both purchaser and manager should be able to view (READ).
- Only a purchaser can raise an escalation (CREATE).
- Only a manager can modify an escalation (UPDATE).

Let's modify the Escalations entity definition by adding the @restrict annotation, as specified in Listing 6.15.

```
entity Escalations @(restrict : [
  { grant: ['READ','CREATE'], to: ['purchaser_scope'] },
  { grant: ['READ','UPDATE'], to: ['manager_scope'] }
]) as projection on db.Escalations;
```
Listing 6.15 Fine-Grained Authorization Using "@restrict - grant -to"

Because you're not defining any new scopes or roles, you don't need to update the security descriptor file. Now let's build and deploy the application.

In the previous step, you had assigned role collection purchaser_role_collection to your user ID. This role collection contains the role purchaser, which in turn contains scope purchaser_scope. Because the current user contains only this scope, once you log in, you can only view and create escalations. You can try modifying any of the escalations, and you'll get a **Forbidden** error. To be able to modify, you need to assign the role collection manager_role_collection to the user as well.

> **Note**
> The preceding code can be seen in the Git repository at *http://s-prs.co/v540901*, branch chapter6/step3.

6.5   Important Terminology

In this chapter, the following terminology was used:

- **AppRouter**
  This is a Node.js library created by SAP. Using this library, you can create a Node.js module to be part of your MTA. Such a module is useful in routing, authentication, and authorization handling for your microservice-based application.
- **Authorization and authentication**
  These are two important enterprise qualities of an application. Authentication verifies the user's or system's claimed identity. Authorization checks if the identified user is allowed to perform a specific action. Authentication is a prerequisite for authorization as authorization can be checked only based on the user's identity.
- **Authorization role**
  Multiple authorization scopes can be grouped inside an authorization role. However, the role can't be assigned directly to a user.

- **Authorization scope**
  A scope is the smallest unit of authorization within SAP BTP.

- **Business user**
  The end users of the applications hosted on SAP BTP are called business users. They perform a business transaction or view business data using the applications hosted on SAP BTP. They aren't aware of how the application is built or provisioned.

- **CORS**
  Cross-origin request sharing (CORS) is an HTTP-based security mechanism that is implemented by internet browsers. It blocks a web page loaded from a particular domain from accessing resources from other domains unless these resource domains permit this action by specific HTTP headers.

- **JSON Web Token (JWT)**
  This is an open standard specifying a data format to pass secure information between multiple entities. JWT used in the security context contains data identifying the user, and details of the user's various authorization scopes are digitally signed to ensure that the intended content isn't tampered with.

- **Platform user**
  Users such as administrators, developers, and security administrators who maintain and configure the SAP BTP are called platform users. They aren't actual users of the applications hosted on the SAP BTP; rather, they make SAP BTP available for those end users.

- **Role collection**
  As the name suggests, a role collection is a collection of roles. Withing the SAP BTP cockpit, you can assign role collections to the user. By doing this, the user indirectly gets access to the authorization scopes.

- **Security descriptor**
  This is a file called *xs-security.json*, which contains the security objects relevant to the application such as roles, role templates, and role collections. Whenever an XSUAA instance gets created, a security descriptor is given as the input, and these authorization objects get created on the XSUAA instance.

6.6   Practice Questions

1.   What is the file name of the security descriptor?

☐   **A.** *xs-app.json*

☐   **B.** *manifest.json*

☐   **C.** *security.json*

☐   **D.** *xs-security.json*

2. What are the two types of users in SAP BTP? (There are two correct answers.)

☐ **A.** Platform users

☐ **B.** Technical users

☐ **C.** Service users

☐ **D.** Business users

3. Which of these are features of AppRouter? (There are two correct answers.)

☐ **A.** Routing of incoming requests to various microservices

☐ **B.** Providing language translations

☐ **C.** Authenticating users

☐ **D.** Creating a secure tunnel with cloud connector

4. Which files are mandatory in a standalone AppRouter module? (There are two correct answers.)

☐ **A.** *destinations.json*

☐ **B.** *xs-app.json*

☐ **C.** *package.json*

☐ **D.** *manifest.yaml*

5. Which is assigned to a business user?

☐ **A.** Scope

☐ **B.** Role

☐ **C.** Role collection

☐ **D.** Attribute

6. Consider an incoming POST request coming to the AppRouter module. Which of the following specifications is required to be specified for this route? (There are two correct answers.)

☐ **A.** destination

☐ **B.** localDir

☐ **C.** target

☐ **D.** service

7. In the OAuth flow, what does the SAP Authorization and Trust Management service act as?

☐ **A.** OAuth resource server

☐ **B.** OAuth authorization server

☐   **C.** OAuth client

☐   **D.** User-agent

8.   An authentication token (JWT) is created by which of the following?

☐   **A.** SAP Authorization and Trust Management service server

☐   **B.** Identity provider (IdP)

☐   **C.** Resource server

☐   **D.** AppRouter

9.   When authentication is enabled via annotation for testing the application locally (without actually authenticating with the IdP), which of the following authentication strategies can you use? (There are two correct answers.)

☐   **A.** SAP Authorization and Trust Management service authentication

☐   **B.** Basic Authentication

☐   **C.** Dummy authentication

☐   **D.** JWT-based authentication

10.   _____ is the smallest unit of authorization in the context of the SAP BTP, Cloud Foundry environment.

☐   **A.** Role collection

☐   **B.** Role

☐   **C.** Scope

☐   **D.** Attribute

11.   In a codebase, code `req.user.is("manager")` is used to check the authorization. What `manager` refer to?

☐   **A.** Scope

☐   **B.** Attribute

☐   **C.** Role

☐   **D.** Role collection

6.7   Practice Question Answers and Explanations

1.   Answer: **D**
     File *xs-security.json* is the security descriptor. It describes the security artifacts required within an application. When you deploy the application to Cloud Foundry, an SAP Authorization and Trust Management service will be created with settings specified in *xs-security.json*.

2. Answer: **A and D**

   Users who develop, administer, and troubleshoot applications are called platform users. These aren't end users of the application. However, business users are the actual target personas for whom those applications are developed.

3. Answer: **A and C**

   The AppRouter module helps you route incoming requests to various microservices, either within the MTA or outside. AppRouter also redirects unauthenticated users to Identity providers and sends the authentication token to other microservices based on the configuration.

4. Answer: **B and C**

   The *package.json* package descriptor is a mandatory file for a Node.js application. As AppRouter is a Node.js application, *package.json* is a required file, containing the start command, dependencies, and other settings. *xs-app.json* is the routing configuration file for the AppRouter. It defines various sources (incoming requests) and targets (where to send) for URLs. In addition, this file also specifies the authentication types and other settings for various routes.

5. Answer: **C**

   A scope is assigned to a role. One or more roles are assigned to a role collection. Only a role collection is assigned to a business user. You can't directly assign a role to a business user.

6. Answer: **A and D**

   Within the routes array, you specify all the valid routes for the application. For each route, one among `destination`, `service`, or `localDir` is mandatory to be specified. The incoming request will be sent to one of these locations. However, `localDir` can serve static files only, thus supporting only `GET` and `HEAD` request types. If the incoming request type is of type `POST`, then one of the `destination` or `service` specifications is mandatory.

7. Answer: **B**

   In the OAuth authentication flow, the AppRouter module acts as an OAuth client. The resource that the user (or the AppRouter) is trying to access can be considered as the OAuth resource server. SAP Authorization and Trust Management service acts as the OAuth server orchestrating the entire authentication flow.

8. Answer: **A**

   Upon user authentication, the SAP Authorization and Trust Management service server receives SAML assertion from the IdP, along with user attributes. The SAP Authorization and Trust Management service server acts as an OAuth server and creates an authentication token with the received attributes. Within the authentication token, it adds details about the user and his authorizations. This JWT token will be used for SSO for various microservices.

9. Answer: **B and C**

   For running the application locally, you can use the dummy authentication strategy to disable the authentication. If you need to test the roles, you can use Basic Authentication along with mock users having the required roles.

10. Answer: **C**

    The scope is the smallest unit of authorization possible. It can define an operation (from CRUD) on an entity. Multiple scopes are included in a role using a security descriptor file. Multiple roles are grouped in a role collection and are assigned to an end user.

11. Answer: **A**

    API `request.user.is` is used for checking the user's assigned scopes. However, when an *xs-security.json* file is generated from CDS (using command `cds compile`), it will contain the scope and role with the same name as the role specified in CDS. Therefore, it might give an impression that you're using a role along with `request.user.is`. However, in this chapter, you saw that the API uses the authorization scopes by naming scopes and roles differently.

6.8   Test Takeaway

At the subaccount level, we specify the trust configuration to specify an identity provider. The JWT token is widely used as an authentication token to propagate identity and to pass authorization details. The SAP Authorization and Trust Management service is central to carrying out authentication and authorization functionalities.

As we model the data and service models, we can also specify the requirements of authentication for an OData service using the annotations `@requires` and `@restrict`. These specifications are stored in the security descriptor, and when deployed, they create security artifacts within SAP BTP. You can also programmatically enforce authorization checks.

AppRouter is a node module is central to your SAP Cloud Application Programming Model application and plays an important role in routing, authentication, and authorization. `xs-app.json` is the AppRouter's configuration file that contains routing rules, authentication specification and many other configurations.

6.9   Summary

We started with the challenges of microservice architecture and how the AppRouter module solves them. You learned how to configure the AppRouter module and host the SAPUI5 files on the HTML5 host application repository service. We covered authentication and trust management topics by discussing the configuration of the SAP ID provider, the SAP Authorization and Trust Management service, and authentication services. Next, you learned about authorization, specifically the required authorizations, how to programmatically and statically check authorizations, and how to assign these authorizations to the users.

In the next chapter, we'll discuss continuous integration and continuous deployment techniques.

Chapter 7
Continuous Integration and Delivery

Techniques You'll Master

- Understanding the CI/CD process
- Discovering various CI/CD tools
- Configuring the CI/CD pipeline for your SAP Cloud Application Programming Model application in SAP BTP

As software's lines of code and scope increase, it will become more difficult for developers to maintain software, and every production release will take longer due to increased scope and end-to-end manual testing. With continuous integration and continuous delivery/deployment (CI/CD) of software, you can continuously build, test, and deploy code changes to production in minutes. (See Figure 7.1 for an example.) This approach will have fewer manual operations and more automated processes to achieve faster deployments of the software to production.

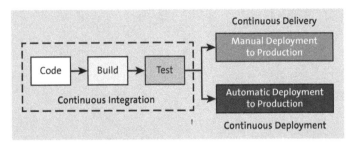

Figure 7.1 A Typical CI/CD Process

Let's take an example of an organization that maintains a large software. Developers in that organization use Git to save the code and release the new features to that software quarterly. Every quarter, all the changes and features developed are cumulated and deployed to production. With this kind of model, there should be a lot of manual testing done for all the changes created in the whole quarter, and many bugs are expected due to cumulated changes. With CI/CD, this can be avoided by moving the small changes frequently in a matter of minutes with automated testing and builds created, which can be deployed to production automatically or by an administrator.

CI/CD consists mainly of three methods:

- Continuous integration
- Continuous delivery
- Continuous deployment

We'll cover these topics, as well as configuring and using the CI/CD pipeline, in later sections in this chapter.

Real-World Scenario

You're developing new applications or maintaining the existing applications, and you want to ship the code to production environments quickly and efficiently by getting immediate feedback on the code with the help of automated tests.

7.1 Objectives of This Portion of the Test

This portion of the test checks your understanding of the CI/CD process for the SAP Cloud Application Programming Model application. You need to understand various steps in the CI/CD process and how to configure the CI/CD pipeline for your SAP Cloud Application Programming Model application using the SAP Continuous Integration and Delivery service in SAP Business Technology Platform (SAP BTP). You'll also learn to create unit test cases, a required part of the CI process and the Git repository to connect it to the CI/CD pipeline.

> **Note**
> CI/CD topics make up 8%–12% of the total exam.

7.2 Continuous Integration, Delivery, and Deployment

In the following sections, we'll cover the three different methods of CI/CD in detail: continuous integration, continuous delivery, and continuous deployment.

7.2.1 Continuous Integration

Continuous integration (CI) is part of the CI/CD that automatically processes the building, packaging, and testing of the application. With CI, the developers will submit and integrate the changes multiple times a day. After each submission, the code changes are moved to source code management systems such as the Git repository. Then, the dedicated CI server will fetch these changes to build and test using the predefined test scripts. If there are any build or test failures, developers will be notified. Once the issues are fixed, the process is repeated (see Figure 7.2).

All developers should push the changes to the main branch (Git) as frequently as possible to ensure that any issues with the integrations can be detected early and fixed. If the changes aren't supposed to be moved to production, feature flags can be used to hide the execution of the new code. If they are **ON**, the code will be executed; otherwise, the execution will be skipped.

Testing is the most important process of this stage and should be automated and run in parallel to speed up the process. The developers must invest more time while writing these unit test scripts as the code provides them with direct feedback, and once it's successful, it's ready to be deployed. Along with the unit tests, static code analysis should also be automated to check if deprecated libraries or code are in use, which can cause security issues.

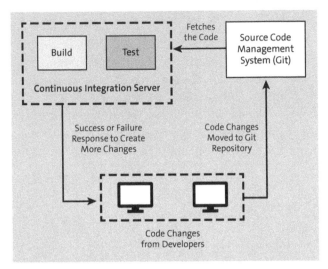

Figure 7.2 Continuous Integration Process

7.2.2   Continuous Delivery

Continuous delivery (CD) is the process of deploying the application to the production environment. In this stage, the application will always be ready to be deployed to the production environment. Instead of automatically deploying the application to production, it will wait for human approval (press of a button) after the acceptance testing to deploy to production (see Figure 7.3). This is because many customers prefer to trigger the deployment manually, as there will be manual testing involved or due to the complexity of the application.

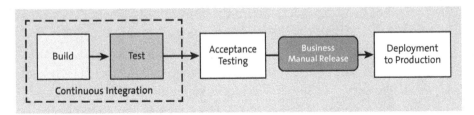

Figure 7.3 Continuous Delivery process

7.2.3   Continuous Deployment

Continuous deployment is similar to continuous delivery, but the only change here is that deployment will be automatic instead of manual deployment to production by the customer (see Figure 7.4). In this process, the application will be deployed after every commit and successful testing.

The key difference between continuous deployment and continuous delivery is the deployment mechanism. Based on the customers' preference or the project complexity, you can choose to automatically deploy the application to production using continuous deployment or manually using continuous delivery.

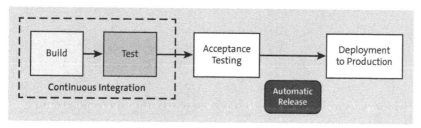

Figure 7.4 Continuous Deployment

7.3   Configuring the CI/CD Pipeline

The CI/CD pipeline is the process or workflow that implements different methods of CI/CD using various tools. Developers or architects maintain and configure the services that are needed to build the CI/CD pipeline. A CI/CD pipeline consists mainly of two components:

- **Job**
  Here you define the job-related information such as the repository where the code should be fetched, the job's frequency (can be based on a timed trigger or automatically triggered based on the commit), and stages that are part of the job.
- **Stages**
  You'll define various stages of the CI/CD process, such as build, test, acceptance, release, and deployment.

Many CI/CD tools are available in the market to configure your CI/CD pipeline; some are open source, and others are offered based on subscription. In the open-source world, Jenkins is a famous free automation tool, and another open-source project is called project "Piper", specifically for the SAP ecosystem. SAP has a subscription continuous integration and Delivery service to configure the CI/CD pipeline using an interactive user interface (UI) or by maintaining the configuration in your application. It also integrates with SAP Cloud Transport Management service to deploy the code to other environments after successful job completion.

You'll configure the CI/CD pipeline for the SAP Cloud Application Programming Model application you created using the continuous integration and Delivery service in SAP BTP. First, you'll create a test file to perform the unit testing for your SAP Cloud Application Programming Model service. Then you'll connect your SAP Cloud Application Programming Model application to a Git repository and later create the CI/CD pipeline to automate the testing and deployment of your SAP Cloud Application Programming Model application on every commit. We'll cover these steps in the following sections.

7.3.1   Unit Testing

Why do you need to test your applications? With every new release, the total number of functionalities will increase along with the code base, and there will be possible bugs that might have been introduced by the developers unknowingly in the
existing or the new code. So, with the unit tests created by developers, old functionalities will be automatically tested by the old unit test cases, and the new unit
test cases will test the new functionality.

In the CI/CD process, unit testing is a critical phase where the code will be continuously tested after each change. Developers need to create multiple test cases that
test every piece of functionality before deploying to various environments. Various open-source tools, such as Jest, Chai, Mocha, and so on, are available to test
your application. For testing SAP Cloud Application Programming Model services,
you use the *cds.test* library, which internally uses Jest and Chai.

Let's start by installing the libraries required to test your SAP Cloud Application
Programming Model project. Open the terminal for your project in SAP Business
Application Studio, and use the following command to install the testing depen-
dencies:

```
npm add -D axios chai chai-as-promised chai-subset jest
```

In the SAP Cloud Application Programming Model application root folder, create a
new folder named **test**, and create a file called **unittest.test.js**, as shown in Figure
7.5. When you run the tests, the Jest testing framework will pick all the files with the
pattern **.test.js* to execute the defined test cases.

Figure 7.5 Testing Folder Structure

Add the following script in *package.json* so the unit tests will run when you execute command npm run test:

```
    "scripts": {
............
        "test": "npx jest",
............
    }
```

Add the function cds.test() in the unit test file to start the SAP Cloud Application
Programming Model application, as follows:

```
const cds = require('@sap/cds');
const { expect, GET, POST } = cds.test.in(__dirname, "..").run(
    "serve",
    "--with-mocks",
```

```
      "--in-memory"
);
```

`cds.test` will test various functions and variables that can be used to execute the tests. `expect` allows you to access numerous matchers that can be used to match the expected and actual results of the test cases. `POST` and `GET` are aliases to corresponding methods from the Axios framework used to execute the HTTP requests.

> **Note**
>
> `__dirname` contains the root project folder path, and passing it to `cds.test.in()` will run the tests in the project root folder. Pass the additional commands such as "serve", "--in-memory", and "--with-mocks" to start the mock server with an in-memory database.

To run a test case, you need to call the function `it` to execute the test. You'll pass two arguments to the `it` function. The first argument is the name of the test case; the second argument is the function, where you write the code to execute the test case. Let's test if the status codes you passed statically to the SAP Cloud Application Programming Model service return the data as expected.

```
it("test status codes", async () => {
  const { data } = await GET`/ems/Statuses?$select=code`;
  expect(data.value).to.eql([
    { code: "CMP" },
    { code: "DRF" },
    { code: "INP" },
  ]);
});
```

The `GET` method fetches all the statuses, and `expect` compares the result with the expected data that we passed to the `to.eql()` method.

Write another test to check if the `resolve` action updates the status of the escalation as expected (see Listing 7.1).

```
it("test action resolve", async () => {
    // Step 1: Create the draft data
    const { data: draft } = await POST`/ems/Escalations ${{
      description: "test",
      purchaseOrder_ID: "9000000001",
      expectedDate: "2022-05-27",
    }}`;

    // Step 2: Save the draft to create a new escalation
    const { data: post } = await POST(
      `/ems/Escalations(ID=${draft.ID},IsActiveEntity=false)/
EscalationManagementService.draftActivate`
    );
```

```
  // Step 3: Read the escalation before executing the resolve action
  let {
    data: readBeforeAction,
  } = await GET`/ems/Escalations(ID=${post.ID},IsActiveEntity=true)`;

  // Step 4: Check if the initial status is 'INP - In process
  expect(readBeforeAction.status_code).to.eql("INP");

  // Step 5: Perform Resolve Action
  await POST`/ems/Escalations(ID=${draft.ID},IsActiveEntity=false)/
EscalationManagementService.resolve`;

  // Step 6: Read the escalation after executing the resolve action
  let {
    data: readAfterAction,
  } = await GET`/ems/Escalations(ID=${post.ID},IsActiveEntity=true)`;

  // Step 7: Check if the escalation is updated to the status 'CMP' -
Completed
    expect(readAfterAction.status_code).to.eql("CMP");
  });
```

Listing 7.1 Unit Test for the Resolve Action

The preceding test case is divided into the following seven steps:

1. A new draft entry is created with the initial mandatory data, which uses the Axios POST method to send the HTTP POST request.
2. The draft is activated by calling draftActivate, which will create a new escalation from the draft entry.
3. The newly created escalation is read, which will be used to check the initial status.
4. The status of the escalation is checked to see if it's **In Process**.
5. The resolve action is executed on the escalation.
6. The status is updated to **Completed**.
7. Finally, the status of the escalation is checked to see if it's updated to **Completed** after executing the resolve action.

In a production application, you'll create many tests to ensure the delivery stability in the application in production with as few defects as possible.

To group various test cases per their category, you can use the describe method, which takes the group's name as the first parameter and the function with all the test cases as the second parameter, as shown in Listing 7.2.

```
describe('Testing OData APIs', () => {
    it('test status codes', async () => {
        ...........................
```

```
      ........................
    })
    it('test action resolve', async () => {
        ........................

    ........................
    })
})
```
Listing 7.2 Unit Test: "describe"

Go to the terminal and execute the following command to run the test cases:

```
npm run test
```

If all the tests are run successfully, the output is displayed as shown in Figure 7.6.

```
PASS  test/unittest.test.js
  Testing OData APIs
    ✓ test status codes (92 ms)
    ✓ test action resolve (116 ms)

Test Suites: 1 passed, 1 total
Tests:       2 passed, 2 total
Snapshots:   0 total
Time:        2.07 s, estimated 3 s
Ran all test suites.
```

Figure 7.6 Unit Test Output

7.3.2   Git Repository

Git is the most common version control system to help developers work collaboratively. You can store your code in a Git repository and track all the changes done on the code, allowing you to revert to the older versions seamlessly in case of any issues with the newer updates. We use GitHub in this chapter to save our code.

> **Note**
>
> GitHub is a code hosting platform used to create Git repositories to store your code.

In the following steps, you'll create a Git repository and upload the code:

1. Create an account at *https://github.com*, and sign in.
2. Create a new Git repository by clicking the **New** button, as shown in Figure 7.7.

Figure 7.7 New Git Repository

3. In the **Repository name** field, enter a unique name (here, "capescalation"), and click **Create repository** to create the Git repository, as shown in Figure 7.8.

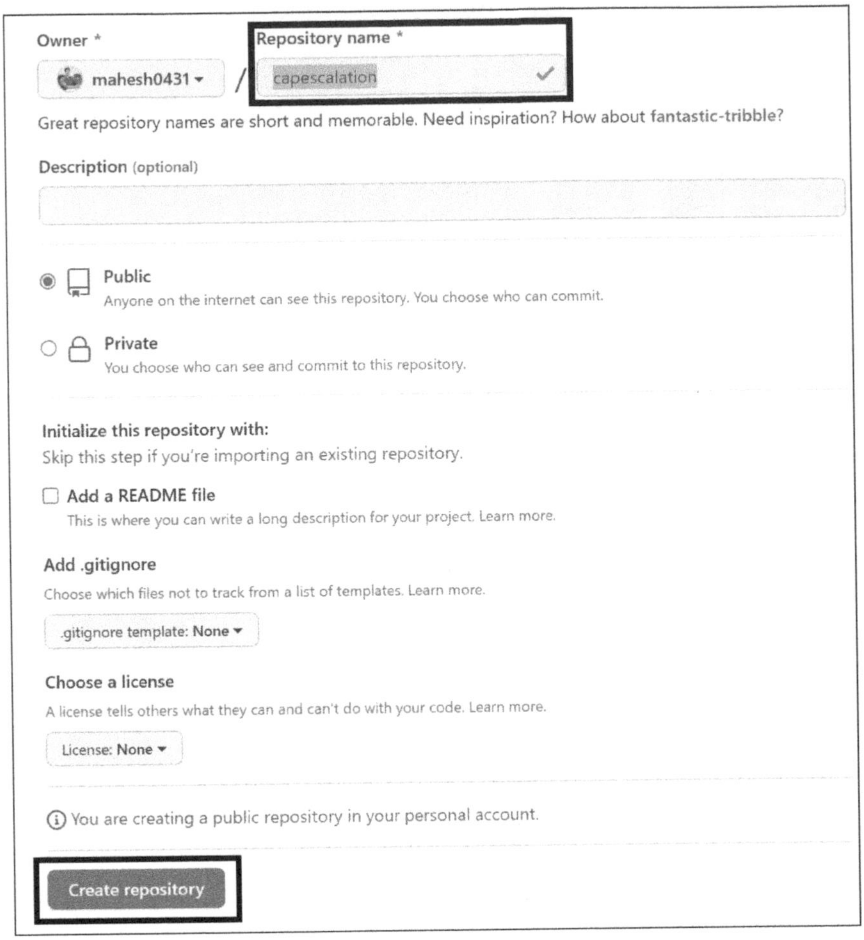

Owner *

🐙 mahesh0431 ▾   /   **Repository name ***

capescalation   ✓

Great repository names are short and memorable. Need inspiration? How about fantastic-tribble?

Description (optional)

◉ 🖥 **Public**
     Anyone on the internet can see this repository. You choose who can commit.

○ 🔒 **Private**
     You choose who can see and commit to this repository.

Initialize this repository with:
Skip this step if you're importing an existing repository.

☐ **Add a README file**
     This is where you can write a long description for your project. Learn more.

Add .gitignore
Choose which files not to track from a list of templates. Learn more.

.gitignore template: None ▾

Choose a license
A license tells others what they can and can't do with your code. Learn more.

License: None ▾

ⓘ You are creating a public repository in your personal account.

Create repository

Figure 7.8 New Repository

After successfully creating the Git repository, a new page will be opened, where you can get the URL for your newly created Git repository (see Figure 7.9), which you'll use to push your code to GitHub.

Quick setup — if you've done this kind of thing before

🖳 Set up in Desktop   or   HTTPS   SSH   https://github.com/_____/capescalation.git   ⧉

Get started by creating a new file or uploading an existing file. We recommend every repository include a README, LICENSE, and .gitignore.

Figure 7.9 New Git Repository URL

4. You need to use the GitHub credentials to push your code to this repository. Only the Personal Access Tokens (PAT) are used to authenticate the user. (Follow the tutorial at *http://s-prs.co/v240928* to do this.)

5. Open the SAP Business Application Studio terminal by choosing **Terminal • New Terminal**, as shown in Figure 7.10.

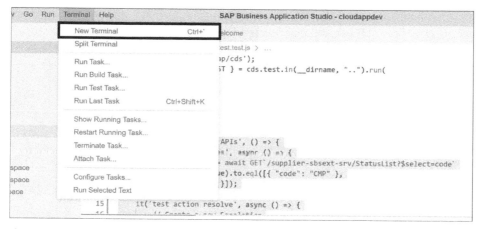

Figure 7.10 New Terminal

6. Initialize the Git repository using the following command in the terminal:

   ```
   git init
   ```

7. Stage and commit all the changes to the local Git repository:

   ```
   git add .
   git commit -m "initial changes"
   ```

8. Update the branch name to the main branch:

   ```
   git branch -M main
   ```

9. Connect the local repository to the GitHub repository using the following code:

   ```
   git remote add origin GITHUB_REPO_URL
   ```

10. Replace "GITHUB_REPO_URL" with the GitHub URL from Figure 7.9, shown earlier.

11. Send the local commit data to the GitHub Repository main branch:

    ```
    git push -u origin main
    ```

Note

If it asks for user ID and password while pushing the changes to GitHub, enter your user ID and PAT (password) to validate the identity before pushing.

7.3.3 Configure CI/CD with SAP Continuous Integration and Delivery Service

SAP Continuous Integration and Delivery lets you configure your CI/CD pipeline in the cloud to automatically build, test, and deploy your code with an easy-to-use configuration tool. It also has a built-in integration with the SAP Cloud Transport Management service to transport the code from one environment to another. This tool is available in your SAP BTP trial account under Extension Suite, and in the upcoming steps, you'll subscribe to this service and configure your CI/CD pipeline. The different stages of the pipeline can be configured in two ways:

- **Job Editor**
  An interactive UI offered as part of SAP Continuous Integration and Delivery in SAP BTP to easily configure the different stages of the pipeline.

- **Source Repository**
  Pipeline configuration will be manually entered in the *.yaml* file, which is based on SAP's open-source project "Piper."

In the following steps, you'll configure the CI/CD pipeline using the graphical-based Job Editor:

1. Open your SAP BTP trial account, go to **Service Marketplace**, and search for "Continuous Integration and Delivery", as shown in Figure 7.11.

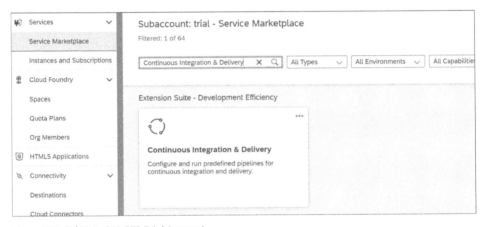

Figure 7.11 CI/CD in SAP BTP Trial Account

2. Click on the tile to open the service, and click the **Create** button to subscribe to the service, as shown in Figure 7.12.

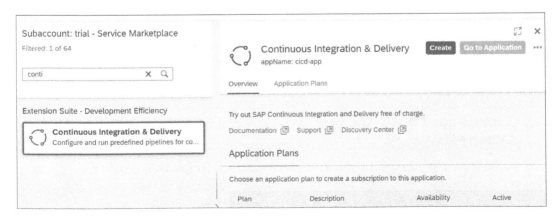

Figure 7.12 Subscribe to the Service

3. Click **Create** in the popup to finalize, as shown in Figure 7.13.

4. Navigate to the **Users** node under **Security** to add SAP Continuous Integration and Delivery roles to your user in the SAP BTP account, as shown in Figure 7.14.

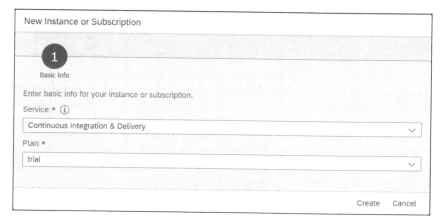

Figure 7.13 CI/CD: Click Create in Popup

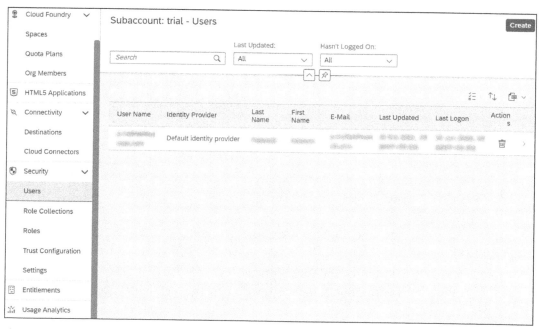

Figure 7.14 Users

5. Click the user to navigate to the detail page, click the three-dot button, and choose **Assign Role Collection**, as shown in Figure 7.15.

6. Select the **CICD Service Administrator** role, and click **Assign Role Collection**, as shown in Figure 7.16.

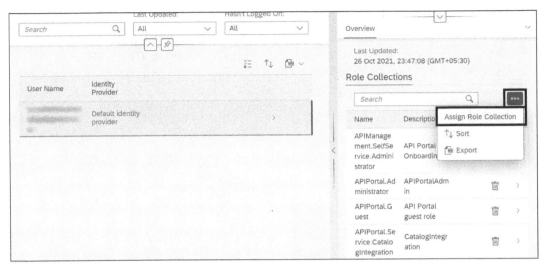

Figure 7.15 User Role Collection

Figure 7.16 Assign CI/CD Administrator Role

Now you have the authorization to access SAP Continuous Integration and Delivery.

7. Navigate to **Instances and Subscriptions** in your SAP BTP trial account, and open **Continuous Integration & Delivery** by clicking the highlighted icon, as shown in Figure 7.17.

8. You must add your GitHub credentials to connect to your repository from SAP Continuous Integration and Delivery. Open the **Credentials** tab, and click the plus icon, as shown in Figure 7.18.

   SAP Continuous Integration and Delivery will use these credentials to access your private GitHub repository.

9. Enter the GitHub **Username** and **Password** (PAT), and then click **Create**, as shown in Figure 7.19.

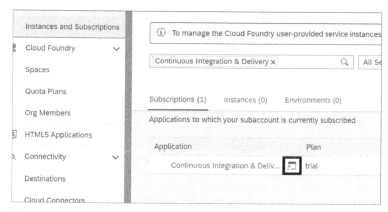

Figure 7.17 Open SAP Continuous Integration and Delivery

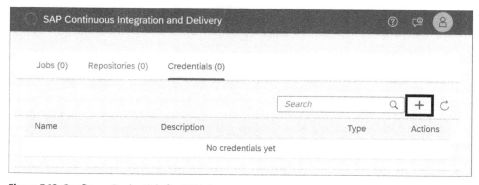

Figure 7.18 Configure Credentials for GitHub

Create Credentials ⑦

*Name:	github
Description:	
Type:	Basic Authentication ∨
*Username:	mahesh0431
Password:	•• 👁

Create   Discard

Figure 7.19 GitHub Credentials

10. Add another credential for your SAP BTP account to automate the SAP Cloud Application Programming Model application's deployment to the SAP BTP, Cloud Foundry environment, as shown in Figure 7.20. You need to enter your SAP BTP account credentials here.

Figure 7.20 Deployment Credentials

11. Navigate to the **Repositories** tab, and click the plus button to add your GitHub repository, as shown in Figure 7.21.

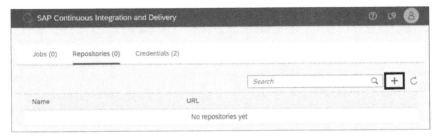

Figure 7.21 SAP Continuous Integration and Delivery Repository

12. Enter the GitHub repository URL, and select the GitHub credentials you created in the previous steps, as shown in Figure 7.22. Leave the other details as they are, which will generate a webhook that GitHub will use to trigger the CI/CD job. Click **Add** to create the repository.

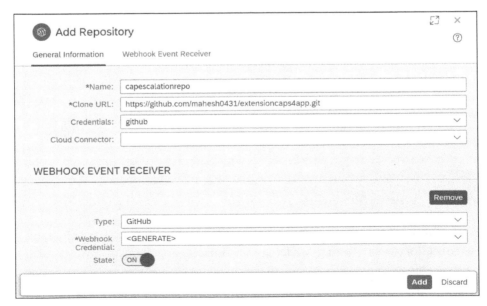

Figure 7.22 Repository Details

13. Navigate to the **Jobs** tab, and click plus button to create a new CI/CD job.

14. Make the following configurations in the **General Information** section, as shown in Figure 7.23. When the job is run, the service will fetch the source code from the Git repository capescalationjob from the branch main.

   - **Job Name**: Enter a unique Name for your CI/CD Job.
   - **Repository**: Select the GitHub repository you created in the **Repository** tab.
   - **Branch**: Enter "main" (branch name of your Git repository).
   - **Pipeline**: Select SAP Cloud Application Programming Model.

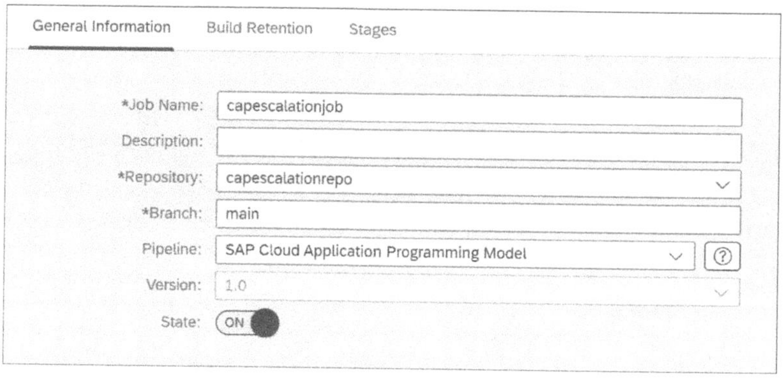

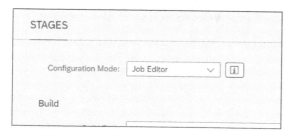

Figure 7.23 CI/CD Pipeline General Information

15. In the **STAGES** section, ensure the **Configuration Mode** is set to **Job Editor**, which gives you the option to maintain the CI/CD pipeline using the UI editor from SAP Continuous Integration and Delivery. The other option is **Source Repository**, where you can maintain this configuration in your source code (SAP Cloud Application Programming Model application) instead of using the UI editor, as shown in Figure 7.24.

STAGES

Configuration Mode: Job Editor

Build

Figure 7.24 Configuration Mode

16. For **Build Tool**, leave **mta** as preselected.

17. Switch on the **Additional Unit Tests**, and leave **test** as the preselected value in the **npm Script** field. This will run the unit tests when the job is run. If the unit test fails, the job status will be set to **Failed**, and any further stages in the CI/CD pipeline won't be executed (see Figure 7.25).

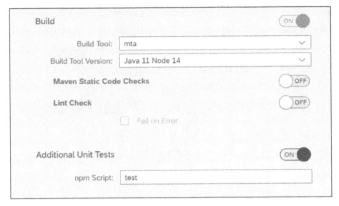

Figure 7.25 Build Tool and Additional Unit Tests

18. Ignore the **Acceptance** and **Compliance** stage, and switch the **Deploy to Cloud Foundry Space** to **ON** in the **Release** stage. So, when the unit tests are run successfully, the application will be deployed to the Cloud Foundry space in SAP BTP, as shown in Figure 7.26.

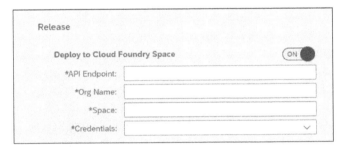

Figure 7.26 Release Stage

19. To enter the details, navigate to your SAP BTP trial subaccount, and copy the **Org Name**, **API Endpoint**, and **Spaces** to the **Release** section in SAP Continuous Integration and Delivery, as shown in Figure 7.27.

Subdomain:	Provider: **Amazon Web Services (AWS)**	Used for Production: **No**
Tenant ID:	Region: **Europe (Frankfurt)**	Beta Features: **Disabled**
Subaccount ID:	Environment: **Multi-Environment**	
Created By:		
Created On: **1 Aug 2021, 14:49:32 (GMT+05:30)**		
Modified On: **2 Jun 2022, 04:00:08 (GMT+05:30)**		

Cloud Foundry Environment

Org Name:

API Endpoint: https://api.cf.eu10.hana.ondemand.com

Org ID:

Manage environment instance

Spaces (1)

Name	Applications
dev	2

Figure 7.27 SAP BTP Account Details

20. Select the **cfdeploy** credentials that you created in the earlier steps, which will be used to authenticate the deployment of the application to the SAP BTP, Cloud Foundry environment. Click **Create** to save the job configuration, as shown in Figure 7.28.

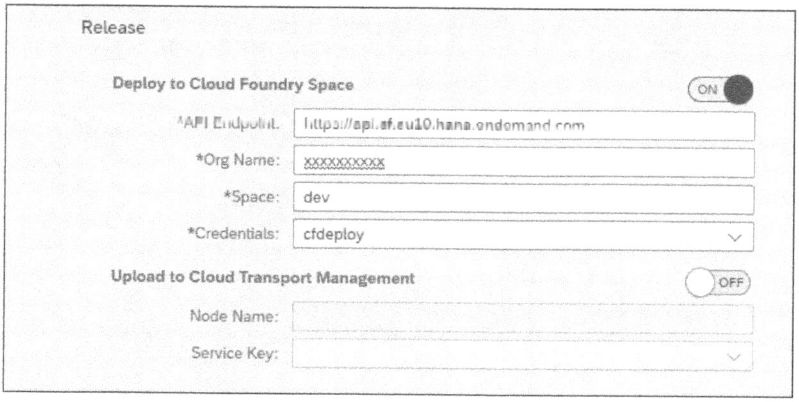

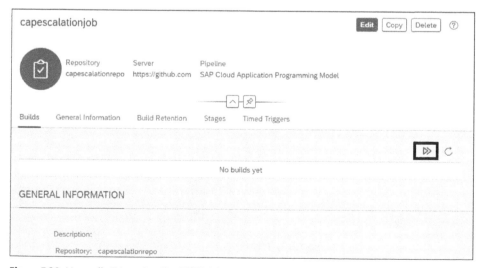

Figure 7.28 Release Stage Filled with Data

For the Continuous Delivery process, you have the option to switch on the **Upload to Cloud Transport Management** to deploy the code in multiple environments (e.g., quality or production). For this example, leave this option switched off.

21. To manually trigger this job, click the **Trigger Build** button in the **Builds** section, as highlighted in Figure 7.29.

capescalationjob

Figure 7.29 Manually Triggering the CI/CD Job

22. Click the build to open the log and wait until the status is successful, as shown in Figure 7.30.

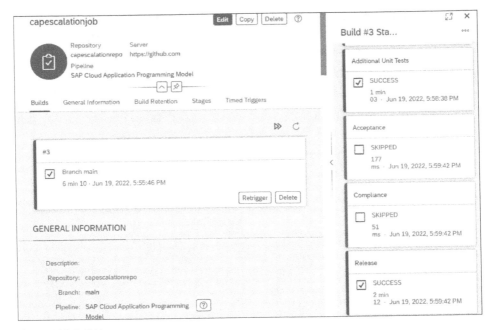

Figure 7.30 Build Log

23. Instead of running the CI/CD job manually every time after you save your source code in Git, you'll configure GitHub to trigger the CI/CD job automatically using webhooks whenever the source code is updated in the Git repository. Navigate to the **capescalationrepo** in the **Repositories** tab, and choose **Webhook Data** to get the webhook details, as shown in Figure 7.31 and Figure 7.32.

Figure 7.31 CI/CD Repository Webhook Data

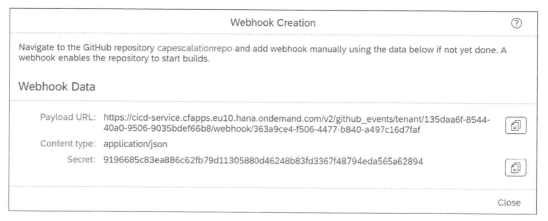

Figure 7.32 CI/CD Webhook Data

24. Go to your Git repository settings, click the **Webhooks** node, and choose **Add webhook** to add the webhook details from the previous step, as shown in Figure 7.33.

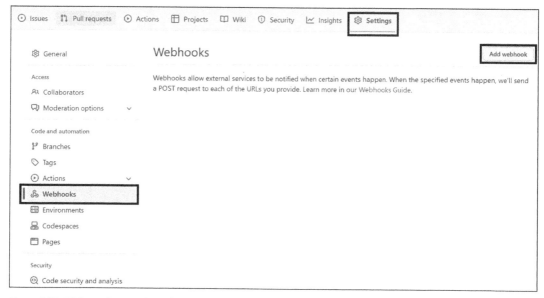

Figure 7.33 Git Repository Webhook Details

25. Copy all the details from the previous step, and click **Add webhook**, as shown in Figure 7.34.

26. To test this, let's go to your source code in your SAP Business Application Studio development space and add a comment in your unit test file for pushing the code to the GitHub repository, as shown in Figure 7.35.

Webhooks / Add webhook

We'll send a POST request to the URL below with details of any subscribed events. You can also specify which data format you'd like to receive (JSON, x-www-form-urlencoded, *etc*). More information can be found in our developer documentation.

Payload URL *

```
https://cicd-service.cfapps.eu10.hana.ondemand.com/v2/github_ev
```

Content type

```
application/json                    ⬍
```

Secret

```
xxxxxxxxxxxxxxxxxxxxxxxxxxxxxxxxxxxxxxxx
```

SSL verification

🔒 By default, we verify SSL certificates when delivering payloads.

◉ **Enable SSL verification**   ○ Disable (not recommended)

Which events would you like to trigger this webhook?

◉ Just the push event.

○ Send me **everything**.

○ Let me select individual events.

☑ **Active**
We will deliver event details when this hook is triggered.

[Add webhook]

Figure 7.34 Creating a GitHub Webhook

```
1  const cds = require("@sap/cds");
2  const { expect, GET, POST } = cds.test.in(__dirname, "..").run(
3    "serve", "--with-mocks", "--in-memory");
4
5  // New changes to push the code to github
6  describe("Testing OData APIs", () => {
7    it("test status codes", async () => {
8      const { data } = await GET`/ems/Statuses?$select=code`;
9      expect(data.value).to.eql([
10       { code: "CMP" },
11       { code: "DRF" },
12       { code: "INP" },
13     ]);
14   });
15
```

Figure 7.35 Adding a Comment

> **Note**
> In real-time, you'll perform actual code changes to enhance or implement new features and push them to the Git repository to trigger the CI/CD process. For testing purposes, you'll just add a comment to push the changes to the Git repository.

27. Commit the changes, and push them to GitHub:

```
git add .
git commit -m 'added a comment'
git push
```

28. Open the job in SAP Continuous Integration and Delivery, and you can see a new build triggered, as shown in Figure 7.36.

Figure 7.36 Automatic Triggering of CI/CD Job

If you want to configure the steps from the source code, choose **Source Repository** instead of **Job Editor** in the Configuration Mode field shown earlier in Figure 7.24. Then you need to manually add the pipeline in your code by executing cds add pipeline in your project terminal, which will create a folder with the name *.pipeline* with the file *config.yaml*. You need to configure the CI/CD pipeline and its stages in this configuration file.

Congratulations!! You've now successfully configured your SAP Cloud Application Programming Model application's CI/CD pipeline using SAP Continuous Integration and Delivery in SAP BTP.

7.4 Important Terminology

In this chapter, the following terminology was used:

- **Chai**
  Chai is a behavioral-driven development (BDD)/test-driven development (TDD) assertion library for Node.js and browsers.

- **CI/CD**
  This acronym stands for continuous integration and continuous delivery/continuous deployment. Continuous integration automatically processes the building, packaging, and testing of the application. Continuous delivery is the process of deploying the application to the production environment. Similarly, in continuous deployment, the deployment will be automatic instead of rewuiring manual deployment to production by the customer.

- **CI/CD pipeline**
  The process or workflow that implements different methods of CI/CD using various tools.

- **Git**
  A Git repository tracks and saves the history of all changes made to the files in a project.

- **GitHub**
  GitHub is a code hosting platform for collaboration and version control for your Git repository.

- **Jest**
  Jest is a JavaScript-based end-to-end unit testing independent framework without other library dependencies.

- **Mocha**
  Mocha is another popular JavaScript test runner framework with dependencies on other libraries such as Chai.

7.5   Practice Questions

1. What is the definition of CI/CD?

   ☐ **A.** Continuous integration

   ☐ **B.** Continuous deployment

   ☐ **C.** Continuous integration and continuous deployment

   ☐ **D.** Continuous integration and continuous delivery/deployment

2. Continuous integration involves which of the following processes? (There are three correct answers.)

   ☐ **A.** Building the application

   ☐ **B.** Packaging the application

   ☐ **C.** Deploying the application

   ☐ **D.** Testing the application

3. Which one of the following is true?

☐   **A.** The application will be waiting for human approval in the continuous deployment process.

☐   **B.** The application will be deployed automatically in the continuous deployment process.

☐   **C.** Neither are true.

4. What are the components of the CI/CD pipeline? (There are two correct answers.)

☐   **A.** Stages

☐   **B.** Job

☐   **C.** SAP Cloud Application Programming Model application

5. Which of the following tools are used to configure your CI/CD pipeline? (There are two correct answers.)

☐   **A.** SAP Fiori elements template

☐   **B.** Jenkins

☐   **C.** SAP Continuous Integration and Delivery in SAP BTP

6. Which Node.js modules are used to test your SAP Cloud Application Programming Model application? (There are two correct answers.)

☐   **A.** Chai

☐   **B.** SAPUI5

☐   **C.** Jest

7. What is unit testing useful for? (There are two correct answers.)

☐   **A.** To test the code for bugs before deploying to the various environments

☐   **B.** For running the application in the development environment

☐   **C.** To offer continuous feedback to the developers while making changes

8. Which function do you use to run the unit testing for your SAP Cloud Application Programming Model application?

☐   **A.** CDS.RUN()

☐   **B.** CDS.TEST()

☐   **C.** CDS.MOCHA()

9. Which function do you use to execute a unit test?

☐   **A.** it()

☐   **B.** run()

☐   **C.** describe()

10. Which function do you use to group the unit tests?

☐   **A.** it()

☐   **B.** run()

☐   **C.** describe()

11. Where can you store your SAP Cloud Application Programming Model application source code?

☐   **A.** Personal laptop

☐   **B.** Production server

☐   **C.** Git repository

12. Which tools are used to create a CI/CD pipeline?

☐   **A.** Project "Piper"

☐   **B.** Jenkins

☐   **C.** SAP Continuous Integration and Delivery

☐   **D.** All of the above

13. What are the available ways to configure the pipeline using SAP Continuous Integration and Delivery?

☐   **A.** Source Repository

☐   **B.** Job Editor

☐   **C.** Both of the above

14. To use SAP Continuous Integration and Delivery for your SAP Cloud Application Programming Model application, which of the following do you have to perform? (There are two correct answers.)

☐   **A.** Create a Jenkins project.

☐   **B.** Subscribe to SAP Continuous Integration and Delivery in SAP BTP.

☐   **C.** Assign the role collection related to SAP Continuous Integration and Delivery to the user.

☐   **D.** Create a new subaccount and subscribe to SAP Continuous Integration and Delivery.

15. What command do you use to create the CI/CD pipeline using the Source Repository?

    ☐ **A.** cds add cicd

    ☐ **B.** cds add pipeline

    ☐ **C.** cds run pipeline

16. While configuring the webhook details in GitHub, which of the following details are required?

    ☐ **A.** Payload URL

    ☐ **B.** Content type

    ☐ **C.** Secret

    ☐ **D.** All of the above

17. Which of the following files are needed in your SAP Cloud Application Programming Model project to run the CI/CD pipeline using Source Repository?

    ☐ **A.** *.pipeline* folder with *manifest.yml* file

    ☐ **B.** *.pipeline* folder with *mta.yml* file

    ☐ **C.** *.pipeline* folder with *config.yml* file

7.6   Practice Question Answers and Explanations

1. Answer: **D**
   CI stands for continuous integration and CD stands for both continuous delivery and continuous deployment, so the definition is continuous integration and continuous delivery/deployment.

2. Answer: **A, B, and D**
   In the CI process, the application goes through the building, packaging, and testing processes.

3. Answer: **B**
   The application will be deployed automatically in the continuous deployment process and wait for human approval in the Continuous Delivery process.

4. Answer: **A and B**
   The main components of the CI/CD pipeline are Stages and Job.

5. Answer: **B and C**
   Jenkins and SAP Continuous Integration and Delivery in SAP BTP are two of the many available tools to configure a CI/CD pipeline for your project.

6. Answer: **A and C**
   Chai, Mocha, and Jest are different Node.js modules that can be used to test your SAP Cloud Application Programming Model application.

7. Answer: **A and C**

    Unit testing is useful for offering continuous feedback on the code to check if any bugs are introduced while doing code changes.

8. Answer: **B**

    The cds.test() function is used to run the SAP Cloud Application Programming Model application locally and to test its functionalities.

9. Answer: **A**

    The it() function expects a function, where you'll write the code to test the SAP Cloud Application Programming Model functionality.

10. Answer: **C**

    The describe() function is used to group multiple tests together.

11. Answer: **C**

    You store your SAP Cloud Application Programming Model application in a Git repository using tools such as GitHub.

12. Answer: **D**

    You can use Jenkins, Project "Piper," or SAP Continuous Integration and Delivery to create the CI/CD pipeline.

13. Answer: **C**

    You can configure the CI/CD pipeline using SAP Continuous Integration and Delivery via the Job Editor or Source Repository.

14. Answer: **B and C**

    You need to subscribe to SAP Continuous Integration and Delivery in SAP BTP and assign the relevant role collections to your user.

15. Answer: **B**

    The cds add pipeline is used to configure the CI/CD pipeline using Source Repository.

16. Answer: **D**

    You need the Payload URL, Content Type, and Secret to configure the webhook in GitHub.

17. Answer: **C**

    The *.pipeline* file will be created with a file named *config.yml* after executing the cds add pipeline command.

7.7   Test Takeaway

CI/CD practices help developers develop and maintain the code by providing them with early feedback from unit tests and by continuously deploying the code to production in small chunks instead of gigantic yearly or quarterly releases. Continuous delivery and continuous deployment aren't the same; continuous delivery means that the code build is always ready to be deployed to production at a click of a button, whereas continuous deployment automatically deploys the code to the production landscape.

SAP Cloud Application Programming Model allows you to choose JEST, Mocha, or Chai syntaxes for writing your unit tests. You integrate the CI/CD pipeline created using SAP Continuous Integration and Delivery with GitHub, so if you push any change to the Git repository, the pipeline will run and execute all the configured stages.

Using a Job Editor to define the CI/CD pipeline via SAP Continuous Integration and Delivery isn't necessary. You can also use Source Repository-based configuration where you must manually write the configuration file in your SAP Cloud Application Programming Model application.

7.8   Summary

In this chapter, we started by discussing the CI/CD process and its importance. Then, you learned about the CI/CD pipeline and the tools available to configure it. Later, we added unit testing to our SAP Cloud Application Programming Model application as this is the crucial step in the CI process. Then we pushed our code and configured the CI/CD pipeline using SAP Continuous Integration and Delivery in SAP BTP, which is then configured to be triggered in the Git repository `commit` using the webhook. We then tested the pipeline by pushing a dummy `commit`. Finally, you also learned about the other Source Repository-based configuration.

The Authors

Krishna Kishor Kammaje is a passionate developer and application architect working at ConvergentIS. He is a recognized SAP Community contributor and was named as an SAP Mentor. He is also an author of the book *SAP Fiori Certification Guide*. His latest interests are in SAP Business Technology Platform, cloud computing, machine learning, and teaching.

Mahesh Palavalli is a senior developer at SAP Labs in Bangalore. He has more than 9 years of experience working with customers from government and private sectors in the areas of SAP Fiori, SAP Business Technology Platform, and ABAP. He was also recognized as a top contributor and a member of the month by SAP Community.

Index

- Learn about SAP's new technology platform

- Explore products, services, and tools for data management, application development, integration, analytics, and more

- Walk through customer use cases to see how SAP BTP can bring value to your business

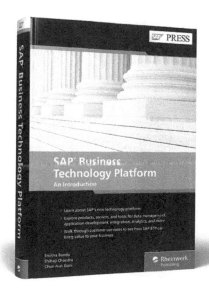

Banda, Chandra, Gooi

SAP Business Technology Platform

An Introduction

What is SAP Business Technology Platform, and what does it offer your organization? Answer these questions and more with this introduction! See how SAP BTP serves as your complete technical foundation and learn about its capabilities for application development, integration, data management, analytics, and more. Identify business use cases and follow practical examples that show how to use SAP BTP's portfolio to its full potential. Envision how SAP BTP enhances your business!

570 pages, pub. 05/2022
E-Book: $74.99 | **Print:** $79.95 | **Bundle:** $89.99

www.sap-press.com/5440

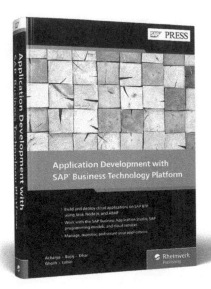

- Build and deploy cloud applications on SAP BTP using Java, Node.js, and ABAP

- Work with the SAP Business Application Studio, SAP programming models, and cloud services

- Manage, monitor, and secure your applications

Acharya, Bajaj, Dhar, Ghosh, Lahiri

Application Development with SAP Business Technology Platform

Develop cloud applications customized for your business needs! Master the basics of SAP Business Technology Platform (SAP BTP) and its development environments; then get step-by-step instructions for developing and operating your own applications. Build your backend with Java, Node.js, or ABAP, and set up your frontend using SAPUI5 and SAP Fiori. With detailed code examples throughout, this book is your complete guide to building cloud applications on SAP BTP!

approx. 625 pp., avail. 01/2023
E-Book: $84.99 | **Print:** $89.95 | **Bundle:** $99.99

www.sap-press.com/5504

- Configure security for the Neo and Cloud Foundry environments

- Set up secure connections with the cloud connector

- Protect key cloud services like SAP Business Application Studio and SAP Integration Suite

Martin Koch and Siegfried Zeilinger

Security and Authorizations for SAP Business Technology Platform

Learn what it takes to protect SAP Business Technology Platform! Walk through the cloud security mechanisms of SAP BTP (formerly SAP Cloud Platform). See how to set up users and permissions for your unique circumstances and configure secure connection to cloud and on-premise systems. Work with SAP BTP's administration tools, including the command line interface and APIs. With information on safeguarding key cloud services, this guide will leave you confident in your cloud system's security!

approx. 400 pp., avail. 12/2022
E-Book: $84.99 | **Print:** $89.95 | **Bundle:** $99.99

www.sap-press.com/5627